Punishment and Shame

Punishment and Shame

A Philosophical Study

Wendy C. Hamblet

LEXINGTON BOOKS
A division of
ROWMAN & LITTLEFIELD PUBLISHERS, INC.
Lanham • Boulder • New York • Toronto • Plymouth, UK

Published by Lexington Books
A division of Rowman & Littlefield Publishers, Inc.
A wholly owned subsidary of The Rowman & Littlefield Publishing Group, Inc.
4501 Forbes Boulevard, Suite 200, Lanham, Maryland 20706
http://www.lexingtonbooks.com

Estover Road, Plymouth PL6 7PY, United Kingdom

British Library Cataloguing in Publication Information Available

Library of Congress Cataloging-in-Publication Data

Hamblet, Wendy C., 1949–
  Punishment and shame : a philosophical study / Wendy C. Hamblet.
    p. cm.
  Includes bibliographical references and index.
  ISBN 978-0-7391-4936-2 (cloth : alk. paper) — ISBN 978-0-7391-4937-9 (pbk. : alk. paper)
  1. Punishment—Philosophy. 2. Punishment—Moral and ethical aspects. 3. Shame—Philosophy. I. Title.
  HV8693.H36 2011
  303.3'6—dc22

                            2010039526

⊖™ The paper used in this publication meets the minimum requirements of American National Standard for Information Sciences—Permanence of Paper for Printed Library Materials, ANSI/NISO Z39.48-1992.

Printed in the United States of America

The heavens do not say anything.
Confucius.

Table of Contents

Introduction

In Plato's *Republic*, the stark political realist Thrasymachus ridicules the idealist Socrates:

> You think that the shepherds and the neatherds are considering the good of the sheep and the cattle and fatten and tend them with anything else in view than the good of the masters and themselves. (343b)

What is named "justice" in our states is simply the good of the stronger. Thrasymachus recognizes that what matters in state politics is not that rulers *have* justice but that they *have the appearance* of justice. What matters for preserving public trust in the rulers is that the people be convinced that those rulers are just, that they are making the right use of power—making laws that are just, giving defendants just trials, and punishing social offenders justly. Thrasymachus appreciates the power of the public gaze in determining political legitimacy, despite the fact that the democracy, like every other political form, unswervingly serves the interests of the ruler.

> And each form of government enacts the laws with a view to its own advantage, a democracy democratic laws and tyranny autocratic, and the others likewise, and by so legislating they proclaim that the just for their subjects is that which is for their—the rulers'—advantage and the man who deviates from this law they chastise as a lawbreaker and a wrongdoer. This then, my good sir, is what I understand as the identical principle of justice that obtains in all states—the advantage of the established government. (338e)

Socrates insists that justice is an ideal, a condition of soul that is purchased by right conduct, a condition that evidences moral health and brings happiness wherever it is found. Rulers must rule rightly—justly—if they are to be deemed legitimate rulers or true "statesmen." Socrates is not disagreeing with Thrasymachus' realpolitik account of what actually happens in states: rulers as they currently rule (i.e., according to their own advantage) do not truly exemplify the ideal to which they invariably lay claim. Socrates knows the reality, but he is arguing in favor of a better form of rule, a rule oriented by, and serving, true justice, a rule that he will later reveal to be possible only when philosophers assume the helm of power. Socrates argues for real justice, not its counterfeit form in current practice.

What is curious in this interchange between the realist and the philosopher is that they both appreciate the distinction between the political reality and the ideal. That is, their argument is no argument at all. Socrates sees that Thrasymachus is right about how rulers currently rule, how their justice serves their interests alone. But Thrasymachus appreciates too that Socrates is right: that the ideal must exist and the people must internalize it (believe that the "justice" that rules in their state evidences moral health and brings happiness to all that it touches) for the political system to achieve its ends (the interests of the ruling class). People must believe in the philosopher's justice for the realist's justice to have the force that it has to serve the interests of the ruler. Philosophy serves politics.

Millennia later, Michel Foucault will look back over the evolving history of forms of justice in the Western world and will declare the advent of modern penal forms to compose a veritable "revolution" in justice, the culmination of public sensibilities about the right use of power and the connection between political legitimacy and humane forms of punishment. Foucault will see the shift from cruel public spectacles to more human forms of punishment, concealed behind prison walls, in ship galleys, and in the fields of far-off colonies, as evidence that Enlightenment ideals have taken root in the public mind and forced a change in penal policy. Foucault is claiming that politics serves philosophy, rather than the other way around.

Brilliant philosopher that Foucault undeniably is, I will challenge his explanation for modern penal forms, showing that a stark economic pragmatism underlies the modern penal revolution. While what are accounted as right rule, just laws, and fitting forms of punishment are shaped by a people's "penal temper," that temper fluctuates with the politico-economic circumstances of the times. Across the history of the Western world, the logic of punishment has softened or hardened, grown subtle and discretely concealed or cruel and shamelessly displayed in the public square, not according to evolving moral sensibilities (as Foucault claims), but according to economic forces and political realities. In particular, how *this* offender will be punished when found guilty of crime will depend largely on the social value placed upon him, the shame or honor attached to his social position or condition of life.

Ideas about justice and punishment and the connection of these ideals to the realities of politics and economics fluctuate along a spectrum of forms. The two poles of this continuum emerge in the cradle of Western ideas—with the archaic Greek princes on the one hand and the Greek philosophers on the other. Thrasymachus voices the archaic view of justice: what matters is how people view me, the honor I am accorded in the public gaze, the social status I enjoy relative to my peers. Socrates represents the philosophical counter-thesis to this construction of justice: what matters is how nobly, honorably I act, the condition of my soul, regardless of the (mis)perceptions that others may hold about me or my position on the social scale.

In the fifth century BCE, Plato offers an alternative to the already timeworn aristocratic construction of justice, grounded in calculations of honor and claims to social place, that culminates in a vengeance (*dikephoros*) penology, with its inclination toward punitive excess. He recommends that injustice is an inner state, a sickened condition of soul, which calls for the therapy of a healing (*therapeuma*) justice.

Justice and punishment are institutions, legitimated by time and tradition. People tend in general to take for granted the rightness of the institutions of the system into which they are born and the traditions by which they are raised. Many families in many societies see the primary task of parenting to be guiding their offspring in the successful absorption of the ideas and practices that constitute what they deem as not merely the local preferences of their group, but the "right ways" of doing things, the "right modes" of behaving, and the "right strategies" for taking one's proper place within a civilized society.

Rarely do people challenge the rightness of the system itself, the logic that orients the system, or the values that underpin it. This is because it is extremely difficult to step outside the reigning worldview, to gain perspective on its merits and critically assess its shortcomings. In fact, everyday life, as Martin Heidegger brilliantly points out, is largely a matter of "falling." We mostly tumble through our everyday existences, taking for granted our reality postulates as simple "common sense" because our worlds make sense for us. We are early on teethed on the logic of the system, then we comprehend all else within its terms.

The tendency to fall uncritically in line with the system that envelopes us is understandably strong for those members of the system whose interests are best served by it. There is simply less reason or motivation to question what works perfectly well *for me*. What comes into view *as a problem* depends upon social status. A thing emerges into view *as a problem* in my lifeworld because it is a problem *for me*, something that harms *my* interests. From the summit of the social ladder, few problems will be seen to arise, except perhaps in the annoying threats to social peace launched at the base of the system. At the foot of the social ladder, we may expect the case to be the opposite. We may expect those persons least advantaged in the society—the poor and the marginalized—to recognize more aspects of system traditions and institutions *as problematic*, since the socio-economic distance suffered by the poor grants them a greater "critical distance" from the benefits that blind the wealthier classes to the flaws of the system. That is, we may expect the poor to enjoy a greater capacity for clarity of vision on matters of social justice. But, in actuality, those marginalized by the system are often its most fervent defenders rather than its detractors, for who so loves a system and yearns to be enfolded in its accommodating embrace as desperately as those who are excluded from it?

Thus, breaking away from the everyday "falling" within our systems is exceedingly difficult for people at every level of their system. In this work, I am suggesting that we do just that—take a philosophical break from the everyday. This work forces a deliberate step back from the comfortable assumptions that ground our understanding of the world, by asking some important questions about certain fundamental ideas that we take for granted, ideas whose "good sense" seems so self-evident that their rightness rarely comes into view as questionable. These are ideas that appear *absolutely* valuable, that is, "natural" for all human beings, the only alternative for rational minds. The ideas I am calling into question in this study are our ideas about justice, crime, and punishment.

These ideas are so archaic and timeworn as to compose veritable institutions that frame the lifeworld of the West, so it is exceedingly difficult to accomplish a critical view of them. Friedrich Nietzsche and Michel Foucault have pioneered an effective approach for undermining the sense of self-evident timeless validity that attaches to traditions and institutions. Bringing a thing into the discerning light of history and exposing its origins in time has the freeing effect of undercutting an institution's sacred, eternal, and universal flavor. When we witness the strange and foreign world in which a tradition came to be, we find it easier to question its timeless eternality, as well as its validity and applicability in the present. The power of histories is circumvented by merely exposing the historical roots of the thing.

The current study leads the reader through an historical exploration of the ideas of justice, crime, and punishment, as they arise in the cradle of the Western world among the archaic Greeks; then we follow these concepts as they evolve and devolve into the Greek democracy, then across the Christian feudal world. Finally we rediscover in modernity the persistent logic that connects the trinity of ideas; disguised but persistent, they reappear, heavily loaded with new metaphysical and psychologico-ethical assumptions.

The extensive attention that I devote in early chapters to the heroic worldview of the Greek princes serves the purpose of laying the conceptual foundations of a configuration of justice, crime, and punishment that will be shown to enjoy remarkable longevity throughout the history of the Western world. But the extended treatment of the Greeks is also meant as an occasion to view the radical foreignness of the archaic worldview, the better to enable us to question the fitness of ancient understandings for the modern world situation.

Ancient ideas about justice, crime and punishment took shape within a particular worldview, the cult of the Greek warrior-hero. The heroic idea of justice was rigorously focused upon the outraged victim (*atimos* or "one deprived of honor"), who felt dishonored (*atimastos* or "without honor" but also "unrevenged" or "unpunished") by the "crime" (*atimia*), which threw into question his elevated status as deserving of highest respect. The victim's (and the community's) anger at the affront that upset the social order became the "measure" of compensatory penalty (*atimia*) that was due to the offended. Since the aristocrats' entire worldview was grounded in distributions of honor and since mistreatment by a peer was seen to dishonor or degrade, justice constituted a "giving back" of what was taken. The work of justice was to "give and take" honors such that the social register was rebalanced in light of the offense.

However, in the heroic worldview, affront tended to stimulate exaggerated anger in the victim, a feral fury that often sought, not merely a reasonable pay-back, but the utter destruction of the offender. Therefore archaic justice, though modeled as a "give and take" of honors, tended to give more (shame and pain) to the offender than he had originally taken.

Focused on the outraged victim, justice assumed the exaggerated economy of vengeance. The excesses to which an economy of vengeance
could lead were mirrored in myth by the goddesses who doled out the
archaic justice (prior to the institution of trials by jury). The Furies (Erinyes), Daughters of the Night, were horrible to look upon, with their
hair of snakes and eyes dripping blood, but even more horrible was the
punishment they brought to offenders, pursuing them relentlessly and
driving them to insanity.

If the Greeks prized measure and balance as qualities divine, it was
because they appreciated all too well how difficult it is to realize these
high ideals in the life of human beings. The quick-tempered warrior
princes were merciless in exacting revenge upon their offenders. When
they meted out justice to friend and foe alike, they tended toward punitive excessiveness. Against their peers, "taking justice" meant exacting
penalties that degraded and humiliated, just as in battle, they crushed and
disgraced their enemies, with a vengeance as ruthless and relentless as
the Furies.

The vengeance model of justice, with its punitive logic of shaming,
has remained with the Western world for thousands of years, despite the
fact that the flaws in this form of justice were identified very early in the
history of the West. The archaic Greeks recognized the problems associated with the vengeance model of justice, and their myths and tragedies
grappled with this failing, warning against disproportionate penalties and
the cycles of vengeance that they could incite, and proposing a new form
of justice system to mitigate against its flaws.

The trial by jury, initiated by the founding goddess of Athens, the
wise Athena (according to myth), built safeguards into the system to fun-
nel the hair-trigger responses, typical of hot-tempered warriors, into an
extended *process* that granted expression of all sides of the case. The
offended could express his rage before an audience who shared his moral
code, but his testimony had to be marshaled within strict boundaries—
channeled into the formal language and rational argument of the court.
The hope was that the victim's fury could be placated by venting before
the sympathetic community, but also that the offender's testimony could
balance the victim's understanding of the crime. The trial by jury justice
system strove toward a fair and evenhanded resolution, imaged in the
scales of justice. Moreover, following the goddess' example, the Athenian courts preferred to err on the side of generosity: where doubt remained of the offender's guilt, after a day-long trial, punishment was
foregone.

Myth and tragedy testify to the Greek insight that justice must be as generous as possible. The Greeks had a deep appreciation for the fact that punishment exacted in shame is never happily paid. Shame is a debilitating negative affect that has a tendency to run toward excess. Unlike guilt, which is simply the *empirical* fact of having committed a crime, shame is as an *ontological* event, which gnaws away at the very being of the culprit, shattering his *arête* and eroding his humanness. In the long run punishments that shame can do more harm than good, undermining the values that ground the community and compose the objective of the justice system—balance, order, harmony, and integrity.

So with the advent of written codes of law and the jury trial in Athens, justice, crime, and punishment become systematized, rationalized, and ordered. Often the trials end generously without further cycles of shaming. But reasonableness could not be guaranteed, because generosity was optional, and justice remained focused on the victim, so the degree of victim outrage continued to be a strong determinant of the kind and intensity of penalty exacted of offenders. As long as justice maintained an economy of vengeance, the polis remained at risk for rebounding cycles of violence.

The vengeance economy of justice was as archaic as the early Hellenic kings, and though the justice system of Athens underwent a great many changes through the classical era and into the later democracy, the vengeance economy of justice, grounded in the "give and take" of honors among powerful peers, endured throughout the politico-economic changes. Plato recognized the dangerous economy of the Athenian justice system and challenged the logical foundations of the Greek notions of justice as vengeance, crime as dishonor, and punishment as shame. No one can strip a good man of his honor, Plato asserted; doing shamefully alone brings shame. The focus had to be removed from the offended victim and placed squarely upon the offender, who had shamed himself in behaving badly. The work of justice is to locate the soul-sick, who suffer from injustice in their souls, and the work of punishment is to heal the soul-sickness and make the offender a just man again.

Plato was the first to appreciate that people harm others because they are morally sick, out of sorts with their society's standards, dishonorable in a society that defines itself on the honor system. The morally sick cannot be shamed; they are incapable of shame, because shame is witness to moral learning, which the unjust undoubtedly lack. Offenders must be educated to justice, not humiliated by shameful punishments. Cruel punishments, he figured, would only make the sick sicker, the dishonorable

less honorable. Plato reconfigured the language of justice to revolution-
ize the economy of justice. The *dikephoros* (avenging) justice of the archaic world Plato advised be abandoned in favor of a *therapeuma* (healing) justice that promotes the moral health of the soul-sick offender.
Justice's work became a rehabilitative process focused upon re-educating
offenders and healing their twisted souls, rather than stripping them of
the last shred of their dignity that might be called upon to motivate noble
behavior.

With these two opposing models of justice broadly defined, we will
scan the history of Western penal practices, to determine how the prevailing understandings of justice fit within the cultural and socio-political
climates of the changing times and to gauge to what degree people's
evolving ideas and practices follow the Greek princes vengeance economy of justice or Plato's healing economy. The degree of outrage or
sympathy that people direct toward their social offenders will vary with
the times. What they see as criminal or pitiable fluctuates with the evolving circumstances of their lives. Societies have "penal tempers" that ebb
and flow with politico-economic conditions.

Offences that shamed and humiliated social peers posed a serious
challenge to social order in the ancient world, so such acts were considered criminal. On the other hand, no import was placed upon shaming
social inferiors. The *hoi polloi* deserved all the contempt that aristocrats
could heap upon them. The early democracies of Athens represent attempts by the nouveau riche to crack open the sedimented social system
of the well-born, to allow the wealthy poor-born access to social place.
But the poor remained contemptible and deserving of their slavish life-
styles. However, in the tight-knit, ordered world of feudal Europe, governed by the principle of the "Great Chain of Being," the poor found
their place and grew less despised. Church teachings on *karitas* and the
paternalistic system of feudalism allowed the lowly to be seen as providing opportunities for demonstrating one's generosity and piety. This is
not to say that punishments became less cruel. On the contrary, penal
tempers flared in the cruel spectacles of the medieval era, called upon to
demonstrate the power of divine kings and clergy, and to deliver a fore-
taste of the torments of Hell.

Ultimately the spectacular cruelties of medieval tortures gave way to
the more subtle and hidden tortures of the modern prison. Michel Foucault attributes the penal change to a new sense of shame shifted from
the criminal to the executioner, which in turn reflected badly upon the
power behind the gallows—the king and the church fathers. Foucault

credits Enlightenment ideals for a newfound sense of shame that drives punishment into seclusion. However, I challenge Foucault's generous explanation for the shift in penal forms, and offer an alternative explanation for the penal revolution, by rethinking its dating. I argue that the shift was already well underway hundreds of years earlier than Foucault allows and is explicable not in terms of a growing sense of shame in the punishing powers, but in terms of a new worldview being propagated by the bourgeois middle class, rising across Europe in the budding capitalist era. In this new vision, shame is attached not to the powers that punish too cruelly, but to the condition of poverty and the profitless squandering of labor power on the gallows.

On the whole across the history of the West, ideas about crime, justice, and punishment follow the vengeance economy. When times grow difficult and jobs are scarce, poverty and homelessness increase. As poverty increases, so does petty crime (petty property theft, vagrancy, prostitution, and begging), often the only survival option for the indigent. As petty crime increases, social sympathies wane and the public cries out for harsher penalties, thinking erroneously that cruel punishments will deter criminality. Politicians respond to the public demands and punishments become harsh, more degrading and more dehumanizing. Rarely across the history of Western penal practices do societies give serious attention to curing social deviants of their ills. Rarely across the history of global capitalism do societies make the logical connection between crime and poverty, which would recommend that better conditions for the least fortunate would mitigate crime in their society. But then, as I argued at the outset of this chapter, what comes to be seen *as a problem* in a society is what is a problem *for those with a social voice*, so what comes to be seen *as a crime* in a society is what undermines the best interests of the propertied classes.

Exposing the origins of modern ideas about justice, crime, and punishment will free us to consider these things as products of histories, hundreds and thousands of years old, rather than seeing them as the product of the evolution of Western moral sensibilities and a "history of progress." Our ideas have their foundation in a particular past of a particular people; they are not timeless, self-evident truths that every civilized society should embrace. The difficult histories of our ideas will help us to take a fresh look at how we treat our poor, what we consider criminal, and how we prefer to punish our fellow citizens when they go astray.

For the ancient philosophers Plato and Aristotle, justice is a noble quality of soul that must be nourished by the parent-city. Sound statesmanship is so critical because establishing strong exemplars that model good habits is the best way of educating the ignorant and cultivating the virtues that keep people from going morally astray. Since the human tendency is to become what we behold, good leaders leading citizens in the direction of excellence is crucial to their (the citizens') moral development, and far more efficacious than correcting people by painful punishments after the fact of their going morally astray. Justice is a noble faculty that is lovingly and painstakingly nurtured in the fertile garden of the soul, by wise and compassionate gardeners.

Yet, today in the vast majority of states, justice remains modeled on the "due recompense" economy of outraged, offended princes, still modeled by the set of scales that balance punishment with crime. Focused on shaming offenders and robbing them of their dignity, justice remains a redistribution of honors, a pay-back of the dishonorable act of crime with the dishonor of a shaming punishment. Plato's curative model of justice, as education in excellence, never really caught on, in the legal and political arenas of Western states, as a serious response to crime. The retributive economy of Western justice systems remains true to the archaic vengeance model. Indeed in some modern states, the state sets the appalling moral example of killing its offending citizens to underscore the prohibition against killing and other serious offenses. At best, modern states are largely content to herd their offender populations into overcrowded and under-funded prisons, where they are dehumanized and trained in criminality, rather than cured of their injustice. This method has grown so popular in the United States that punishment has become big business, contracted out to clever entrepreneurial third parties to do with the prisoners what they will at the lowest cost they can manage.

Penologies have traditionally been written by penologists, so they suffer from the general tendency to begin from the unacknowledged presupposition that punishment is a social and political good, which serves a number of sound objectives in a society, the primary one being the maintenance of social order. A philosopher writes from a philosophical tradition that questions presuppositions. The philosophical task composes exposing unacknowledged assumptions that underpin systems of truth, and challenging their viability for producing good effects in the world. Philosophers expose the assumptions that inhere in the language (*logos*) that frames the accepted truths, and in the logic (*logos*) that underpins and structures the arguments (*logoi*) called upon to defend prevailing practices and traditions.

Punishment is held generally to be a social and political good, in accord with the penologist's prejudice. But it is a good which is by definition evil, after Thomas Aquinas' definition of punishment as "the infliction of a penal evil by a legitimate authority upon one who has committed an offense."[1] So the definition of punishment throws us into the dilemma of equating an evil with a good. What distinguishes the good evil of punishment from other forms of evil? The answer is encrypted within the definition: *who enacts* this evil—a legitimate authority—and *who suffers* it—an offender. When bad things happen to good people, those things are accounted evil; when bad things happen to bad (offensive) people, those things are accounted good, the good evil of punishment. But Aquinas' definition begs the question: what renders an authority "legitimate" and what renders an actor offensive? Might it simply be the case that the punisher has power, while the offender is offensive for his lack thereof, for the miserable condition of his life?

The ancient tragedians ask just these questions. They raise the challenge that authority is legitimated, not simply in the fact of holding power—any tyrant can do that—but in the fact of *right* rule, a great aspect of which is *right* punishing. Do we rightly punish today? Those people who see punishment as vengeance which visits evil upon those who offend their interests and oppose the social order will be happy that the justice systems in many countries are herding their offenders into dehumanizing detainment centers, exiling them from civilized society. But to those who believe that those who fall into crime are unfortunate victims of a social order that generally fails them, social justice responses may emerge as the fitting response to crime. Our attitudes to crime and punishment depend upon whether we follow Plato in his healing response to injustice, or we follow the ancient Greek warrior princes who, sometimes obsessively and with furious vengeance, humiliate and shame those who offend them.

Notes

1. Thomas Aquinas, *Summa Theologica* Art. 1, Obj. 5.

Part One
Ancient Ideas
about Justice and Punishment

Chapter 1
Justice and the Cosmic Order
in Greek Mythology

Trevor J. Saunders, in his *Plato's Penal Code*, argues that there is no punishment in Homer's *Iliad*.[1] In the tradition of Aquinas' definition of punishment as *the infliction of a penal evil by a legitimate authority upon one who has sinned*, Saunders argues that penalties may not be named "punishments" until the great Athenian statesman, Solon, overhauled the Athenian institutions early in the sixth century BCE. Solon established the formal state mechanisms that made official the state's authority over its offenders, carving up among the state authorities the various functions of law-making and designing appropriate reprisals for law-breaking.[2] After Solon, justice became formalized: cases were judged by ten elected military generals in the Areopagus Council and the Assembly of 6,000 male citizens who impaneled juries with anything from 200 to 6,000 citizens.[3]

Saunders relies upon Aquinas' definition of punishment in making his argument against punishment in the *Iliad*, but in doing so, he finds himself trapped in the circular argument noted in the Introduction of this work. If legitimacy is itself determined according to the rightness of rule, a crucial aspect of which is right punishment, then political legitimacy is as dependent upon right punishment as right punishment is dependent upon legitimacy. Whether or not we accept as punishments the penalties imposed in the pre-Solonic world, the fact remains that institutions of justice and ideas about rightful punishment did not spring into being *ex nihilo* in fifth century BCE Athens. Thus, in this work, I find it more useful to apply the terms justice, crime, and punishment to speak of the prevailing practices employed in any society to manage the conduct of its citizens and penalize its deviants, in the interests of maintaining social order.

The punishment practices of classical Athens have their roots in a particular history of a particular people, and are a reflection and culmination of that history. The policies and institutions of the Athenian democracy, including its penal practices, take on the forms that they do, because they fit well within a worldview and a self-understanding that developed over an extensive prehistory. The democracy in Athens was born of longstanding social arrangements that were aristocratic, that is meritocratic, after the Ancient Greek word, *aristos*, which means literally "the good." Rule by the best is taken for granted within the archaic Hellenic cosmology that views goodness as embedded in the logic of cosmic order, where cosmic harmony is purchased moment to moment by maintaining the fragile balance among powerful contesting forces.

The archaic Greeks that we find in Homer's epic tales, the *Iliad* and the *Odyssey*, were a warrior society, with the usual rankings and orderings that any warrior society must have to battle successfully. The individual's rank on the battlefield determined his rank in the society, or to be more precise, the individual's birth into a family of old wealth determined his social and his military rank. The wealthiest members of the society, who could afford the luxuries of horses and armor, formed the hoplites (cavalry); they were leaders on the battlefield, just as they were the leaders in the polis.

People of lesser wealth, who fought in the rank and file with whatever weapons or farm tools they could muster, formed the lower classes of the society. Landless citizens were restricted from the higher offices in the city but in theory they enjoyed the same rights as the wealthy and highborn. But in the reality of their everyday lives, few were able to leave their fields to claim those participatory rights and political voice. Furthermore, their rights and freedoms were fragile, and before Solon, the poor could be sold into slavery if they fell upon hard times. However, with the democratic reforms of the fifth century BCE, debt slavery was no longer a worry to the poor and the property restrictions for public office were removed, so all citizens enjoyed political equality and bodily freedom.

Nevertheless, as Jacques Rancière rightly highlights throughout his corpus, even during the Athenian democracy of the classical period, the claim that the political system of Athens was characterized by citizen equality is a shameless ruse.[4] There exists little equality among citizens wherever great extremes of wealth and poverty coexist. The lifestyle of the poor citizen of ancient Athens at the height of the democracy was more "equal" to that of a slave, than to the lifestyle of the wealthy noble. Whether the poor citizens found themselves in the frontlines of battle defending themselves with pitchforks and hoes, or were landed in the fields miles outside of town, laboring in the hot sun, when court was in session, the poor surely felt the gap between their lot and the lot of their wellborn and wealthy counterparts. The poor were impoverished in the honor and respect afforded them, in the physical and material security they enjoyed, and in the freedom for active participation in city affairs that their lowly lives permitted.

As one might readily imagine, the poor were too powerless to offer much trouble to the wealthy class during the aristocratic age. The greatest challenge to social order in the early warrior culture lay in maintaining a careful balance of power and honors among the hot-blooded, sensitive-tempered, hypermasculine princes. Balance was a great virtue in the Greek mind, for precisely this reason. Later in the evolution of the polis, less well-born upstarts would challenge the elites for a share of the political power. But the poor remained for the most part infrequent visitors to the public places where citizenship was reified.

Earliest Greek cosmology expresses and struggles with the problem of balancing honors, rights, privileges, and responsibilities to maintain harmony among powerful and competitive individuals and myth points the way toward an ideal solution for managing these often arrogant and volatile egos. The Greek pantheon was a broad alliance of gods and goddesses each with his or her own unique powers, domain of influence, and rights of privilege.

For the ancients, the universe made sense—it is *cosmos* (literally, order) rather than *chaos* (literally, disorder)—because the individual components of reality, though distinctive in their potencies, fit neatly together, each in its most natural place, and performed the duties to which nature most suited it. Together all the pieces form a beautiful, reasonable, comprehensible whole, a single *uni*verse, a *cosmos*.

In distinction from the monotheistic worldview, pantheistic cosmic harmony is not guaranteed in advance by some greater dominating superforce, but remains always fragile and tenuous, and thus order and harmony are highly valued in pantheistic societies. Order is not seriously challenged from below, although the least of beings deserves some respect. Grave threats to the order of things are launched on the common power plane. Balance is highly prized and dearly loved, because it is only ever purchased one moment at a time through constant struggle, coalition, and deal-making. Hesiod's *Theogony* permits a gaze into the archaic Greek pantheistic worldview. It is worthwhile to consider Greek cosmology here, as it offers telling insight into the common mental world of the archaic Greeks.

Hesiod's Theogony

First a word is needed to dispel certain common misconceptions and anachronisms about mythological civilizations. One finds a persistent prejudice in literature, classical history, and philosophy, contrasting between the "rational systems of inquiry" pursued by philosophy and science, over against the "irrational beliefs" of mythology, legend, and religion. G. S. Kirk, famed Cambridge philosopher, echoes this prejudice and opens his book, *Myth*, with precisely this contrast.[5] The contrast is simply erroneous and misleading because it characterizes mythological thinking negatively and anachronistically. To describe mythology as irrational is to say what it is not, rather than what it is; it is to say that mythology is not a later mode of thinking, with the implication that myth is, therefore, inferior.

F. M. Cornford too, in his *Before and After Socrates*, commits a similar anachronism with his notion of "projection" in ancient intuitions about the world. Cornford argues that mythological civilizations projected onto nature analogues of human personality and will, thereby creating anthropomorphic divinities. This way of explaining mythological thinking is anachronistic because it presupposes a notion of non-anthropomorphic nature as the rationally sophisticated screen for human projection, a notion grounded in the distinction between the capricious "invention" of fictitious divinities and the supposedly objective "fact" of nature as the object of scientific investigation.

Cornford and other classical scholars also charge mythological civilizations with being concerned only with the past, focusing upon the beginnings of the universe to the downplaying of the import of present and future. This is a misrepresentation of the Greek view of the significance of beginnings for all aspects of human time. For the ancients, the key to understanding the present and the future lies locked in the mysteries of the past. Just as the Greek aristocrats placed enormous importance on birthline as indicative of individual worth, character, and destiny, and saw themselves as extensions of their family lineage, so too they understood all things to be rooted in their beginnings, their essential nature and their destiny tied up in their ancestry and their histories. In the Greek intuition, the stories of the past encrypt timeless truths that are equally valid for the present and the future. Origin myths are the most important myths because they lay out the enduring blueprints of lawfulness—the patterns, forces, and principles—that govern the cosmos and regulate and integrate the whole of earthly existence.

It is exceedingly difficult for people to avoid the common trap of measuring other people's beliefs and values through the lens of their own, which always appear as right and natural and common sense, causing others to appear as deviant, irrational, and unnatural. Looking across the globe to foreign ideas is all but impossible to do accurately and fairly. But looking back upon the past with unprejudiced eyes is exponentially more difficult, because we have been schooled all our intellectual lives in the myth of "history of progress" that places our ways of doing things and seeing the world at the summit of the ladder of human creative potential. We always see our ideas and practices as the evolutionary best, the mature fruit of natural selection.

However, philosophy and its offspring sciences are relatively recent ways of describing reality, recent ways of using our reason. We moderns compose a mere footnote in the history of the human species on earth. Our ideas and prejudices are so recent as to encompass fewer than a couple of millennia of human time, a brief episode in the hundreds of thousands of millennia during which human beings have lived on the earth. Human beings, across their long pre-philosophical, pre-scientific history, have always survived by virtue of their rational faculties—by studying their environment, identifying the challenges therein, imagining how their lives could be better, and creating the tools that would make it so. Their very success proves that their thinking had some intricate texture of rationality, different to be certain from later rational forms, but decidedly deserving of positive characterization.

The distinction between the irrational world of myth and the rational, dispassionate, objective world of philosophy and the sciences is a faulty distinction. Our modern ideas about important things, including justice and punishment, are derived largely from the classical Greeks, and their worldview is grounded in previous millennia of mythological truth. We have much to learn if we approach mythology as rational *in its own way* instead of a degraded precursor to our own reality postulates.

Henri Frankfort's *Before Philosophy: The Intellectual Adventure of Ancient Man* is a far fairer treatment of the pre-philosophical mind than those of Kirk and many other scholars.[6] In this work, Frankfort tries with great success to get at the distinctively "rational" quality of mythological thinking. Frankfort helps us to appreciate that the mythological works of the ancient Greek world map out a sophisticated logic that captures the enduring nature of patterns of existence.

Ancient Greek myths inquire into the perennial questions of nature, the sacred, and the human condition, and they look into the natural world, to oak and stream, to unlock the secrets of the heavens and things below. They do not simply invent fiction, as the "irrational" reading of myth suggests. Engaging with myth positively and on its own terms can help us to see how people of a different era oriented themselves both conceptually and practically, in order to make sense of their world. One of the founding cosmological myths is the *Theogony* of Hesiod. Hesiod hailed from Boiotia, on the central Greek mainland, and wrote at the close of the eighth through the beginning of the seventh century BCE. Richard Lattimore states that Hesiod's work, and especially the *Theogony*, incorporates themes from very ancient legend, not only from Boiotia and southern Thessaly, but from the whole mainland of Greece. For this reason, it is fair to consider this seminal work a broad report of the Hellenic mythological worldview.

The *Theogony* catalogues the coming-into-being of the Greek pantheon, mapping the genealogy of each power as it comes into being and assumes its place in the cosmos. Hesiod opens by attributing the proem to the inspiration of the Helikonian Muses. The three daughters of Zeus breathe voice into him, he reports, ordering him, a lowly shepherd of the wilderness, to "sing the race of the gods everlasting." Straightway, they warn him to always put them, "the three" [Muses], at the beginnings and ends of his singing. Hesiod's tribute to his divine sources is an early indicator of the importance of boundaries in the ancient Greek worldview. The fault seen as most reprehensible among the ancient Greeks was overbearing pride, a character flaw which drove individuals to overstep their proper bounds, the bounds of common decency and custom. *Hybris* was seen as a most dread moral failing that could upset kingdoms, dethrone kings, and throw the cosmos into chaos. If Hesiod had told his tale in his own name, his act would have constituted an instance of *hybris*. A mere mortal cannot know that truth of heavenly things, so the poet must open with a declaration of his ignorance, and an expression of his gratitude for the divine inspiration that grants him knowledge he could not possibly claim as his own.

For the Greeks, all things derive from the combination of four divine forces—fire, air, earth, and water. Hesiod's genealogy tracks the birth of each of these original forces as divine personalities, with their own

unique powers and spheres of influence. The order of the births is significant since, for the Greeks, the older is always the more powerful
force. Thus it is striking that of all divinities, Chaos arises first. Chaos
gives birth to Erebos (Darkness or Night), who in turn produces the gods
who rule the fate of human beings: Nemesis (the inescapable law of just
desserts that follows wrongdoing without mercy) and the three sisters,
the Moirai—Klotho (spinner of the thread of life), Lachesis (disposer of
lots), and Atropos (unchanging, inflexible).

Gaia (Earth) and Tartarus (Hades) are next on the scene and parent-
less. Then Gaia bares Ouranos, the fiery heavens, and with him, she con-
ceives a great generation of monster-gods, the Titans. But Ouranos tries
to suppress the birth of this next generation, fearful of being deposed by
his sons. Gaia then conspires with her sons to murder their father. Kronos
(Time) castrates his father and from the patriarch's blood springs forth
the Furies, Giants, and Nymphs, and from his severed genitals, Aphro-
dite. Kronos then lies with Rheia and begins a new generation. But he in
turn suppresses his sons. Once again with the collusion of the mother, the
father is violently overcome and the Olympians are born. Zeus takes the
helm of the cosmos after a vicious confrontation with the Titans. But
Zeus is no mere tyrant who rules by force. He makes every attempt to
seduce the Titans through crafty words and alliance. Those he cannot
persuade to his support, he drives into Tartarus with his thunderous
might, aided by the Titan, Prometheus, the Far-seeing.

Hesiod's myth expresses a number of aspects of the Greek experience of world. A fundamental intuition of the Greeks is that the world is
a cosmos—an ordered *uni*-verse, a whole composed of many parts. The
divine is a basic principle of the cosmos, an ontologically privileged, indwelling aspect of the world, which grants to the whole its order, intelli-
gibility, and predictable lawfulness, expressed in political terms. The
order of the cosmos, however, is not achieved by a simple hierarchy of
might. Similarly, Zeus, though the leader of the Olympians, is by no
means an all-powerful hegemon. Still older forces have helped to secure
him his position of leadership, so there are privileges to be observed,
debts to be paid, and reverence to be given on account of their archaic
status. Only where rule is fair and balanced will the ruler be considered
legitimate. Only where boundaries are properly observed, will the monster-gods remain at bay.

In the Greek intuition, the cosmos is a network of interlocking powers, each god and goddess representing an individual ontological privilege point, the peculiar powers of each immanent and concealed in the

aspects of the natural world. The notion of intricate interconnection, spatially ordered, matches the Greek view of the physical world. For the Greeks, there is no sense of "dead matter" to be animated by indwelling gods, but the gods compose the immanent ingredients of life. The earth, a solid round disc, holds the center position, around which water flows in a perfect circle. Above her rises the great brazen sky in a heavenly dome, and equally far below her stretches the dark underworld. The great masses of earth, sea, sky/air/light, and underworld/dark represent spatial domains of the great divinities—Gaia and her daughters, Okeanos and his children, Ouranos and his offspring including Zeus, and Hades/Tartarus. In this worldview, several facets of the Greek intuition of cosmos find expression—the whole is an intelligible, ordered scheme, perfectly symmetrical and thus beautiful. Up and down, far and wide, "the gods are," as Thales declared, "in all things."

The harmony of the whole is never guaranteed but depends upon the will and whim of the ruling divinities, each a unique personality. Keeping the fragile peace is a matter of observing proper boundaries and granting to each of the divine aspects of existence their due respect, honor, and privilege. Since the gods themselves are many and often embroiled in intrigues and torn by conflicted interests, Chaos and the dark powers of Night and the underworld are ever threatening to engulf the cosmos. For the Greeks, balance and boundaries are determined at the cosmic level, embedded in a system of justice and recompense that undergirds the entire cosmic structure. The divine forces stand in an ordered relation to one another. Not only do each of the four major divinities rule within each elemental domain, but they are accompanied and aided by a great number of lesser divinities, from the winds that whip the mainland and the rains that feed the sea, to the well in the garden and the hearth inside the house. Each thing in the Greek world is empowered by its own hidden divine substance, and all are entwined in an elaborate political system of greater and lesser powers.

Human life is lived at the very center of the equally poised polarities of high and low, light and dark, at the very interface of the four great elements of earth, water, fire, and air. Humans stand in a fascinating relation to the divine, according to the Greek worldview. On the one hand, they are utterly powerless against the vacillating whims of the gods. On the other hand, humans can influence the divine, through their religious rites, prayers, and sacrifices, so they do have an ambiguous sort of persuasive power. Myth images the fragility of the cosmic order and the tenuous status of human beings as victims of divine caprice. Perhaps humans could fare better if they could only figure out the logic of the cosmic order and attune their actions with the laws of destiny, but the rules seem to shift and change, just as they align their acts. Artemis refuses favorable winds to blow the Greek fleet toward Troy, until Agamemnon sacrifices his daughter. But since killing kin is a grave offense, Agamemnon brings generations of tragedy upon his family by agreeing to the fatal sacrifice.

Greek relations with the divine were essentially directed toward concrete effects, not idle contemplation. Survival depended upon getting along with these often fickle powers, winning their favor, or at the very least avoiding their wrath. The myths allowed humans to cultivate a knowledge of the individual gods to make their interactions with them more profitable, and less dangerous. The knowledge that the owl is Athena's sacred bird was not merely a quaint piece of folklore, but a grim warning that Athena sees everything. Killing or disturbing a creature of nature was to launch an attack upon a divine realm. Prayers, sacrifices, and other rituals and observances are not so much customs of worship as practical strategies for staying out of trouble and preserving the vital relationship between the human realm and the divine.

The *Theogony* offers a model of justice as communal harmony, which is still worthy of contemplation these long millennia after its writing. First of all, Zeus brings peace to the heavenly throng by two diverse approaches: he uses compulsion to contain the undisciplined forces of monstrousness that will not listen to reason, but he secures the consent of the orderly gods, binding them to him through alliances, respect, and benevolence (line 700 ff.). Monsters keep no boundaries, but the orderly respect laws and boundaries. So Zeus "of the Counsels" sets up a cosmic system where each orderly god exchanges loyalty for the king and respect for her peers for sovereignty in her own domain.

The *Theogony* not only models justice on the macro level as a balance among reigning powers, but it stages a model for communal justice, as the administration over conflicts that arise within society. When disputes or quarreling break out among the immortals, a trial process addresses the cosmic imbalance. From the outset the problem of justice is framed as one of conflicting truths. Zeus sends Iris, daughter of Thaumas (Wonder), "to carry the many-storied water" for the gods to swear upon so that he may determine who is telling the truth about the matter and who is lying (line 780). The untruthful gods, swearing upon the water, are simultaneously revealed as liars and punished for their injustice by being "laid flat without voice or breath" for an entire year. Deprived of ambrosia and nectar, "the evil coma covers him" (line 797-98). Upon awakening from the deathly slumber, the offending god undergoes a second trial, still harsher, where he is ostracized again from the orderly and honest gods and denied part in their counsels and their festivals for nine long years. On the tenth year, the offender is finally permitted reentry to the divine fold and he may at last "[mingle] in the assemblies of the gods" (line 803–804).

The model of justice among the divine community presented in the *Theogony* teaches us a great deal about how the Greeks viewed justice, crime, and punishment. The pantheon is a complex community composed of individuals of great diversity. The least imposing god has a special place and a unique power to influence the rest. This also means that each has special obligations toward the others. And it means that if one individual is not happy, the rest are caught up in her unease. Social order does not mean mere compliance to the mightiest party. Zeus may be the king of the gods, but his influence is not extensive of the cosmos. Justice is dished out by the king, but it is not a simple matter of imposing his might to get what he wants from his social inferiors. Even Zeus cannot overstep his bounds. He must humor the fickle, accommodate the demanding, and respect even the weakest goddess, if the divine chorus is to function with any degree of harmony.

The *Theogony* witnesses the Greek conviction that no community is healthy where even one of its members is discontent. Justice is the tricky business of balancing the fragile egos of powerful individuals. The divine community is a delicate web of interrelations, founded upon mutual respect. One of the primary ways of showing respect to one's fellows and maintaining bounds of propriety is through truthful dealings. Hence oaths and allegiances are given enormous import in the myths. The trials of the gods depict justice as the intervention between conflicted parties for the primary purpose of sorting out the truth from the lies. When a liar is found, the appropriate penalty is separation from the company of his honest fellows—in the solitary confinement of a coma or in exile from the heavens. Deceitful parties are excluded from the divine fold for a substantial period of time, and only readmitted to the community when they have been successfully rehabilitated to moral health.

Homer's Hymn to Demeter

Hesiod's myth demonstrates from a variety of angles that peace is a matter of strict observance of appropriate boundaries. The most powerful god must tell the truth, honor the least powerful, and respect the separate domains of power. Homer's "Hymn to Demeter" echoes many of the themes of justice we have just witnessed in Hesiod's *Theogony*. But where Hesiod draws the grand macro-picture of a web of divine relations, Homer demonstrates in the micro-instance the power of a single offended god. Havoc befalls the entire cosmos when one god disrespects another, reminding the listener of the fragile balance of power that holds the cosmos intact, and the limited power of the most powerful king to hold back the forces of chaos, when the bounds of *timē* have been offended.

First, a word about "Homer" is needed. Homer is named the author of the two epic poems, the *Iliad* and the *Odyssey*, which draw upon a series of events that date to (or were imagined to have occurred) during the Bronze Age, that is, no later than the twelfth century BCE.[7] Thus these works are dated as having been written slightly later than those of Hesiod, during the eighth century BCE, and although they address the earlier era when a "great king" still reigned in Mycenae, they reflect the worldview and political realities of the later period, "when Greece was fragmented into small communities presided over by hereditary aristocrats known as kings."[8]

Homer's name is also uncritically assigned to thirty-three anonymous poems celebrating individual Greek gods. These, known as the Homeric Hymns, were probably written in the seventh century BCE. The Homeric Hymns are "Homeric" only in the sense that they are written in much the same style as the earlier epic poems; that is, they use the same epic meter, the dactylic hexameter, that was employed in the *Iliad* and *Odyssey*, they repeat many similar poetic formulae, and they are written in the same Hellenic dialect. They were uncritically attributed to Homer in antiquity, and the label has stuck to this day.[9] But there is little doubt in scholarly minds that these poems were written by a number of different bards.

The "Hymn to Demeter" gives us a compelling glimpse of the complex dialectic of independence and obligation that the Greeks understood to characterize relations among the powerful—both in the human world and among the gods that made up their pantheon. Though the pantheon is framed as a monarchy under the powerful king Zeus, this was no simple top-down coercive model of absolute governance. Let us consider the crisis that Zeus finds himself facing in this telling myth.

The tale opens with Zeus having affronted the earth-mother Demeter, by giving the goddess' daughter, Persephone, as wife to their brother

Hades. Hades lives in the dark netherworld below the earth, far from the
mother's green and sunny realm. The poet names Hades "the lord, Host
of Many," demonstrating the Greek reluctance even to directly name the
underworld or its sovereign deity. The dark god has violently seized Persephone and carried her away to the lower world. The poet describes the
abduction as *akon* (without consent). Queenly Demeter becomes aware
of the crime when she hears her daughter's cries ringing, from the
heights of the snowy mountains to the depths of the watery sea. Demeter
sets out in search of Persephone, wandering across the earth, refusing
"ambrosia and nectar" (i.e., the company of the gods) until her quest is
ended. Her fellow gods finally take pity upon her and inform her of her
daughter's fate. The problem is not that the marriage is unacceptable, as
the Son of Hyperion argues: "the Ruler of Many is not an unfitting husband and [is] born of the same stock" (line 11.86). The problem is that
Demeter has not consented to the marriage. The crisis centers about the
akon nature of the marriage. The offense has encroached upon her prerogative to herself choose a fitting husband for her daughter.

Demeter is not to be placated; in her sorrow, she ceases to carry out
the queenly duties attached to her position as Earth Mother. She with-
draws life from earth. "[Sitting] apart from all the blessed gods [she]
stayed, wasting with yearning for her deep-bosomed daughter" (line
11.308-10). For a year, the earth refuses to take seed, and ploughing is in
vain. As a result, the race of men are cast into a cruel famine. Blaming
the gods of Olympus for their predicament, they withhold their custom-
ary sacrifices. Now all the divine choir is dragged into the crisis, angry
and upset that the sacrifices have ceased. They then decide it is high time
to intercede and pressure Zeus to put things right.

Zeus then displays the craftiness for which he was made king of the
gods in the first place; he devises a compromise that placates both Hades
and Demeter. Persephone will spend part of the year on the sunny earth
with her mother, and part of the year with her husband in the dark underworld (the myth thereby explaining the barrenness of the earth during
the winter months). Demeter ultimately gives her consent (*hekon*) and
peace returns to the heavens as does fruitfulness to the earth.

The hymn is notable for a number of different insights it grants us
into the archaic Greek worldview. The poem demonstrates that the gods
are not contained by, or circumscribed within, their natural domains, but
enjoy a sovereignty and independence that stretches well beyond their
material substances and their cosmic territories. The myth is didactic,
teaching the lesson so fundamental to the Greek worldview: the impor-

tance of observing boundaries, disciplining one's actions, avoiding *hybris*, and respecting the other's domain. The hymn witnesses the tragic consequences of dishonoring a powerful peer. It displays as well how a community of powerful forces can act as a united force to pressure the mightiest leader into changing his ways. The poem provides a model for democratic action to influence the outcome of a crisis in the direction of peaceful resolution and a model for legitimate governance in managing conflict. As I have indicated, the gods of the Greek pantheon form an interlocking system. When they stick together in upholding the *timē* of a single member, they all win, because they all get to live in a more just and democratic society.

The hymn also demonstrates the aristocratic ideal of justice as *dikephoros* since justice is focused upon placating the anger of the offended party. Only the offended, in this case Demeter, can say when the penalty is just and the payment is complete. She must grant her consent (*hekon*) to the settlement of her daughter's fate, before the matter can be put to rest. She must put aside her anger, if the community is to return to peace.

Each of the gods and goddesses of the Greek pantheon has its domain of power and privilege, but the law against *hybris* and in respect of lawful boundaries holds sway over all individuals. Impersonal, objective moral forces hold sway in the background of the divine drama. Moira (Destiny), Dikē (Justice), Tūchē (Fate, unfathomable and dark), and Ananke (Necessity) help to maintain the delicate balance of power among the volatile divinities, as they also do in human affairs. No individual, not even Zeus, can upset the scales of *timē* without having to pay recompense. The cosmic balance is fragile, precarious at best, and regularly falls apart. When this occurs and cosmic harmony is lost, the entire community suffers. The guilty and the innocent alike endure the consequences of injustice, rendering it crucial that the entire community take part in the work of justice. Until the scales have been rebalanced and due recompense has been paid to the offended, none can function effectively.

Another important feature of the Greek worldview, revealed in Homer's Hymn, is that all the gods are "Janus-faced." That is, they have a terrible beauty, a beautiful power. This view of the divine tells us several things about the Greeks who admired them. First, it shows that the Greeks had a very positive attitude toward strong passions, despite the trouble they can cause. The Greeks seem to have considered anger, vindictiveness, jealousy, resentment, hatred, and especially moral outrage to be entirely necessary and appropriate responses to situations of injustice.

Passions, even excessive ones, have their proper place and function in the full human life.

I have said that the hymn shows clearly the fragility of the cosmic order. This fragility has enormous implications for the human world as well, given the non-symmetrical relation between the divine and the human. If the stable order of the heavens is as precarious as the poem suggests, resting on the fluctuating relations among capricious and unpredictable gods, how much more tenuous is the lot of mere human beings? Humans are in the ancient tales depicted as simple victims of the divine drama, pawns in celestial games of intrigue, privilege, and sanction. They appear in the myths only in fleeting glimpses and they enjoy very few champions among the pantheon.

Yet humans are not without power in their own small way, if power is the ability to influence the actions of others. The gods do not *need* human sacrifices, but they are certainly happier for them. Divine privilege means little without the counterpart of the lowly; divine lives are clearly impoverished when humans cease to sacrifice to them. However humble and helpless, we humans do matter in the great scheme of things. Inferior beings may compose a relatively inconsequential aspect of the cosmic whole, yet because a common *logos*, a reasonable order, runs through the entire universe, the human world too enjoys its little share of reason, its own simple beauty and wisdom.

Notes

1. Trevor J. Saunders, *Plato's Penal Code* (Oxford: Clarendon Press, 1991); Contra A. W. H. Adkins, *Moral Values and Political Behavior in Ancient Greece* (London, Eng.: Chatto & Windus, 1960) and M. M. Mackenzie, *Plato on Punishment* (Cambridge: Cambridge University Press, 1981).

2. Thomas Aquinas, *Summa Theologica* Art. 1, Obj. 5.

3. By the fourth century, the wealthy elites of the Areopagus had been subordinated to the authority of the *demos* and Athens became a truly radical democracy.

4. Jacques Rancière, *Disagreements: Politics and Philosophy*, Julie Rose, trans. (Minneapolis: University of Minnesota Press, 1999).

5. G. S. Kirk, *Myth* (Cambridge, MA: Cambridge University Press, 1970), 1-51.

6. Henri Frankfort, *Before Philosophy: The Intellectual Adventure of Ancient Man* (Harmondsworth: Pelican Books, 1949), especially 11–35, 137–165, and 237–263.

7. Michael Gagarin and Paul Woodruff, eds. and trans., *Early Greek Political Thought from Homer to the Sophists* (Cambridge, Eng.: Cambridge University Press, 1995), x.

8. Ibid.

9. A. W. Verrall, "The Hymn to Apollo: An Essay in the Homeric Question" in *Journal of Hellenic Studies*, Vol. 14: (1894:1-29), 2.

Chapter 2
Justice and Punishment in Greek Tragedy

Greek tragedy gets its name from *tragoidia* (from *tragos* or "goat") and *aeidein* ("to sing"). The origin of the odd name of this specific form of drama is traced to an archaic practice of giving a goat as the prize in competitions of choral dancing. Or it may simply be that the goat was the unfortunate animal sacrificed at the festival where tragedies were performed.[1] Greek tragedy offers another rich opportunity to contemplate archaic notions of justice and punishment. The tragedies of the classical period retell the old myths, yet, written many centuries after Hesiod and Homer were writing, they grant us a glimpse into the worldview of the Greeks in the classical era.

Tragedy meditates extensively upon the nature of justice and the place of punishment in human life and communal affairs. Danielle S. Allen catalogs thirty-eight instances of punishments or attempts to punish in Aeschylus, forty-three in Sophocles, and eighty-four in Euripides.[2] These dramas take up from many angles the eternal question of the relationship among justice, legitimacy, and punishment. The relenting focus upon these crucial notions may be explained by the fact that Greek tragic drama finds its apex in times when ancient societies were in a state of highest unrest. The tragic poets reflect upon their changing world with disappointment, doubt, pride, and (given the depth of paradox highlighted in every tragedy) sheer philosophical wonder.

There was certainly much to excite people's wonder in the Athens of Aeschylus' lifetime (c. 524-456 BCE). He witnessed the reform of the Athenian constitution to allow full participatory citizenship; he saw both the dark and the beneficent sides of tyranny under the thirty-six year rule of the house of the Peisistratids. He beheld Athens' fleet gain dominion of the Aegean, and her armies take command of a united Hellenic league, leading them to permanently expel the Persian "*barbaroi*." He watched her lead her friends to triumph, roust her enemies, and expand her material prosperity and her prestige as an international power and a world center of culture and commerce.

Aeschylus himself fought in the battle of Marathon so he knew fortitude in battle, heroic sacrifice, courage against overwhelming odds, and the sweet taste of victory against overwhelming odds. He watched brave men from diverse cities bond together as "Hellenes" to defeat barbaric insolence. Then he witnessed as Athens showed the cruel face of power. She turned into an empire, began dictating policy to her allies, seized league funds for her private interests, bullied her friends, enslaved and slaughtered neutral neighbors, and ultimately betrayed the values by which she defined herself; Athena, the patron goddess of Athens, is the divinity of justice and wisdom, as well as war.

Aeschylus reports, but he also brings to philosophical reflection and challenges, Attic national life, as well as prevailing assumptions about justice, power, freedom, the rights and responsibilities of leaders and sovereign peoples, and the obligations of the powerful to their citizens and neighbors. The eternal themes that Greek myth explores in its elusive imagery—the mysterious agencies of destiny and fate, the rights and limits of the mightiest ruler, the meaning of suffering and its value in the formation of heroic character—Aeschylus brings to philosophical fulfillment in his brooding analyses of the workings of power and the miseries of powerlessness. He appropriates the timeless, universal truths regarding human greatness and folly, sketched out in the myths, and brings them to pointed philosophical reflection in the microcosm of the polis.

Aeschylus' *Prometheus Bound*

Aeschylus' tragedy, *Prometheus Bound*, directly investigates the relationship among justice, political legitimacy, and punishment. It explores questions such as: does might make right, what constitutes just rule and loyal citizenship, and what is the right response to wrongdoing? The tragedy raises a challenge to the legitimacy of a ruler in failing to punish rightly, denies justice to his subjects. In this tragedy, Aeschylus stages a face-off between the political ideology of "might is right" and statesmanship as the science of "appropriate measure."

The tragedy is set at the opening of the reign of the mighty Zeus, just after of his ascent as the leader of the heavenly throng. Prometheus, the Far-Sighted, of the first generation of monster-gods, had helped Zeus to overcome his brothers, the Titan monster-gods. But once Zeus' rule was secured through strategy and alliance with the orderly gods, the king is not so generous with human beings. He determines from the outset to annihilate the human race.

Prometheus has a special love for the human race, feels pity for their weakness, and comes to their aid. Stealing fire from the gods in the heavens, he makes of it an ambiguous "gift" to humankind—ambiguous because the gift is not his to give and far from being a blessing, it will elicit toward them even greater bitterness from the powerful king of the gods. Prometheus greatly improves the lowly lot of humans, who, before this, had had a most difficult time scraping a decent life from the earthly hollows where they crouched. Fire brought the arts and all manner of *techne* (craft), including tools for cultivating crops and weapons to fight their enemies. But Zeus is furious about Prometheus' impertinence; he sees this gift as a theft that blurs the boundaries between divine and human realms, upsetting the balance of the *timē* of heavenly privilege—fire is for the gods alone! Zeus feels dishonored by the willful betrayal of this impudent lesser god.

This is the point where the play opens. There has been no trial before a jury of Prometheus' peers; no counsel has advocated for his defense; he has had no public hearing. Zeus has simply declared Prometheus guilty and condemned him to a cruel sentence: he is to be riveted, by the divine smith Hephaestus, to the rocky wall of the Scythian mountain overlooking the broad Ocean, in the most remote limits of the earth and in the dead of winter. The incarceration in lands and weather entirely forbidding ensures his utter isolation, far beyond all possibility of company or sympathy, especially human companionship. This is emphasized as an important aspect of the punishment: "No voice nor form of mortal man shall meet thy ken" (lines 22–23). Prometheus will have no witness to his suffering, no sympathetic ear for his wailings. There will be no hearing for his case.

The offense is *hybris*, the sheer arrogance that oversteps the bounds of propriety, and this *hybris* has been treacherous, challenging the sovereign dictate of the king. Kratos (Power) and Bia (Force) are sent to oversee that the sentence is carried out. Kratos confirms the dual nature of Prometheus' crime: "Such is his offence; [Prometheus has] brook[ed] the sovereignty of Zeus" (line 10–11) and "he hath betrayed [the king's] pre-rogative to mortals" (line 38). Kratos and Bia have not the slightest doubt about the just nature of Zeus' dictate. They are satisfied that the king's word is right. When justice is calculated according to power and force, a sovereign's dictates are by definition just. Justice is the act of a sovereign, justified by the fact of his power and sovereignty. Might is right.

Kratos argues that the punishment is fair; thus Zeus is not a tyrant. Zeus punishes rightly and thus he is rightly king. Bia, on the other hand, argues that the punishment is fair *because* Zeus is king and the king decides what constitutes justice. Might is right. Hephaestus, by contrast, is not at all certain that this punishment fulfills the demands of justice. Playing the role of advocate, he alludes to Prometheus' defense: "I cannot nerve myself to bind a kindred god upon this rocky cleft" (lines 14–15). The implied argument upon which Hephaestus questions the justness of Prometheus' punishment is the special consideration owing to kin.

Ultimately and despite his misgivings, the divine smith acquiesces and carries out his duty out of fear for his own safety, explaining that "it is perilous to disregard the commandments of the Father" (lines 16–17). Hephaestus protests and complains the entire while that he carries out the task assigned him, concluding with a statement that underscores the infancy of Zeus' reign: "Everyone is harsh whose power is new," the smith declares (line 35).

Hephaestus' mention of a "new king" is meant to remind Aeschylus' audience that Zeus fits the definition of a tyrant. He has taken cosmic power by force; he has not succeeded legitimately to the throne or been invited to it by willing subjects. "New" power always raises the question of whether the ruler is a tyrant. Just as in the "Hymn to Demeter," Zeus must secure the agreement (*hekon*) of the gods, if his dictates are to be legitimate and find support among the heavenly throng. A new god must take great pains to rule rightly and secure consent for his edicts. By dishing out justice harshly and arbitrarily to a fellow god and former ally, Zeus puts in question his right to rule. Hephaestus launches a formidable defense in connecting the infancy of Zeus' reign with the justness of Prometheus' punishment.

Hephaestus' charge is echoed by Prometheus: "I know that Zeus is harsh and keepeth justice in his own hands" (lines 189–90). Playing upon the connection Hephaestus has drawn between legitimacy and right punishment, Prometheus insists upon a hearing, a fair trial before his peers, and not an arbitrary punishment. He wants his day in court. He calls upon his fellow gods and the Chorus as his judges. He pleads his case and his defense is a familiar aristocratic argument of peer obligation, honor, and prerogative: he is a victim of dishonor, tyranny, and ingratitude. He recounts his services to Zeus during his ascent to power and explains his reasons for assisting the pitiable mortals (lines 199–243).

At the close of his testimony, another mighty god of the older generation enters; the mighty Okeanos too expresses sympathy and pity for Prometheus and asks how he may aid him. Again the newness of Zeus' reign is recalled, as Okeanos counsels pragmatism: "Adapt to thyself new ways, for new likewise is the ruler amongst the gods" (lines 311–312). He does not say that Zeus is right. He only says that he is king now, and can dictate the terms of justice. The sympathetic Okeanos, affirms that might is right.

Then the play takes a curious turn. Aeschylus introduces a long-suffering victim of the mighty king Zeus. The maiden Io enters and recounts the tale of her woes, and begs Prometheus, the Far-seeing, to foretell her fate. The tale serves as a further commentary upon Zeus' brand of arbitrary and cruel justice. But it also reminds us of a curious irony: Prometheus is the trickster, hence his ambiguous gift/theft. But he is also the far-seeing god. He must have known in advance what fate would befall him if he crossed the mighty king. This changes our way of looking at his punishment, suggesting he wagered in full awareness of the price that he has come to pay.

Io tells her tale. Against her wishes Zeus has lusted after her for long years. Yet now Zeus' jealous wife Hera blames the girl for her husband's attentions. She cruelly torments her and drives her across the wide lands of the earth. "Gadfly-hunted," she is besieged by a maddening heaven-sent plague. Though the girl is innocent and Zeus professes to love her, he does not intercede to help her. Prometheus' prophecy does not reveal happier times ahead for her. Rather, the girl's story resonates with Prometheus's predicament: they are both victims of powerful gods who are quite content to watch them suffer.

Prometheus is riveted to the rocky crag but he is not without counsel and defense. In keeping with his epithet, "the Devious-Devising," he has managed to launch a defense, argue his case, draw supporters from his peer group, and sway the sympathies of the audience (representing public opinion). At this point in the tragedy, he reveals a further weapon, a secret up his sleeve. His mother has disclosed to him a piece of foreknowledge that is enormously important to the king who chains him. The knowledge can save Zeus from his father's fate of becoming unseated from power by a future son. Prometheus can save the dominion of Zeus, but he will not reveal the secret until he is released from his punishment. The tables of the contest seem to turn on Zeus.[3]

Prometheus' final visitor is Hermes, the winged messenger. Hermes enters the scene and advises Prometheus against overconfidence in contests against Zeus. The king too has more secrets up his sleeve. Zeus, as all strong monarchs, can weather contestation in proportion to his strength, and he has quite an arsenal of punishments at his disposal to wait out Prometheus' compliance. Hermes warns:

> First, the Father will shatter this jagged cliff with thunder and lightning-flame, and will entomb thy frame, while the rock shall still hold thee clasped in its embrace. But when thou hast completed a long stretch of time, thou shalt come back again to the light. Then verily the winged hound of Zeus, the ravening eagle, coming an unbidden banqueter the whole day long, with savage appetite shall tear thy body piecemeal into great rents and feast his fill upon thy liver till it be black with gnawing. (lines 1016–1025)

Prometheus is faced with a full battery of punishments—binding, exile, public shaming, exile to Tartarus, and endless torture. Subtle accents of contested truths separate Prometheus from Zeus in their understanding of the conflict between them—socio-political values, notions of sovereignty and legitimacy, rights and responsibilities of kinship, political allegiance, the obligations of friendship, the special privilege due on the basis of social status and honor, the rigors of political expedience, and the simple urgency of maintaining social order under a new regime.

The confrontation between the powerful Zeus and his weaker prisoner, Prometheus, while it raises many compelling questions, ultimately highlights the arbitrary nature of justice, as a handmaiden of political power. It reminds us of Socrates' question to Euthyphro, in Plato's *Euthyphro*: Is a thing good because the gods love it, or do the gods love it because it is good? The confrontation urges us to think beyond the play, beyond myth, beyond history's conundrums, to our own systems of justice, pressing us to consider: what makes for what people come to name "justice" in their states? Do their laws and systems of justice reflect the interests of the dominant person or class of the society, those who enjoy social power and political voice? Do the laws and courts uphold minimal safeguards put in place by the enlightened few to ensure that the weakest and least powerful citizens have some recourse against the strong? Or are they a reflection of higher, more universal interests—the common good, the decent thing to do, rules of propriety that would be agreed upon as the most rudimentary moral standards applicable to all individuals within any civilized society?

The tragedy *Prometheus Bound* forces us to take a fresh look at the relations among justice, punishment, and legitimacy. We rarely stop to question the workings of power in the exercise of justice or punishment. We tend to accept as unimpeachable the laws that impose order. But laws (*logoi*) are simply words (*logoi*), bound by a logic (*logos*) that generally serves power. The tragedy demands that we pay attention to the language and the logic we use when we think and speak about justice, and to consider whom our justice serves, and who is left hung out to dry without a fair hearing.

In the opening lines of the work, justice is presented in its traditional imagery, a set of scales—give and take, honor and responsibility. Relationships must be balanced for order to reign. In taking fire from the gods and giving it to lesser creatures, Prometheus shown disloyalty to his king—loving what Zeus hates. But he has also upset the fragile balance of *timē* (honor) which holds the cosmos intact. Fire is the property of the gods. Prometheus does not simply owe recompense to Zeus, but he is "bound to make requital to the gods" (*dei theois dounai dikēn*), literally "give to the gods justice" (line 9). A single member within a society of peers, who oversteps the bounds of propriety and tips the scales of *timē*, harms the whole of the society by undermining its stable foundations, its tightly balanced integrity. The offender must make recompense (*didonai dikēn* or "give justice") if those scales are to find balance once again.

Aeschylus demonstrates how the archaic model of *dikephoros* justice is simple retribution or vengeance. The "give and take" of honors is, in reality, a "give and take" of shame. Zeus felt dishonored by Prometheus' disrespect for him, his orders, and his power; Prometheus is now dishonored in this spectacle of shame, hung out on the rocks like a piece of dirty laundry. The lonely setting signifies that the one who offends the social peace is unfit for society, and must be exiled from it until he learns his lesson. Yet, we cannot help but notice that the play stages the trial that Zeus denied Prometheus, where we, the audience and the Chorus act as Prometheus' jury. The plot of the play enacts the drawn-out trial process, permitting us to hear all sides of the story. Despite the remoteness of the setting, Prometheus' case is heard, and sympathetically. We, the audience, find ourselves sympathizing with Prometheus and wondering at the cruel judgment of the king of the gods. The Chorus represents both the contemporary audience of classical Athens and the social conscience of the divine peer group, and they too are sympathetic to Prometheus' plight.

The language of shame/dishonor (*atimos*), threaded through the tragedy, persistently highlights the importance of honor and shame in the ancient rendering of justice. It demonstrates that justice is agreed by all to be about the *right* distribution of honor and the conferring of *appropriate* respect to peers. But the conflict between the Titan and the King show too that calculations of *rightness*, in the minds of gods (and men), can depart very far from each other, when emotions color reason. The problem is that in matters of justice, there is generally so much at stake— honor, family name, ancestral pride, political legitimacy—that a common rendering between defendant and prosecutor is an enormous challenge with grave consequences.

The tragedy also highlights another crucial ancient assumption: innocent or guilty, just or unjust, the shame inheres in the being wronged, and not in the doing wrong. Prometheus is innocent, he claims, yet he is "blasted in these shackles of shame" and suffers a "shameful disgrace"; his torture is "a spectacle of shame." He is warned by the Chorus: "'Tis shameful for the wise to persist in error" (line 1039). On the other hand, the far-seeing god recognizes that "For foe to suffer ill from foe is no disgrace" (line 1041–042).

Shame is given a great deal of attention in this tragedy about divine justice and punishment, because shame plays a crucial role in the workings of justice within the Greek society of powerful peers before whom the tragedy will be staged. Justice is thought through, weighed up and dished out, in archaic Greece, just as the play has depicted it—according to distributions of honor and shame. The trial (*timesis*) will hear, measure, reassess, deny, or redistribute honors among the conflicted parties. If the offender is declared guilty, he will be dishonored by some form of punishment (*timoria*). Punishing (*timoresthai*) names the process whereby honors are properly apportioned once again, rebalancing the peer relationships that have been damaged by the crime. Punishment can alternatively be expressed in the language of justice. Punishing is "taking justice" (*lambanein dikēn*) from the offender; accepting punishment is a "giving justice" (*didonai dikēn*).

Aeschylus, in *Prometheus Bound*, is exploring the give and take of honors that compose justice in the Greek intuition. He is also demonstrating the ambiguous fact that what is accounted as due honors to each in a society of peers is both determined and challenged from within the arrangements of power. In *dikephoros* justice, social equals can lay claim to the social conscience and claim their due. But the less powerful, such as Io and Prometheus' human beneficiaries, are powerless against the powerful gods. Having no honor of their own, they can make no claim to justice.

On the other hand, sometimes a victim's very powerlessness composes her power to influence the social body. The victim's helplessness can call forth pity and stimulates the intervention of other powerful personages. Pity and generosity toward the weak are clearly valued qualities of character in the ancient world of aristocrats. They compose the worldly demonstrations of noble-mindedness. However, the weaker cannot count in all circumstances upon the generosity of the powerful. As witnessed in the *Iliad*, with Odysseus' harsh treatment of the commoner Thersites (lines 243–269) who dared to speak up his opinion on the matter of war strategy, lesser men can be punished sorely for the *hybris* of intervening in the counsels of better men.

The *Prometheus Bound* closes with a stand-off between the weak and the strong, the wit and foresight of the seer against the dogged will of the mighty Zeus. The stand-off signals to the audience that matters of justice are never simple, clear and easily resolved. That is precisely why the trial must be in the form of a process, which gives voice to all accents and subtleties of the matter, and not be settled simply with a sweeping command of a powerful king. A king, as all his subjects, must observe the traditions and customs of their group. They must weigh up each and every testimony, in light of timeworn expectations of the community, honoring past practices, weighing present unique circumstances, and considering too future exigencies and vulnerabilities, which will ultimately affect the entire community, if the trial does not conclude to the satisfaction of all.

Aeschylus' *Oresteia*

Aeschylus' *Oresteia* is a tragic trilogy that gives expression to the mythical tale that traces the fate of the house of Atreus, following its heroes, the kings of Argos, from Argos to Troy and back again, across Greece to the "far country" of Phocus, to Delphi and ultimately to Athens, where Athena will intervene to bring a formal system of justice into being.

In the first book, the "Agamemnon," we find the Kings of Argos, Menelaus and Agamemnon, about to set sail for Troy to reclaim Helen, Menelaus' wife, who has been "stolen" by the prince of Troy, Paris, during his visit to the court of Menelaus. The offense is an outrage on a number of levels, at the highest level, an affront to Zeus, who is the divine overseer of host/guest relations, guardian of the rights of hospitality and protector of strangers. The powerful king Menelaus has been disgraced by the young Paris, and is honor-bound to pursue the culprit and reclaim his wife, though there is some question as to whether this was a willing abduction on the wife's part.

However, the goddess Artemis opposes the mission to Troy to reclaim the wife. This is curious since Artemis is the goddess of both midwifery and the hunt—guardian of both the hunter and the forest creatures that they hunt. Since Artemis is goddess of the hunt, one might expect that she would readily throw her support behind this seemingly just hunt for the offender and rescue of the (ambiguous) victim. However, not only does she not rally for this cause on the expected side, she, goddess of midwifery, demands for her support of the mission the sacrifice of a child. Artemis sends adverse winds that hold the kings' thousand ships at Aulis, until a child ransom is paid. To appease the goddess and reverse the winds, Agamemnon has been directed to sacrifice with his own hands his young daughter, Iphigenia. Agamemnon completes the sacrifice, alienating his wife Clytemnestra. Then, winds in their sails at last, the warships sail away, and, in the fated tenth year of their siege of Troy, they make good their victory and decimate the kingdom of their enemies.

The war may have ultimately proven successful for the king brothers, but its tragic consequences long outlive its victors. Agamemnon's wife Clytemnestra, having kept herself occupied during the war years plotting with her husband's cousin Aegisthus, no sooner welcomes her husband home from the war but takes her revenge for her daughter's murder. She kills her husband and his war-prize mistress Cassandra, and assumes rule in the land of Argos.

The second book, the "Libation Bearers," sees Agamemnon's son return from the far country, Phocis, where he has long been living with his uncle Strophius. When he is grown, Orestes is divinely commissioned by Apollo to exact revenge upon his mother for his father's betrayal and murder. Again the ironies of divine justice abound. If he does not revenge his father, he will suffer assault from the cruel Erinyes (Furies), the daughters of dark Night who see to it that blood murders are revenged. However, once he returns to Argus and dishes out the vengeance he is commissioned to apply, killing his mother and her lover Aegisthus, the Erinyes then are drawn to chase and torture him—for spilling the blood of a mother. "Damned if he does; damned if he doesn't" is the law of blood vengeance that rules the archaic world and torments the hapless Orestes. Aeschylus seems not to make much of this fatefulness that victimizes even those who comply with their laws of vengeance. On the other hand, he is setting the scene for the final book in the trilogy, where the problem will be highlighted precisely in its finding resolution.

The third book, the "Eumenides," finds Orestes, the tortured victim of the Erinyes, at the shrine of Apollo at Delphi, throwing himself on the mercy of the god who had gotten him into this problem in the first place. Orestes begs the god of prophecy for his support in escaping the fearsome Furies. Apollo, in his far-seeing wisdom, sends Orestes to Athens to submit his case to the goddess Athena, deity of wisdom and justice. Pallas Athena, most telling in her wisdom, asserts that the case is too difficult for a goddess alone to decide. So she proposes to judge the case, not alone, but with the assistance of a chosen group of her best citizens. Significantly, she must secure the consent of the Erinyes, reminding us of one of the core messages of Homer's "Hymn to Demeter."

The Erinyes grant their consent, and the first formal "trial" of the archaic world is begun. In this third book of the trilogy, we witness the trial process in its perfect form. The Furies are the plaintiffs (though for the modern reader, the victim and persecutor roles may seem to be reversed). They render their charge. The defendant's counsel responds. Apollo shows up to play the role of counsel for the defense. He defends the accused Orestes, explaining that the slaying of the mother was at his direct behest, for her prior murderous and treacherous acts; the accusers, the Erinyes, should have taken vengeance upon the mother, saving Orestes from that task. The Erinyes answer the counter-charge, rejecting it on the grounds that Clytemnestra was not a murderess of a blood relative, as was Orestes. Apollo responds with a most insight-rendering argument— that a son is not a blood kin to his mother because the mother is the simple receptacle of the father's implanted seed. The vote is cast and the vote even. Athena renders final judgment in favor of the plaintiff.

The Furies are angry at the acquittal and charge the "younger gods" with having "contravened ancient laws" against familial blood-letting.

But Athena pleads with them "not to bear it with sore lament" (line 794). "Proud honors" and a home alongside her in Attica, the goddess promises to them, if they will but grant their consent. Finally, their anger subsides and they give their broad blessings to the city of Athens and then, against their ancient charge, they ban "deadly and untimely fate for men" (lines 56–7). At this moment of goodwill when their anger has softened to blessing, their cruel names are suddenly changed to Eumenides, the fair-minded ones, witnessing again the importance of the consent of the victim in settling matters of justice. Now that their consent and support for the court has been granted, the matter under judgment has reached a happy conclusion, the conflict put to rest, and the community healed.

Aeschylus is showing us a number of important things about justice and punishment in the *Oresteia*. He is demonstrating through the convoluted twists of the plot of this trilogy that when victims seek out justice in their own cases, their anger is excessive, relentless, merciless, and persistent, and until the anger has been healed, the conflict remains an open wound in the society, resulting in resentment, misery, and bloodshed that floods across multiple generations.

The court system permits the opportunity for a healing of this wound. By exposing the injury before a court of the victim's peers, the victim's outrage is granted a public airing. Often this is all that is needed to calm the excessive passion of the enraged victim. However, the trial then allows an opportunity for a public defense of the offender's reasons for his actions. This too is an important part of the process, not only for the sake of winning over the mercy of the jury, but in helping the victim to understand any special circumstances that framed the offender's behavior.

The trial is an intricate and elaborate process. In ancient Athens a trial might take an entire day to decide. Its process quality is what made it work so well. Simply through the slow and determinate progression of the series of hearings, all the parties are in turn allowed to speak their position, give their reasons, and plead their cause. This process channels the victim's rage, while it also forces them to move beyond mere passion to the frame their complaint in the language of the court. So reason must intervene to make sense of their claim. Similarly, the defendant must direct her pleas for mercy in the terms, form, and language of public debate. In this simple requirement that the court places upon the victim and the defendant, that they reframe their side of the issue into reasonable and logical argument, much of the work of justice is achieved.

Aeschylus is showing his audience that the passions have their fitting place in the human drama. Outrage must be voiced if it is to be ultimately soothed, and pity is called upon to temper the overbearing punishing hand. Indeed, the court itself always strives to err on the side of generosity, and a split vote is taken to be an acquittal. In the final accounting, it is ordered, controlled reason that must triumph to bring justice to human affairs, but reason that has a human face, a gentle ear, and a generous, sympathetic spirit.

In the context of a society of powerful peers, the heroic ethos can favor an egoistic individualism, but the system of trial by jury models a higher ethos that favors mercy, altruism, and service of the common good. The jury trial expresses the Greek trust in reasoned public debate as curative of social unrest. The object of the trial is to give hearing to all parties and show public concern for individual misery. Punishments are levied on social offenders only as a last resort, where the trial process has proven incapable of allaying the victim's outrage and putting the community to rest.

Among the arsenal of potential punishments available to the court system—death penalty, exile from the city or from all or some public places within the city for varying periods of time, public shaming, monetary penalty, or mercy—the latter is accepted as the most divine response to wrongdoing. Preferable is the public trial that ends generously, where the dishonored secures through persuasive speech, the support of his community and the return of his honor, without having to bring dishonor to another citizen.

Greek tragedy takes the questions myth posits at a cosmic level and applies them explicitly to the life of human beings as they act freely among their fellows and suffer the consequences of their actions. The heroic adventures staged in tragic poetry bring into relief the impulses that make human beings great, as well as the passions and impulses that cause their downfall. Tragedy portrays individuals at their finest and at their most degraded, as they struggle against the backdrop of the mysterious agencies of destiny and fate.

Myth's cosmic fatalism provides a compelling arena for the dramatization of the universal human struggle. In *Prometheus Bound*, the Chorus asks the Far-Sighted god "Who is the steersman of Necessity?" Prometheus answers, "The Fates, three-formed, and the mindful Furies" (lines 515–16). The daughters of dark Night and the maddening Erinyes have power greater even than the king of the gods; "he cannot escape what is foredoomed," tells the sure-sighted Titan (line 518).

Prometheus' tortures at the solitary ends of the earth beg comparison with Orestes' lonely torment, as he is pursued by the relentless Erinyes across the broad landscape of Greece. Prometheus has been denied a trial among his peers, and suffers at the hands of the arbitrary dictates of a jealous king, so he makes of his punitive spectacle an informal trial. His "hearing" finds ready reception among his divine peers and their compassion for his predicament mirrors his own pity for lesser creatures, the substance of his crime. His true judge, the powerful Zeus, is conspicuously absent from the trial, however.

By comparison, Athena's trial by jury staged in the *Oresteia* appears a healthy alternative. The trial represents a careful process that allows voice to all interested parties. Each is "heard" and then the details of the case are deliberated at great length among the community of peers. Most importantly, the trial finds closure in an ethos of generosity that chooses to forego punishments, and since the defendant's prosecutors have granted their consent to its decision, both the rage of the victim and the resentment of the defendant are put to rest, no longer to threaten communal integrity and peace.

The comparison between the two trials is stark. Both original crimes involve the contravention of an ancient law. Prometheus has upset the balance of *timē* in granting the heaven's fire to a lesser ontological realm. Orestes has killed his mother and brought pollution on himself and his progeny. The divine response to the two crimes is utterly opposed. Zeus grants no hearing to his accused and so his punishment appears arbitrary and cruel, the dictate of might, rather than right. The goddess Athena, on the contrary, shows both wisdom and humility, in declaring Orestes' case too great for a goddess alone to decide, and calls upon the community of peers to deliberate the matter.

At the close of *Prometheus Bound*, nothing has been resolved. Prometheus still suffers, Zeus is still angry, and the pantheon is torn apart by conflicted loyalties. Fear, resentment, and rage govern the final scene. Where might is right, justice capricious, and punishment harsh, discord continues to plague the entire community. On the other hand, the *Oresteia* closes with gods and humans attuned, all parties satisfied with the conclusion, and communal peace restored. The formal trial in Athens offers a higher brand of justice, which overcomes the dangerous passions in victim and accused. The trial by jury is not simply a more merciful response to wrongdoing than the response of an arbitrary king; it alters the fundamental nature of justice, signaled in the Erinyes' transformation into the Eumenides (well-minded ones).

The Erinyes and Zeus share a history. The three maddening sisters are chthonic deities of blood vengeance, born of the drops of blood spilled during Zeus' gory castration of his father Kronos. Like Zeus, they care nothing for the individual circumstances of singular crimes.[4] The Erinyes pursue their victims with cruelest intention and the relentlessness of blind necessity, whatever the mitigating circumstances of the original offence, just as Zeus, in his unyielding anger, punishes Prometheus mercilessly, applying cruel tortures on the Scythian crag at the ends of the earth and then throwing him into Hades. In each case, individuals are pursued but punished, but they are not heard *as individuals* with separate stories to tell and unique reasons to explain their acts. As a result of both excessive punishments, whole communities are made to suffer, across familial generations and across geographical space. The *Prometheus Bound* gives private hearing but only to illuminate that no public hearing was given and thus nothing was resolved. Athena's trial by jury lets every concerned party have their say, and as a result, it leaves the parties and the community at peace. By comparison, the rage that drove the Erinyes has been utterly transformed into goodwill and right-mindedness, signaled in their new name, the Eumenides. It is significant that the Eumenides have a shrine dedicated to them, which protects the weakest members of the society, the slaves.

Just as the gods of Greek myth enjoyed a special justice grounded in the balance of *timē* that excluded lesser beings, so the Greek *aristoi* of the ancient world enjoyed a system of justice that was not extended to those without aretaic status and privilege—women, children, and slaves. Even in the budding democracy of Athens, class distinctions rigorously separated the have's from the have-not's. Whether the decaying *ancien regime*, or the *nouveau riche* merchant class of merchant fleet owners and commercial dealers, only the wealthiest Athenians enjoyed the full benefits of citizenship and could take advantage of the protections afforded by the institutions of justice.[5]

The volatility of heroic passions around questions of honor and shame explains the ancient Greeks' profound appreciation for justice as balance. The princely peers shared a special sense of identity as a "higher" race of men, the noble *aristoi*. They shared a common language and interlocking interests, but they also possessed a common fragility of temperament; they were easily outraged and flew into murderous tempers, when the general balance of power was upset or their individual sense of honor offended. Across the Greek mainland and beyond to the colonies, at every level of Greek society, a great appreciation for fairness helped to maintain an uncommon level of fraternity among the hot-tempered, war-loving, status-sensitive males. But when things went wrong and the balance of honors was offended, then chaos could tear apart their world.

Notes

1. Oscar G. Brockett and Franklin J. Hildy, *History of the Theater* (Columbus, OH: Allyn and Bacon, 2003), 13.

2. Danielle S. Allen, *The World of Prometheus* (Princeton, NJ: Princeton University Press, 2000), 326-331.

3. Trials in Greek are *agones* or contests, and prosecutor and defendant are named *agonista*, or contestants.

4. Oedipus witnesses the fact that innocence of intention does not remove the stain of guilt from bloodied hands.

5. See Jacques Ranciere, *Disagreement: Politics and Philosophy* (Minneapolis: University of Minnesota Press, 1998). Ranciere argues that poor citizens of democratic Athens lived lives no better than those of slaves, so democracy, as promising citizen equality, was nothing more than a ruse.

Chapter 3
Honor and Shame in the Heroic Worldview

The Greek cult of the hero represents the best and highest ideals of the ancient Greek world. Like the pantheon whose relations they mirrored, the Greek princes inhabited a closely knit world of interlocking domains of power, maintained by the strict observance of respect and obligation toward peers. Honor and shame are the sentries posted at the gates of the boundaries between domains. Overstepping the boundaries of privilege meant offending a powerful peer. Justice put right such offenses by stripping the offender of honor, humiliating him in turn for having humiliated his victim.

Greek myth and tragedy reveal the dangers of the heroic worldview. They explore a dangerous excess in gods and heroes—an obsessive "will to punish." In highlighting this danger, the poets raise a challenge to the archaic Greek worldview of hot-blooded, highborn princes. Mythological and tragic spectacles of excessive divine punishments expose the paradoxical relationship among justice, legitimacy, and punishment and challenge prevailing assumptions about these critical ideas. The excessive "will to punish" articulated in myth and tragedy represents a challenge from the gentler poetic natures to the fickle and volatile warriors about the moral limitations of their heroic *ethos*.

The age of heroes is most clearly depicted in the epic poems attributed to Homer, the *Iliad* and the *Odyssey*. These works not only represent the worldview of the heroic age and the *ethos* of manly virtue (*arête*) that underpins the "cult of the hero," but these poems, and in particular the *Iliad,* embody the poet's challenge to the hero as well, revealing the tragic consequences of his intemperate *ethos* and the dangers of his unbridled passions and hyperbolic pride, which drove them to self-destructive extremes in their relationships and dealings with their peers and neighbors, as much as against their enemies.

An ancient proverb Diogenes Laertius attributes to Cleobulus (I.93) runs: *Metron ariston*. The maxim is generally translated "Moderation is best" but the phrase could as rightly be read as "the good are measured." But since "the good" and "the noble" are identical terms in the ancient Greek language (*aristos*), the proverb may also be read as a warning to the aristocratic class: "what is [truly] noble is measured" or [truly] good men practice good measure.

The aristocratic tendency toward passionate excess explains the important place granted to the excellence of temperance by the ancient philosophers. Temperance (*sophrosume*) is the virtue assigned to the noble horse of passion in Plato's tripartite soul in his careful study of passion in the *Phaedrus*. Temperance appears again as the essence of the higher type of "measure" that witnesses the science of "right judgment" in the statesman's moral and political stewardship, in the *Statesman*. The virtue is again crowned supreme in Aristotle's doctrine of the Golden Mean in the *Nichomachean Ethics*.

I have said that Trevor J. Saunders, in his *Plato's Penal Code*, argues that there is no punishment in Homer's *Iliad*.[1] His argument is that without a legitimate authority to carry out retribution against an offender, penalties cannot rightly be named punishment. However, we have seen that Aeschylus' *Prometheus Bound* demonstrates not only that punishment is one of the major ways that the powerful assert and confirm their legitimacy, but that excessive punishment can unseat the legitimacy of powerful kings, which undermines the neat logic that grounds Saunders' argument.

I will offer a reading of Homer's *Iliad* that assumes that one of the primary themes of the epic is to chart the fatal consequences of excessive punishment. I argue that Homer is expressing, between the lines of the very poems that extol the virtues of heroes, the warning that no human being or divinity is exempt from the cosmic prohibition against *hybris*. Homer is affirming the four moral norms—Moira, Tuche, Dike, and Ananke—that lie in the background of the cosmic drama, regulating the excesses of gods and men. Homer is demonstrating, in the *Iliad*, that the excellence of moderation is superior to the warrior virtues, older and more universally prized among the ancient Hellenes. Over the portal of the Temple of Apollo at Delphi was inscribed the warning of the all-seeing god: *Mēden ágan* ("Nothing in excess").

The expedition to Troy is not only a heroic adventure, an agon among competitive princely camps. It is the chronicle of the extended efforts of a king (Menelaus) and his princes to exact due recompense upon a foreign king and his entire flock of kin for the dishonor afforded him (the king) by one of their young princes (Paris), who has disrespected the honor of the king by stealing his beautiful wife (Helen). The war effort raised by the Princes of Hellas against the House of Troy seek to dish out a harsh, redistributive justice to avenge the original offense. The goal of the expedition was to punish the perpetrator by levying upon the entire kingdom of Troy and all the people housed therein the harshest retribution they could muster. The mission's violence had to be as radical as the effrontery of the crime, if it was to rebalance the scales of justice that had been upset by Paris's impudence in disgracing of one of Greece's most powerful kings.

One common reading of the *Iliad* interprets the tragedy of war as a backdrop for the demonstration of heroic virtues. Only in the hardest of times does the mettle in great men become fully tested and revealed. However, this seems to me an oversimplistic reading. It is important to note that almost without exception, every last noble warrior in both camps of that grand confrontation ultimately sacrifices his dignity and indeed his and his army's best interests to wild outrage and merciless vengeance. The poet appreciates that unbridled passions drive vindictive warriors toward disproportionate punishment of their enemies, destroying their own best interests in the bargain. Ultimately victor and loser alike are crushed by the experience of the great war against Troy.

It is true that more than anywhere, the manly Greek virtues are displayed on the battlefield. The *Iliad* is nothing if not a tale of competing egoisms, fighting to the death in manly *agon* to demonstrate their manly mettle, defend the reputations of their lineage, and win honors as superior human beings. Thus the themes of honor, shame, and punishment wind throughout the plot of this epic poem. The stage for the contest of manly distinction is set before the poem opens, when Paris (Alexandros), son of Priam, the King of Troy, runs off to Troy with Helen, shaming not only the great king Menelaus, and humiliating and endangering his entire clan, but offending Zeus, guardian of the rights of hospitality. The princes of Greece, having bound themselves in loyalty to Menelaus from the time of his having overcome them all in the contest for the hand of the stunning Helen, raised a force of a thousand ships to compel the return of Helen, and wreak vengeance for the loss of their honor in suffering an affront to their King. They set out to punish (*timoresthai* or "seize the honor" of) the Trojans.

Homer's *Iliad*

As the *Iliad* opens, the Hellenes are found fighting amongst themselves. Agamemnon has been forced to return his war prize, Chryseis, to her father, a powerful priest, to win divine favor for his war and end a god-sent plague. Agamemnon feels shamed by the loss and expresses his outrage (*aitiai*) and reclaims his self-respect by challenging his most powerful warrior, Achilles, son of the goddess Themis and champion of the battlefield. Agamemnon seizes the war prize, Briseis, who had been the prize awarded to the proud Achilles. Agamemnon admits his simple motivation for this injustice, when he crows:

> Thus you may learn well
> How much greater I am than you, and another may shrink
> From likening his to my power and contending against me.[2]

Agamemnon punishes another prince for his ill fate and loss, defending his action not on an argument of justice as fair distribution, but on the claim that might is right.

The proud Achilles is humiliated and retires from the war effort to the whitening waves of the boundless sea, wailing and weeping to his mother for vengeance against Agamemnon. Homer gives us a stark view of the debilitating effects of the overblown love of honor in the sorry image of the great hero crushed to a whimpering child and crying for his mother. Achilles punishes the king and the Greek war effort by withdrawing his forces from the battle.

The gods hear Achilles' cries. The great hero will not wait long for the tide of honor to turn upon the powerful king. Agamemnon's turn for humiliation comes swift upon the heels of his shaming Achilles. A very few days later, the king must humble himself, weeping and pleading with the great warrior to rejoin the ranks of battle. Agamemnon, the supreme commander of the avenging forces of Helen, comes to know the bitter taste of humility as he debases himself in pleading for Achilles' forgiveness.

The *Iliad* records the rise and fall of the tides of war, but it also charts the ebb and flow of heroic outrage and desolation, sketched in the language of honor and shame. This epic is a testimony to the greatness of the Greek warrior class, but also a harsh condemnation

of the raw effects of their overblown pride and hot tempers, the
moral and political blindness of their heroic code of honors. The
ethos of *arête* is on trial in the *Iliad*.

A striking feature of the *Iliad*, and perhaps its most telling mark,
is the way it manipulates the reader's sense of time to stage striking
revelations of truth. Again and again throughout the grand fray and
amidst the dust and din of battle, Homer creates a curious suspension
in the action, much as a Hollywood director might freeze the frame
of a film to register the strange phenomenology of time during fate-
ful moments of the human life. The din of battle is suspended; the
drama of war pauses; time stands still and the stage opens up to reveal a hero confronting his destiny. This is an ultimate test, a singu-
larizing instant, that seems to lift the hero from the fray, a giant of
epic proportions in a limbo of sensibility. The contest is not one with
a second stout hero, a valiant and mighty contender in the *agon* of
war. The hero is confronted by another kind of test, a moral challenge. Before him crouches a broken man, a diminished enemy and
pleading suppliant, begging for his life.

The scene is a singular one but is repeated again and again, representing a universal experience. At the height of his glory, each hero
confronts this challenge, as though fate were extending to him one
divine chance for a superhuman glory, amidst the more human, aretaic glories of war. Each hero is granted this opportunity to break the
epic pattern of shame and honor. He is invited to rise above the destructive and vengeful pride exemplified in the greatest warrior,
Achilles. Each has his chance to set himself apart from his peers.[3]

In each of these still-frame moments, the poet is staging a hercu-
lean test for the human hero. Powerful in body, invincible in valor,
cunning in strategy of war, the hero shows weakness, a weakness
embedded in the heroic ideal, as he plunges his sword into a dis-
armed petitioner, sunken to his knees and pleading for life and
mercy. Time and time again, a hero crushes a defenseless dying man,
delighting in the victory, describing to him in gory details the outra-
geous disgraces his body will suffer after his soul has been dis-
patched. In the moral face-off that is heroic encounter, might is right
and knows no moral bounds, no temperance, no mercy or pity.

The poet thus reveals the Achilles' heel of the heroic ethos. In
the final analysis of this great war epic, the failure of heroes to reach
for the loftier goals of temperance, mercy, and pity, heroism is revealed as base and brutal. Above all, the hero seeks immortality

through his deeds, epitomized in Achilles' choice of a short and glo-
rious life over a long and undistinguished one. Ironically, however,
when heroism is pushed to the extreme, his deeds are but fleeting
atrocities. The glory of Agamemnon over Achilles is short-lived and
debasing; the glory of Achilles over Hector equally so; the grandeur
of Achilles is dwarfed by the gentle courage of the regal old Priam;
the death of Achilles brings but fleeting triumph to the Trojans; the
crushing of the great civilization of Troy brings hollow victory to the
Achaians.

The *Iliad* witnesses the hollowness of the heroic ideal, against
the true challenge—the moral moment. Never does it occur to the
hero that the supreme test of his power occurs in the moment that he
is charged to overcome his brutal might and spare, rather than de-
stroy, his enemy. Never does it occur to the hero that crushing a defenseless suppliant is cowardice, not grandeur. In this reading, the
Iliad, that great epic of war, composes a theatricalization of the
weakness of heroes, not a display of their virile dignity. Intoxicated
by power and bloodlust, heroes ultimately take the path of *least* resistance—driving their weapons into the already defeated, the living
dead. The superb indifference that the powerful feel for the weak is
the profound flaw in the *ethos* of the hero, rendering to each in turn
the just deserts of hollow victory and bitter justice.

In this epic, heroes are shown to be weak and sniveling whiners,
who cry to their mothers and punish their brothers when their play-
things have been stolen; their egos are feeble and volatile, and their
anger misdirected to innocent bystanders. In the *Iliad*, as in all wars,
no one goes home a hero, whatever his valiant boldness in the glori-
ous phases of the war. In fact, we come to see in this tragic tale that
only violence triumphs when the strong crush the weak. And, since
violence has a terrible necessity to repeat itself in ever more ingenious and brutalizing forms, the war does not end when the spoils of
battle are divided and the heroes withdraw to their homelands, but, as
witnessed in the *Oresteia*, continue to rebound in their societies long
after the fray has expired.

The Heroic Ethos

I have said that the aretaic *ethos* of individual distinction among worthy
peers could lead to excesses which were destructive of individual lives,
families, and the peaceful coexistence of whole communities. However,

it is crucial to appreciate the careful balance of individuality and community, particularism and communalism, which characterized the ethos of tribalistic societies at this early moment of the Western civilization, as much as in tribal societies today. Within a community that finds its identity on the basis of honors and regulates behaviors on the basis of shame, distinction of the individual is always distinction *within* a broader human context and *among* one's worthy peers. The system of honors rests on the conviction that the individual comes to greatness as a function of his social learning within a distinguished community and as a chapter in a distinguished lineage. Let us consider the interplay of individuality and community here.

The heroic age revered the individual; the battlefield, the gymnasium, and the political arena staged contests of beauty, intelligence, and prowess, that granted individuals the opportunity to distinguish their unique talents, virtues, and strengths. But the aristocratic thirst for individual reputation was balanced by a deep sense of broader identity. Each saw himself as an episode in a long history of ancestral merit, and, at least after the Trojan War, the Greeks recognized themselves as well as members of a unique people born of a particular history, with a common cultural and linguistic tradition that set them apart from the others, the *barbaroi,* and granted them renown as "the Hellenes."

The "cult of heroic manliness" rested on the precept that a man was more than a single life; he was a link in the chain of ancestral preeminence, a product of a historical line of distinction. Many of the older families of Athens charted their ancestry back to heroes and kings, and some even took this lineage further, citing a god as the father of their line. Socrates, a man known for his humility, took great pride in his ancestral lineage. He claimed to descend from the line of Daedalus, the skillful craftsman of Greek myth and tragedy whose images seemed to move about.[4]

Honorable heritage brought honor, reputation, wealth, social status, and political power, but it also brought obligation. The noble warrior ethos is rooted in the obligation to fight to the death for the honor of family and friend. An aristocrat's class is named for its moral worth; the Greek language makes no distinction between "nobleman" (*aristos*) and "the good" (*aristos*). A noble man must always live up to the high standards set by his ancestors and maintain the reputation and prestige attached to his stock. So a man must conduct himself with dignity, pride, and excellence, fulfill his responsibilities among a community of men of equal stature and renown, and uphold that community's high expectations of him. The great man, according to the aretaic vision, was superior in mind, body, and character, so he courted danger as opportunity in the present to prove his individual worth among his peers, and to prove his worthiness to his ancestral line.

C. M. Bowra, in his *The Greek Experience*, explores the lengthy history of the heroic outlook, charting its beginnings in aristocratic individualism to its development as a national *ethos* adopted by the people who come to call themselves the "Hellenes."[5] Bowra sees the ancient philosophers as explicitly engaging the heroic worldview, locating its first philosophical articulations in the sixth century BCE. philosopher Pythagoras of Samos. Pythagoras (c. 580–500 BCE) distinguishes three kinds of men—seekers of knowledge, seekers of honor, and seekers of gain. These categories he matches to the kinds of men he finds at the Olympic Games—onlookers, athletes, and hucksters, respectively. Pythagoras declares men of honor to be the highest class of men; indeed, they represent the very *raison d'être* of the Games.

Bowra sees Heraclitus supporting the heroic ideal. While Heraclitus expresses disgust at the lack of wisdom among men, he thinks best of those who seek glory, so readily distinguishable from the beast-like majority. Plato continues in this tradition, according to Bowra's reading, maintaining the heroic ideal in his tripartite division of the human soul. In this image, the white horse is high born, beautiful in inner nature, and well-figured in form. It stands out against the black horse in its dignity and grace, as well as for its noble, self-assertive principle that drives it to seek honor through noble action. Its greatest virtue inheres in its natural tendency to align itself with reason. Bowra plays down the philosopher's abandonment of the Pythagorean hierarchy, demoting the lover of honor to the lover of knowledge. Indeed, Plato names the honor-seeker an entirely different species from the lover of wisdom (philosopher), shift to the image of the horse to be brought to the whip by the reasonable charioteer.

Aristotle continues the tradition, according to Bowra, remaining a proponent of the heroic ideal. Yet when he sorts out the kinds of men according to their loves, the *Nichomachean Ethics*, his formulation affirms Plato's hierarchy, rather than Pythagoras' ordering.[6]

Bowra understands the Greek heroic ideal to frame the Greek way of life, and he sees the cult of the hero, shaped by its social context of a warrior society, enduring well beyond the transition from tribal to national politics. The cult of the hero lasted long after the age of princely warriors, Bowra explains, because its ideals were well worth preserving and readily adaptable to changing times. It motivated greatness in every field of endeavor, he argues, inspiring not only greatness on the battlefield, but intellectual, moral, and physical excellence in every arena of human activity. Thus, as Greek city-states evolved into settled nations and shifted their attention from war and the plunder of their neighbors to legitimate commercial activities and trade with their neighboring states, the man of *arête*, who once sought distinction for himself, his family, and his clan in the contests of war, now sought personal fame and glory for his line, his class and his city in less bellicose ways.

In his *After Virtue*, Alastair MacIntyre too stresses the benefits that the heroic ethic afforded to Greek society.[7] Stories of the valor and prowess of ancestral heroes remained the chief vehicle for moral education, the foundational matter for schooling young males in the virtues of duty, courage, shrewdness, fortitude, and loyalty. Like Bowra, MacIntyre sees these virtues readily transferable to changing times, because they remained essential to the security of the household and the *polis*. MacIntyre notes a further advantage of holding onto the beliefs and ideals of earlier times: heroic values granted to early Greek communities a stability, an endurance of worldview and value system, to act as ballast against the troubling flux of changing times. For MacIntyre, heroic warrior ideals evolved in the context of the polis into three essential principles of ideal citizenship: the notion of social duty; the standard of excellence in the execution of duty; and the ideal of dignified endurance under difficult conditions. The cult of the hero accepted the human condition as in every case fragile and death-bound, rendering the matter of *how* life is lived more significant than *how long*.

Werner Jaeger's *Paideia, the Ideals of Greek Culture* agrees that long after the end of the age of heroes that we see depicted in Homer, the ideals of the heroic cult lived on in Greek tradition. But he emphasizes that the ideals that framed the cult of the hero became sublimated and universalized in the ideals of Greek philosophy, with some notable alterations.[8] Rather than these ideals being demoted to a lower station, Jaeger sees them morphing into philosophical concepts and political values. The heroic ideal, he argues, is responsible for *psyche* being reinterpreted by the philosophers as essentially moral. It is responsible for Socrates' understanding of the cultivation of the individual soul as a purification practice and a moral quest. And the heroic worldview bequeathed to later Greeks the idea of statesmanship as an honor and a duty, rather than a burden and a source of profit, ideals of friendship and filial love, and the general contempt for money-making. All these founding ideals that orient ancient Greek philosophy and find expression in myriad ways in everyday Greek life well into the democratic era find their origin in the heroic cult of the masculine. On the other hand, Jaeger notes, the one aspect of the heroic cult that comes to be jettisoned by the later Greeks is the love of glory *for its own sake*. This will come to be seen as shameful.

The scholars of Greek antiquity highlight the many benefits of the Greek ideal of heroic manliness and cite these benefits to explain its endurance across the geographical space of the Greek world and the changing times of Greek politics. MacIntyre insists that the slow but steady moral fall of the Athenian Empire, from the sifting of funds from the Delian League, to the nepotism and graft of Athenian rebuilding projects after the great war, to the bullying of allies and neutrals during the Peloponnesian War, evidence the collapse, rather than the fulfillment of the noble *ethos*. He and others argue that the moral fall of Athens comes from the undermining of the heroic ethical code by the new capitalist ideals characteristic of the rising merchant class in Athens, the sense of shame in the society growing increasingly undermined by the love of money.

However, classicists are prepared as well to admit that the Greek code of manly excellence also has its dark side. Bowra highlights the need among the ancient Greeks for the gentler, softening, nurturing effects that a feminine ethic might have brought to the hyper-masculine. MacIntyre, contra Bowra and Jaeger, argues that the heroic ethos was not only undermined by new capitalist ideals, but being fundamentally competitive, those ideals needed to be abandoned to allow for Athens' commercial evolution. A competitive ethos, he posits, was unsuitable for the context of the democratic *polis*, where cooperation was essential to the smooth running of the administrative machinery.[9]

I have made the argument in this chapter that the heroic ethos finds its extreme fulfillment in an excessive "will to punish" directed at subordinates and insufficiently respectful peers. Because honor is a value that requires a public staging before a community, rather than simply the quiet cultivation of inner moral qualities, an inherent aspect of the heroic ethos is that it is other-related, much like the value of fame in the modern era. People tend to be fickle in their judgments and easily change their mind about the worth of their neighbors. An ethos that grounds self-worth in the opinion of one's peers is fragile, unpredictable, and unstable. It hands over the reins of the noble horse to charioteers who are not necessarily reasonable.

Because the grounds of honor are vulnerable and unstable, so too is the heroic character, as evidenced in Achilles. When offended, the hero can readily put the interests of the community behind personal considerations, and suspend his reasoned judgment out of outrage and an unhealthy thirst for vengeance. His rage against those who dare to question his worth can readily turn obsessive. This too is witnessed in the *Iliad* in the bullying of the commoner Thersites, as in the merciless crushing of Troy. In the archaic past of the Western world, the volatile egos and passions of hyper-sensitive men often led to cruelty, cutthroat rivalries, and bloody feuds. It led to slavery, war, and brutality against social inferiors. Heroic virtues could easily sicken into arrogant elitisms, which promoted and justified cruelty to those deemed unworthy of respect. The warrior's love of excellence had a tendency to deteriorate into callousness and spite toward the weak, and a readiness to humiliate and abuse social subordinates.

The self-assertiveness that was the essence of *arete* could deteriorate into a ruthless thirst for power and for domination of social inferiors and neighboring peoples. Therefore, contra MacIntyre, I see the fulfillment of the Greek heroic cult of manliness in the shameless behavior of Athens in the age of its Empire, in its general treatment of its allies during the Peloponnesian War and in its bullying brutality toward Mytilene and the neutral island of Melos.[10] Critics will argue that it was the abandonment of fundamental heroic values that allowed these disgraces to occur, but I maintain that the seed of excess was long planted in the soil of heroic greatness and its overriding value of honor.

There is no denying that the cult of heroic manliness in many ways helped to stimulate excellence in every endeavor of city life. It promoted a sense of citizen duty conducive to the successful transition to democratic political and judicial forms, and it encouraged respect and willing adherence to city laws. The disgust for dishonor and the vulnerability to public shame proved positive forces in maintaining order in the cities. In theory, a man of distinction would not shame himself by crude behavior, shirking his civic duty, or indulging in petty criminal acts. Indeed, even if unjustly treated by fate, his fellows or the courts, a man's strong sense of self and duty could temper his response to injustice. The model for the hyper-responsibility that the heroic code could inspire is the mythical case of Oedipus, who struck out his eyes and drove himself into exile, administering and indeed welcoming the opportunity for punishment, for the wrongs he had inadvertently committed. Socrates too refused to escape punishment and accepted his sentence with grace and contentment, because of his deep commitment to noble and heroic ideals

Arête was an ethos that valued physical strength, intellectual ability, and moral character. These are timeless virtues that promote high standards in communities during times of peace as much as among armies at war. The ethos cultivated grace, pride, and a sense of calling to moral distinction, alongside a warlike valor. It militated against shameful behaviors. Indeed a man's capacity to experience shame when he behaves inappropriately indicates that social learning has been successfully completed. Thus the many forms of punishment that were employed in classical Athens, from shaming in the city's public spaces to the various degrees of exile that limited participatory citizenship, evidences the moral work accomplished upon the citizens by the ideals of the heroic ethos.

The value of a noble ethic that inspires excellence in all aspects of the human life is difficult to challenge on ethical grounds. It is crucial to our understanding of this ethic that we appreciate that the warrior's love of honor and dread of shame was not simply a love of glory *for its own sake*. To focus upon glory as the warrior's "good in itself" is to miss the point of the cult of the hero. Glory is only the outward signal of an inner moral strength, just as a sense of shame at wrongdoing is the signal that social learning is complete and codes of conduct have been internalized. However, Achilles, the paradigmatic hero, exposes the Achilles' heel of the noble ethic—its tendency toward excess, its debilitating effects on the individual psyche and on the community, and its fragile foundation in popular opinion.

The exaggerated emphasis on honor and shame in the heroic worldview eclipses the practical purpose of justice, to manage the volatile emotions of outraged victims such that communities may live in peace and social harmony. Shame tends to bring only more volatile emotion into questions of right and wrong, and aggravate the already outraged, triggering dangerous responses that further upset social order. The *dikephoros* (avenging) justice of the archaic warrior princes will need to be brought to a more healing and curative (*therapeuma*) formulation.

Notes

1. Trevor J. Saunders, *Plato's Penal Code* (Oxford: Clarendon Press, 1991).
2. Homer. *Iliad*, Book I, 185-186.
3. In Plato, *Phaedrus* (247a), we witness a similar choice. We see a parade of gods march off to the Feast of Being in all their might and glory. But Socrates

notes that the goddess Hestia (literally, "Hearth") forsakes the divine parade to remain at the fireside to tend her earthly suppliants in their times of need.

4. Plato, *Euthyphro*, 11b.

5. C. M. Bowra, in *The Greek Experience* (Aylesbury, UK: Hazzel, Watson, and Viney, 1973).

6. Aristotle, *Nichomachean Ethics*, Book 5: 1095b13-1096a5.

7. Alastair MacIntyre, *After Virtue* (Notre Dame, IN: University of Notre Dame, 1984), 121 ff.

8. Werner Jaeger, *Paideia: the Ideals of Greek Culture* (Oxford: Oxford University Press, 1967).

9. MacIntyre, *After Virtue*, 223. MacIntyre's criticism flies in the face of a truth that has come increasingly into focus with the globalizing of capitalism—that commerce is fundamentally competitive, even at its healthiest, but when it evolves into cooperation among competitors, it results in monopoly and then imperialism, economic tyranny over the consumer and the laborer as foreseen by Vladimir Lenin (1916).

10. Thucydides, *The Peloponnesian War*, Rex Warner, trans., (Middlesex, Eng.: Penguin Books, 1985), 3.36–50; 5.84–116.

Chapter 4
Justice and Punishment in Classical Athens

Despite the geographical disconnectedness of Greek cities, the lack of formal alliances, and the regular frontier skirmishes with which the Greek cities plagued each other, from the time of the Trojan War (c. thirteenth to twelfth century BCE) the Greeks saw themselves as a homogenous group, the Hellenes, bound by a common language and similar cultural traits.[1] The Hellenic sense of shared identity was from the beginning infused with ideals of manly excellence and the cult of the hero. Aristocratic families of "noble birth" (from *aristos* meaning "good" and "noble") traced their lineage back to heroes and gods, hence their general sense of superiority over non-Greeks or "barbarian" races (*barbaroi*) surrounding them.[2] The Greeks were proud of their citizenship in cities (*poloi*), even when political power was still tribally organized, and for this reason, punishments were early on associated with suspension of citizenship rights, the worst of which was exile. Exile was tantamount to being cast out to dwell among the uncivilized, so the penalty carried the connotation of extreme disgrace. For this reason, the threat of exile proved a powerful deterrent to crime.[3]

In archaic Greece during the age of the great princes, social hierarchy was an indisputable fact. Yet, just as in the Greek cosmology, power was never simple dictatorship. Rather, an intricate system of interlocking rights and privileges ensured individual sovereignty while preserving the balance of power among the aristocratic classes. In other words, justice was the balance of interests that preserved social harmony. This understanding of justice was deeply embedded in the Greek worldview—from their cosmology, to their understanding of cultured existence, to their political arrangements, to their strategy on the battlefield, to their ideal of *arête* as manly forbearance whatever the circumstances. Balance and harmony were highly praised in warrior society precisely because of the enormous challenge of keeping their world in balance and managing the bellicose inclinations, the fragile egos, and the passionate natures of the princes.

There were no sudden revolutions in Greek ideas about justice, crime, or punishment from the age of the kings through the democracy in Athens. Laws were grounded in the traditional *nomoi* (customs) understood to be handed down by the gods, as fitting rules for all civilized societies. When the laws were broken, justice remained consistently focused upon placating the accuser and rebalancing the social register by applying forms of punishment that shamed and demoted the offender. In short, despite the plethora of important changes in politics, laws, and social attitudes and practices that brought the Greeks from a tribal aristocracy to a democratic polis, their understanding of justice remained fairly consistent for more than eight hundred years: the function of justice was to repay dishonorable conduct (having the dualistic meaning of shaming oneself and shaming or dishonoring a victim peer) with a punishment that in turn disgraced. Greek justice was a *dikephoros* (avenging) justice.

The traditional laws (*nomoi*) were first laid down in written form (*thesmoi*) by the famous law-giver Drakon (621-620 BCE), during the archonship of Aristaichmos. At this time, the laws still clearly reflected their logical foundations in the archaic system of aristocratic relations. Power relations reflected the hierarchy of command on the battlefield, verifying the prerogative of citizens over non-citizens, males over females, and the aristocratic class of hoplites over common infantrymen. The nine archonships (*archontes*), the treasurers, and even the lesser officials were chosen only from the class of men who were able to provide their own arms and armor on the battlefield, and who had a substantial level of wealth and owned land.[4]

What appears as quite remarkable today is that from the first codification of law in Athens, even the harshest and most "draconian" of laws such as those against homicide, cite disclaimers and alternative penalties that witness a flexible and charitable approach to crime.

> Even if without premeditation [someone kills someone, he goes into exile]. The kings are to judge him guilty of homicide . . . and the *ephetai* [ancient court of homicide alongside the Areopagus] are to give the verdict. [Pardon may be granted if the father] is alive, or brothers or sons, all together; otherwise the one [opposing it shall prevail. If none] of these men is alive, (then by the male relatives) as far as the degree of

cousin's son and [cousin, if all] are willing [to pardon.] The one opposing [shall prevail. If not even any of these is alive,] and the killing was involuntary, and is judged by the [Fifty One, the *ephetai*, that it was involuntary] homicide, let him be admitted into (Attika) by [ten members of his phratry, if they are willing. . . . [Let proclamation be made] against the killer [in the] *agora*.[5]

In faithfulness to the aristocratic formulation, justice is focused on the offended party; that is, the accuser "shall prevail." Even in cases of accidental killing, the justice system remained rigorously focused on placating the offended. On the other hand, there is clear evidence of a spirit of mercy in the approach to punishment: the family might punish its own deviants, and even a murderer could petition for readmission into his phratry, and avoid exile.

From the archaic age through Solon's democratic reforms of the constitution, cases were judged by the ten elected military generals who made up the Areopagus Council, an elite stronghold of the wealthiest male citizens who had previously served as archons, and then "retired" to life-term posts as judges. The Assembly of male citizens impaneled the juries, with anything from two hundred to six thousand citizens showing up on the day of a trial. However detailed the investigation, however convoluted the event, the trial had always to be decided and a resolution reached by day's end.[6]

According to the Greek worldview, everything had its proper place— gods in the heavens, male citizens in the courts and war councils, women in the houses, children in the nursery, and slaves in the fields. Thus, for the Greeks, it seemed most "natural" that those who behaved disgracefully should be exiled from civilized society, hidden out of sight in prison cells, displayed for ridicule in the public squares, or, in the worst cases, executed and their bodies dumped unceremoniously outside the city walls. Social place and social places thus had deep significance for notions of justice and punishments in Athens. Punishment was not, as it is for modern societies, a simple matter of the containment of dangerous social actors. Since crime was understood as *atimos*, a dishonoring of the victim, punishment (*timoresthai*) represented a process that addressed the upset of social status. The goal was to lower the social place of offenders of the society, by shaming them in public humiliations or casting them out for a spell, a most shameful fate. The stripping of honor from the offender redeemed the offended (dishonored) party, and restored the latter to their full social status. The system of justice was a restorative of the complex system of rights and prerogatives that was crucial to social order.

By the time of Solon (594-593 BCE), economic and political crisis threatened, and the justice system was called upon to address imbalances not only among the wealthy, but across the social register. The few wealthy citizens held most of the land and the poor worked the fields and rented plots for their own subsistence, but loans being secured of the borrower's person, the poor easily fell into slavery, along with their children and wives, if the slightest misfortune befell them. A great many poor Athenian families found themselves bound in debt slavery to the few rich by the time Solon assumed archonship.[7] It fell to Solon to avert the crisis and quell the unrest, by revolutionizing the justice system.

Where previously the failure to pay rent had been seen as the great offense, the demos located social deviance in the excessive wealth and greed that brought ruin to those less fortunate. Solon was a member of the middle class, but he was a sympathizer of the plight of the poor. He expresses his sentiments in his elegiac poems, chastising the aristocrats:

> Restrain your mighty hearts in your breasts, you who have pursued every good thing to excess, and let your pride be in moderation, for we shall not succumb to you, and not everything will turn out as you would like.[8]

Solon had democratic sympathies, but he was a balanced and even-handed ruler. He took great pains to be fair with all the classes and not offend the overblown pride of the powerful.

> To the demos I gave privilege enough, neither detracting from their status nor enhancing it. Those who had power and were admirable in their possessions I took care, equally, not to injure. I stood firm, protecting both sides with the enveloping strength of my shield, and did not allow either to gain an unjust victory. . . . I drafted statutes for bad men and for good alike, with justice set up straight for each."[9]

Solon's laws, especially the abolition of debt slavery, brought relief to the poor of Athens. And many of the wealthy and powerful as well supported the democratic changes. The nine *archontes* swore an oath to uphold the new laws, which were committed to wooden tablets at the *Stoa Basileios*, and they pledged that if they failed to keep that oath, they would dedicate a golden statue to the city.[10]

The laws of most significance to the demos included: prohibiting loans on the security of the debtor's person; the provision that any citizen could seek legal redress for any victim of crime; and the right of appeal of any verdict to a jury of citizen peers (*dikasterion*). These laws, according to Aristotle, rendered Athens not merely "master of the courts" but "master of the *politeia*," a stellar model among civilized states.[11]

After Solon, Athens remained peaceful for a few years, but the peace did not last long. Many of the noble families were resentful, and complained of the harm done to them by the cancellation of debts. Many of the demos too remained dissatisfied, because they believed that the changes in the polis did not go far enough in their favor; they hoped to see a redistribution of the wealth, which remained in the hands of the few. Personal rivalries and factional unrest grew increasingly widespread across much of the region of Attica. Thus was the era of Solon followed closely by the Age of Tyrants (650-510 BCE).

By the close of the age of tyrants, the greatest threat to social order was perceived as the existence of arrogant and powerful demagogues, pursuing relentlessly their private interests and forsaking the ancient *nomoi* and the common good of the polis. Thus, from 487 through 417 BCE, a procedure named *ostrakismos*, became the most striking and characteristic feature of Athenian democratic politics. Aristotle reports:

> [The law of *ostrakismos*] had been laid down because of suspicion of those in power, for Peisistratos had established himself as tyrant when he was leader of the demos and a general. And the first man to be ostracized was one of his relatives.[12]

The process sought to crush tyrannical ambitions in its powerful citizens. The custom was for the *Boule* (Assembly) to inscribe upon *ostraka* (pieces of broken pottery) the name of any citizen they felt deserved to be banished. If more than two hundred *ostraka* turned up with the same name, then the person named would be forced into exile for a period of ten years.

The *ostrakismos* law often led to abuses, because powerful individuals could purchase the votes they needed to get rid of their rivals and enemies for a decade. Plutarch confirms that *ostrakismos* was not a "punishment" in the usual sense. To be exiled in this way was not shameful, nor did it carry any connotation of depravity or any assumption of malignant desire on the part of the accusers. It simply meant that someone the people resented must take up residence elsewhere for ten years. According to Plutarch, ostracism simply represented "a way of relieving feelings of jealousy humanely."[13]

One famed case of the abuse of the ostracism law is that of Aristeides the Just. On that occasion (483-482 BCE), Plutarch reports, the citizens were busy marking their *ostraka*, when "an illiterate and boorish fellow" appealed to Aristeides himself to write for him the name "Aristeides" on his *ostraka*. Aristeides was amazed and asked the man in what manner Aristeides had ever done injury to him. "I don't even know the man," was the illiterate's response, "but I am sick and tired of always hearing him called The Just!" On hearing this, Aristeides, true to his reputation, wrote down his own name on the man's *ostraka* and soon found himself ostracized for ten years.[14]

Despite the political and historical changes that Athens underwent across its broad history, its penal practices remained fairly stable for hundreds upon hundreds of years. From the archaic period of the great kings of thirteenth century, through the democratic era, to close of the fourth century, Athens' treatment of its social offenders called upon a broad arsenal of punishments, which recall the armory Zeus levied against Prometheus—public shaming, various degrees of exile, containment in dark, dank places, and various physical tortures. Yet the Athenians tended to temper their punishments in the spirit of moderation recommended by Athena, erring on the side of generosity whenever there was doubt of guilt. Perhaps this helps to explain why Athens' institutions remained surprisingly stable throughout the fifth and fourth centuries, despite fluctuating politics and a good deal of social unrest in the state. The Athenian justice system for the most part managed successfully the delicate balance of relations among an economically diverse population during very unstable times.

The justice system was successful because all its aspects—the trial process, the sentence, and the social places where punishments were exacted—reasserted the society's boundaries—physical, social, and moral. When social deviants upset the distribution of honors in the society and challenged the social order, spectacles of punishment disgraced the offenders and gave public affirmation and redemption to the offended, thus restoring the equilibrium of *timē*. Thus trials returned social actors to their rightful social places.

Solon's *dikasterion* or trial by jury was greatly significant to the workings of justice in Athens: it marked the transfer of penal initiative from the tribe to the state. Drakon's law demonstrates that the custom had always been to leave the punishment of offenders to the clan, wherever possible. Tribal control of punishment was lost with the advent of the jury trial. Individual citizens continued to prosecute their offenders, staging their grievances and airing their outrage before a jury of their social peers (*aikiai*), who then analyzed the case and measured its merit against the ruling norms. The jury was understood to represent the evolving will of the demos. The prosecutor argued for more extreme punishment; the defendant argued for less. The jury was not so much focused on how to handle the wrongdoing, as how to placate the accuser's outrage. The degree of shame the offended experienced at the hands of the offender had to be repaid in exact proportion. If too little shame was exacted of the culprit, the offender and his relatives may not accept the verdict. If the penalty exacted too much shame, the offender may be left with a thirst for retribution. If the anger of all parties was not laid to rest, then the court was not successful, the city remained at risk, and vigilantism remained a concern on both sides of the conflict.

The Greek system of justice, from the age of the kings through the democracy, remained grounded in a logic of retribution. Vengeance is never a healthy affect and has a tendency toward excess. Moreover, exacting vengeance by shaming can have rebounding negative effects in the society. As we shall see in the next chapter, Plato recognized the problems with a *dikephoros* (avenging) justice and tried to effect a revolution concerning these archaic ideas. He challenged the prevailing definition of crime and reconfigured the language of punishment to force a rethinking of justice as a curative of sickened souls.

Notes

1. Thucydides, *The Peloponnesian War*, Rex Warner, trans., (Middlesex, Eng.: Penguin Books, 1985), 1.15.

2. Ibid., 1.3.

3. In Plato's dialogue the *Crito*, Socrates' friends try to save his life by smuggling him from the jail to a foreign city, but he refuses their rescue, arguing that the shame of exile would be worse than death.

4. Aristotle, *Politics*, 4.

5. Drakon, "First Tablet" cited in Michael Crawford, David Whitehead, *Archaic and Classical Greece* (Cambridge, Eng.: Cambridge University Press, 1984), 135.

6. By the fourth century, the wealthy elites of the Areopagus had been subordinated to the authority of the *demos* and Athens became a truly radical democracy.

7. Aristotle, *Athenaion Politeia* 2.

8. Reported by Aristotle, Ibid., 5.

9. Ibid., 11.

10. Ibid, 7.

11. Ibid., 9.

12. Scholars are undecided about whether *ostakismos* was one of Cleisthenes' reforms, as Aristotle claims. Ibid., 22, 1–6. See Crawford and Whitehead (1983), 163–165.

13. *Plutarch's Complete Works: Parallel Lives* (New York: Thomas Y. Crowell & Co., 1909), Vol. I, 506-531.

14. Ibid.

Part Two
Plato's Revolutionary Penology

Chapter 5
From Avenging to Healing

When the jury system of trial and punishment were instituted at Athens as part of Solon's reforms, common notions of justice were understood in the context of the heroic *ethos*. Justice was the virtue naming the correct balance of power and honors in the society. Justice was seen to reign and social order was intact when the appropriate distribution of honors held true among the society of powerful peers. When a wrong was done to a citizen, the victim (*atimos*) felt dishonored or shamed (*atimos*) and sought redemption of his honor in the courts for public affirmation of the debt owed by the offender.

The Athenian trial process in many respects mirrored the trial of the *Oresteia*. It gave a public stage to the conflict through the testimonies of the accuser and the defendant, allowing the victim to express his moral rage (*aitiai*) before an audience who shared his code of *nomoi*, and allowing the defendant to explain his actions and reveal any mitigating circumstances. If the defendant was found guilty by a jury of their peers, punishment was a shaming process (*timoresthai*) that signaled a stripping of the offender's honor and a restoration of honor to the victim.

I have said that this understanding of justice is consistent with the heroic *ethos* that shaped the archaic Greek aristocratic world. We witness the process of justice and punishment as the public redress of imbalances in honor throughout Greek myth and tragedy, and in Homer's epic poems. I have noted a weakness in the Greek heroic ethos in the fact that the volatile warriors were subject to extremes of passion in their responses to injustice, which I have named an obsessive "will to punish." The trial process, imaged in Aeschylus' *Oresteia* and mirrored in the Athenian court system, allowed public expression of victim outrage (with the goal of appeasing the victim) as well as a hearing of the defendant's *apologia* (literally, "defense") for his actions. A broad arsenal of punishments allowed some flexibility as the scales of honor were set aright again. As in the *Oresteia*, the Athenians were committed to placating the victim's rage, but they also preferred to err on the side of generosity, whenever there was doubt as to guilt. They might well forego punishments, once the victim was satisfied, since shaming penalties always risk sparking further cycles of resentment and social unrest.

However, one famous trial stands out against the rest as indicating harshness rather than generosity and leniency. The trial and punishment of the philosopher Socrates, at a ripe seventy years of age, is by any measure an example of punitive excess. The harshness of executing an aged and respected male citizen demonstrates that occasionally, even under the democracy, the excessive "will to punish" that typified the heroic ideal might rear its ugly head. Socrates had shamed some powerful people in Athens, over a lifetime of his gadfly stinging. His execution was payback for their wounded pride.

Socrates' defense as recorded in Plato's *Apology* shows the old philosopher to be charged with corrupting the youth and observing new gods. These are shameful charges that question Socrates' honorable character. Yet in his defense, Socrates reveals that he is actually under attack for "old" reasons and prejudices, the same intolerance that had so often enraged heroes of the past. Socrates seems to have caused an imbalance in the honor system of the city. Affronting prominent citizens of Athens with impertinent questions about their piety, courage, and justice exposed their ignorance in matters to which they lay claim of expertise. They experienced Socrates' questioning as shaming and they wished to shame him in return, to set the honor system back in balance.

The democrats of fifth century Athens believed their political orientation to have overcome the narrow aristocratism of the past. But in respect of their ideas about honor and shame, the democrats remained faithful to the heroic ethos. The merchant class that had recently risen to power demanded honor from fellow citizens as much as did the wellborn of the past. This new breed of men demanded honor, but they did not understand that the honor system is a "give and take" that earned honor through honorable behavior. The democrats indulged in excesses that would have shamed the earlier elites. Plato's meditations on justice and shame will help us see that acting shamelessly is a function of inadequate social learning. People act ignobly, dishonorably, shamelessly, when they fail to appreciate the rights and responsibilities that entwine to underpin conscientious citizenship.

Socrates exemplifies the heroic ethos in his ready submission to the penalty ordered by the court of Athens, just as he had, throughout his life, made it a matter of honor to be faithful to the stringent moral code of noble conduct. His refusal to shame himself through unseemly behavior, even to save his life, typifies the heroic ideal. He tells his friend Crito, in the dialogue *Crito*, that he will not dishonor himself by running away from prison and living in exile in a foreign city. As a good son respects a parent, so Socrates submitted to the dictates of his polis, even when its judgments were wrong, because this, he believed, is the right and noble thing to do. Socrates went to his death honorably and graciously—heroically.

We have no account, in Plato or elsewhere, that suggests that Socrates ever behaved ignobly. We do know that he possessed a strong sense of shame, because many of Plato's dialogues witness his habit of covering his head in shame, when explicating shameful ideas, even though they were not his own. He was true to the heroic worldview in taking pride in his military service in the great wars, slipping mention of his contributions at Potidaea, Amphipolis, and Delium into his defense in the *Apology* (28de). Laches, a warrior of high repute, also confirms Socrates' bravery and forbearance, in dutifully holding any position to which he was assigned (*Laches* 181ab). Socrates' words and his actions, Laches asserts, embody the very spirit of the Doric warrior, which he names the highest form of Hellenic harmony (*Hellenikē harmonia* at 189d).

Socrates was faithful to the heroic ethos in seeking excellence in everything he did, exhibiting noble-mindedness and honorable behavior in matters of love (as Alkibiades testifies at *Symposium* 218c ff.), in prison (as pictured in *Crito*), and in anticipation of his death (as depicted in the *Phaedo*). His frequent expressions of contempt for common men stem not from aristocratic arrogance, but from a heroic disgust for inferior and shameful ideals and behaviors. The Hellenic harmony Laches attributes to him witnesses his internalized social learning, metaphorized as the *daimonion* that whispered warnings to him whenever he was about to go astray. His *daimonion* is the small voice of conscience that saves better men from the moral mistakes of lesser men.[1]

The reader may wonder, if powerful men, such as Laches, recognize Socrates' faithfulness to the exacting heroic ethos, then why was charged with the foul deeds of corrupting the youth and disrespecting the gods of Athens? How is it that a jury of his peers found him guilty of these offenses and had him executed? The timing of the trial tells us a good deal. The democrats had recently returned to power, after a year of brutal rule by the "Thirty Tyrants," puppets of Sparta who sought to reverse the democratic changes Solon had made to the Athenian constitution. The tyrants were expelled in 403 and Socrates was killed in 399. Socrates' harsh sentence reflects the absolute rejection of aristocratic ideals by the commercial classes, moving into seats of power.

The changing political and ethical climate of Athens at the time of Socrates' execution goes far to explain his harsh fate. In his *Seventh Letter*, Plato describes the democratic era of Athens in the early decades of the fifth century.

> There were many things occurring to cause offense, nor is it surprising that in times of revolution, men in some cases took undue revenge on their enemies. Yet for all that, the restored exiles displayed great moderation. . . . Now as I considered these matters, as well as the sort of men who were active in politics, and the laws and customs, the more I examined them and the more I advanced in years, the harder it appeared to me to administer the government correctly. For one thing, nothing could be done without friends and loyal companions, and such men were not easy to find ready at hand, since our city was no longer administered according to the standards and practices of our fathers. Neither could such men be created afresh with any facility. Furthermore the written law and the customs were being corrupted at an astounding rate. (325cd)

Plato describes a shameful situation; "the whirlpool of public life and the incessant movement of shifting currents" characterized the new democracy (325e). He reports closely monitoring the political climate for a favorable moment to enter public life, for the sake of improving the situation, which in his estimation required "reforming the whole constitution" but he finally came to the conclusion that his countrymen had gone too far astray of noble conduct to be saved by a philosopher. "[T]heir system of government is bad. Their constitutions are almost beyond redemption" (326a).

The democratic age in Athens, from that ancient date until the present, has been heralded as a triumph of political reform, celebrated as a revolutionary era of social and political freedom, with superior new ideals of social justice and egalitarianism. Some thinkers are so smitten by the first democratic model that they believe, with Cornelius Castoriadis, that modern representative democracies are sad imposters of the original paradigm.[2] But Plato's testimony and the execution of Socrates evidences that fifth century Athens was anything but a model of political and social justice. The demos may have seized the helm of state and extended political rights to more people, but the grounding values of the democracy, social justice and egalitarianism, were already long present in the heroic ethos, but entwined within a strict code of responsible behavior.

The situation Plato describes in early fifth century Athens demonstrates that the democrats have claimed the political and social honors (previously reserved for the *aristoi*) but failed to adopt the concomitant code of honorable behavior. They were not as schooled in the aristocrats' moral strengths—their strong sense of duty to the community, their loyalty to the timeworn laws and customs, their commitment to the ideals of Doric harmony—as Alastair MacIntyre imagines they were.[3] The execution of Socrates and the decades of lawlessness that Plato describes following Socrates's death suggest that, at the very least, the new leaders of the democracy failed to internalize the prohibitions—the "standards and practices of our fathers"—which would have elicited a crippling sense of shame from a nobler-minded generation.

The movement from the heroic ethos of the warrior to the petty resentment of Socrates' accusers and the corruption Plato describes in the *Seventh Letter* witnesses the new breed of commoner who has found his way to wealth and power in fifth century democratic Athens. New base, pragmatic ideals of the *nouveau riche* are slowly eroding the old aristocratic codes of honor, leaving base men to do as they shamelessly please in the name of their newfound "freedom."

However, if we accept that the full-blown moral and political breakdown Plato describes is the result of the erosion of aristocratic ideals, we must also see the seeds of that erosion in fundamental flaws embedded deep in the heroic ethos. Proud heroes have awful tempers. Their keen sensitivity to peer opinion weakened them morally, by driving them to punitive excesses that undermined social order. Their moral code was so intricately entwined with calculations of honor and shame that their actions against offenders could be merciless and lead the community to disaster.

The excessive "will to punish" that is the mark of the warrior class is witnessed in Athens' treatment of Mytilene and Melos, during the Peloponnesian War, and then again in Athens under the cruel lawlessness of the Thirty Tyrants. After the reign of the Thirty is quashed and the democrats return from exile, someone had to bear the brunt of their anger and be punished for their humiliation. The democrats, like the aristocrats before them, believed that merciless punishment of their enemies was a right of their social station and an appropriate response to shame.

Plato recognized the need to overcome the fatal flaws in the noble ethos that Socrates exemplified. Thus, from the earliest dialogues, he pictures Socrates as having Hellenic harmony and all the virtues of the aristocratic age. However, Socrates has altogether overcome the will to punish. The prestigious old priest, Euthyphro, testifies to this fact. When Euthyphro encounters Socrates on the porch of the Archon-King, he states: "You surely cannot have a case at law. . . . I never would believe that you were prosecuting anybody else" (*Euthyphro* 2ab). To shamelessly prosecute the old philosopher whom wiser men recognize as "the hearth" of the state takes the ignorant audacity of the youthful Meletus, "a hook-nosed man with long straight hair and not much beard" (2b).[4]

Democracy, as a formal system of dynamic, participatory self-governance by a citizen demos, is a revolutionary arrangement born for the first time onto the political scene in fifth century Athens. However, the impetus to democracy is to be located in the heroic ideals that shaped the Greek aristocratic world. Ideals of fairness, equality, mutual respect for one's peers, obligatory participation in the community, political action as a moral duty rather than a burden, and even the princely ideals of warrior *agon*, entwined with values of camaraderie, friendship, and filial love, compose the philosophical backdrop and the existential ground from which emerged the democratic ideals and its balanced political form. An aristocratic tradition, with a long and esteemed history, grounds the democracy at Athens.

The trial and execution of Socrates disgusted the young aristocrat Plato. After this tragedy, Plato abandoned the political life once and for all and became a philosopher in the tradition of the beloved master. Plato's dialogues enact an overcoming of the harsh reality of Athenian justice, by keeping the beloved Socrates alive and well, preserved in living philosophical drama. The experiment in immortality has proven successful; thousands of years later, modern readers can follow the old master as he explores the important philosophical questions—piety, courage, death, friendship, love—whose investigation was the mission of his life.

Since the justice system of Athens so grievously failed in Socrates' case, Plato's greatest challenge is to rethink the meaning of justice and the place of punishment within a healthy state. His speculations around issues of justice and punishment enact nothing short of a revolution in the accepted meanings, language, and penal policies of his day. In the next chapters, I will consider two of the dramatically earliest dialogues, the *Crito* and the *Euthyphro*, where Plato introduces a new conception of punishment that fundamentally challenges the contemporary understandings of the function of judicial penalty. Then, I will analyze the dialogue, *Gorgias*, to show that the fatal flaw in the heroic ethos inheres in the very foundational values that underpin the Greek worldview, in the entwined concepts of honor and shame. Plato's new conception of justice and punishment will need to reconfigure the popular understanding of these ideas. He will need to move his audience from the *dikephoros* (avenging) justice bequeathed by the archaic princes toward a *therapeuma* (healing) justice, which corrects and cures.

Notes

1. Socrates reports that his *daimonion* warns him against shameless behaviors. *Apology* 31d; c.f. *Symposium* 174d ff.

2. See Cornelius Castoriadis, "The Greek and the Modern Political Imaginary," David Ames Curtis. trans., *Salmagundi*, 100 (Fall 1993): 102-29; and "Radical Imagination and the Social Instituting Imaginary" in *Rethinking Imagination: Culture and Creativity*, Gillian Robinson and John Rundell, eds. (London and New York: Routledge, 1994), 136-53.

3. See Alastair MacIntyre, *After Virtue* (Notre Dame, IN: Notre Dame University Press, 1984), 121-145.

4. In the Greek doctrine of "the unity of virtues," the morally good and the socially worthy are also the physically beautiful, so Plato's mention of Meletus' ugly features is meant to reveal that he is ill bred and ignoble.

Chapter 6
Shame as Witness to Education

The Crito

In the *Crito*, Socrates' long-time friend Crito tries to convince Socrates to escape prison and live in exile rather than accept execution. His attempt to persuade Socrates is a moral argument that begins "I don't even feel that it is right" (45c). He lists the moral reasons for Socrates' consideration: it is wrong to throw your life way; you are abandoning your sons; you are taking the path of least resistance in submitting to the court's ruling. He closes:

> Really, I am ashamed (*aiskunomai*), both on your account and on ours, your friends'. It will look as though we had played something like a coward's part all through this affair of yours. . . . Take care, Socrates, that these things be not disgraceful, as well as evil (*kakoi kai aiskura*) besides the suffering there will be all this disgrace for you and for us to bear. (46a)

Crito is appealing to the heroic *ethos* here. In weighing up Socrates' options in the face of execution, Crito's arguments revolve around shame (*aiskuros*) and honor, courage and cowardice. He makes his appeal in reference to others—how will it *look*? *Aiskuros* (shame, the shameful) refers to something disgraceful, but it is also the opposite of *kalos*, (beautiful, the beautiful). Socrates and his friends will appear ugly to their society, if they fail to save Socrates' life. The concern he expresses is for *how they will look*, their reputation and the social prejudice that they will be made to bear as a result of not looking beautiful, by behaving sufficiently prudently, bravely, and gallantly. Plato ironically frames Crito's plea: "Please don't be unreasonable!"

Socrates responds by giving reasons to justify his refusal to escape. These reasons too are moral reasons, and they too speak to the question of shame and honor. But his reckoning of shame is not the same as Crito's—or that of the Greek tradition. "And so in the first place," affirms Socrates, "your proposition is not correct when you say that we should consider opinion (*doxeis*) of the many in questions of what is just (*dikaion*) and honorable (*kalon*) and good (*agathon*)" (48a). The point is so crucial that he repeats it: "we ought not consider what people in general will say about us, but how we stand with the expert in matters of justice (*dikaion*) and injustice (*adikon*)" (48a).

Socrates is here disconnecting the notion of shame and honor from the opinions of their social peers about justice and injustice, and connecting them instead to true knowledge or expert opinion. What matters is what is truly shameful, not what people think of us. Socrates is hereby overturning the heroic and popular notion of shame, arguing that that shame is not other-related, but a self-relation between justice and one's soul. Shame, for Socrates, does not follow from ill repute (particularly from ill repute among "the many" or *hoi polloi*) because people cannot be counted upon to get their moral judgments right. Shame follows from failing to behave well, from doing something morally wrong, not from *being seen* as having done something morally wrong.

Plato is demonstrating from his earliest dialogues that the heroic *ethos* of shame has got it all wrong. The paradigmatic hero, Achilles, makes decisions that are life-altering for himself, his troops, and the whole of the Hellenes, because he feels shamed by Agamemnon's treatment. The great king has dishonored him by failing to treat him justly, and Achilles has accepted that the mistreatment designates his social degradation. Plato is overturning this other-related *ethos* and declaring agents responsible only for what wrongs they commit, not for the wrong judgments of their peers. It matters not what the people find beautiful or ugly; it matters only whether one's soul is beautiful or ugly, according to one's deeds, which beautify the soul or tarnish its beauty. In this radical movement, Plato is reconfiguring the site of justice. Justice inheres not in the opinion of the community but in truth, not in appearance of beauty and ugliness but in the beautiful or ugly state of the soul. Justice is not decided in the community, the marketplace, or the courtroom. It is decided in the rightness, beauty and happiness inhering in the individual soul.

I have said that Plato abandoned his desire for a career in politics after the execution of his beloved old master. His career as a philosopher is launched as the effort to understand how things went so wrong, how the democratic love of good things, such as liberty, honor, and justice, culminated in the killing of a revered old man. Plato's writing style, the use of dialogue, express his desire to reverse this injustice. Socrates would not agree with his friends that their rescue plan for him was just and not disgraceful. But Plato is rescuing Socrates in a just way, keeping him alive and engaged in his beloved philosophical investigations in almost every dialogue he will ever write.

In this scene in the Crito, Plato is rescuing Socrates from the very fate that Crito dreads—social degradation. By reconfiguring shame and honor as the inner relation of the soul with its highest ideals, Plato has severed the connecting thread that holds the heroic ethos intact, the umbilical cord that connects the individual's self-relation to his social fate, determined by the opinion of the peer group. Ironically, Plato is rescuing Socrates from the scandal the old philosopher does not fear. But he is also speaking to an entire ethical tradition. He is telling Achilles that losing his war-prize to the unjust king has no implication for his (Achilles') beauty or ugliness. Achilles has done no misdeed that would suggest his failure to live up to his highest ideals. Plato is overturning a long tradition of other-related ethics.

Socrates responds to Crito's plea for his (Socrates') reasonableness by challenging Crito to consider: If life is not worth living when the body is worn out and health ruined, how much less worthy is a life where the more precious part of the self, the soul, is sullied and disfigured by corruption? Crito does not need to worry what others will think of him (Socrates) or them (Socrates' friends). The good man cannot be harmed by worse, just as the soul cannot be harmed by external forces. What matters is that they all take great care to do the right and just thing. Keeping themselves free from shame (*aiskuron*)—remaining beautiful (*kalon*)—is not a matter decided under the social gaze, but by the inner moral eye, which speaks in the sting of conscience to interrupt the trajectory of injustice.

Shame or dishonor has not become a faulty concept to be ignored altogether; it has become the most crucial aspect in an inner monitoring system that keeps the individual on moral track. Others may have the power to torture people, exile them, and put them to death, but injustices such as these bring shame to the agent, not to the victim. Many a good person has been ill-treated by their enemies. There is no shame in braving their abuse.

The Euthyphro

The dialogue, the *Euthyphro*, offers another opportunity to witness Plato's revolutionary approach to shame and honor, justice and injustice. This dialogue stages the meeting of Socrates with the priest Euthyphro, on the steps of the archon-king, as Socrates is about to present himself for trial. Thus it is the dramatically earliest dialogue. Euthyphro expresses his surprise at seeing the old philosopher at the courthouse, stating, "I would never believe that you were prosecuting anybody else" (3b). One wonders at this statement. It seems to suggest that Socrates has a reputation for avoiding harmdoing to others, and so would never be found trying to bring a fellow, however much a scoundrel, before a court that might punish him. Euthyphro's surprise is not here explained, but neither does Socrates question his assumption that he (Socrates) would not prosecute anyone.

Euthyphro finds himself at the court this day because he is bringing a case himself. The case is quite a scandalous one, because he will prosecute his own father. Euthyphro admits that other citizens consider him to be a maniac for proposing such a case against his own kin (4a). Socrates expresses his surprise at this news and admits that the prosecution would be scandalous and inexplicable, except under special circumstances; the only way one might understand one's doing something this ostensibly maniacal would be if the prosecutor were "already far advanced in point of wisdom" that he knew better than the scandalized crowd.

The fact that the act of prosecuting one's father is maniacal under normal circumstances remains unchallenged by the old philosopher. The mitigating factor which would relieve the act of its maniacal quality resides in the prosecutor's knowledge. Perhaps Euthyphro knows something that the old philosopher does not, which would explain this act, which others would deem scandalous, as right and just. Socrates then proceeds to question Euthyphro to unearth the special knowledge which would explain away the apparent shamefulness of Euthyphro's prosecution of his father.

Euthyphro claims special knowledge of piety, an exclusive understanding of what is pleasing to the gods who oversee the crimes of murder and sacrificial robbery. He explains to Socrates that this special knowledge permits him to understand the situation differently from others. Euthyphro knows that failing to prosecute a family member for these serious crimes is bad for everyone. Failure to exact a "due measure" of punishment in recompense for this serious injustice will bring pollution to his father, as well as to the whole family. You must "cleanse yourself and him as well, by bringing him to justice," explains Euthyphro (4c).

Socrates admits he has no knowledge of this truth, what is holy or unholy to do in this or any case. He asks the priest to teach him all he knows about the gods and their likes and dislikes, so that he might share this special knowledge. As is Socrates' usual aporetic way, all the questions he puts to Euthyphro, to determine the nature of his special understanding of matters divine, run up onto the hard rocks of absurdity and demolish the priest's claims to knowledge. By the end of the dialogue, we understand only one thing—that Euthyphro knows nothing of the things he claims as his expertise. The implication of the failed search for his special knowledge becomes clear by the end of their conversation: Euthyphro cannot, with his present argument, justify prosecuting his father; the act remains maniacal, scandalous, and shameful unless he can come up with better reasons for doing what he is doing. Prosecuting others (and especially family) is an act of wanton hybris. Unless some greater good can be found as being served by the prosecution of even the most heinous crimes, justice as it is currently understood in Athens will have to be abandoned. We must keep this conclusion in mind, as we enter the dialogue with *Gorgias*.

The Gorgias

The *Gorgias* is Plato's dialogue that struggles most pointedly with the idea of shame. The dialogue is named after the famed orator Gorgias, who is its main character along with Socrates. Its dramatic date is 405 BCE, when Gorgias would have been eighty years of age and Socrates would have been about sixty-five, living out his last few years before his execution in 399 BCE. Plato is writing this dialogue at the age of forty, about the time that he definitively removed himself from the political world, opened the Academy, and undertook his great experiment in philosophical education. So he is a middle-aged man, having reflected for twelve years on the scandalous and shameful event that shaped the direction of his life—the execution of Socrates. But Plato has also dated the dialogue at the cusp of the close of a momentous historical era. The Peloponnesian War will come to a close in 404, and shortly thereafter powerful aristocrats exiled from Athens during war will return as a puppet government of Sparta. "The Thirty Tyrants," as they will come to be called,

took power on a moral argument. They declared they would purify the
city of unjust men and reclaim "virtue and justice" in the rest of the citizens. Rapheal Sealey states of the Thirty:

> The fourth-century tradition about the Thirty had a moralistic element.
> It said that at first they seized, condemned and executed evil men, es-
> pecially sycophants or those who had made a profession of prosecuting
> on criminal charges, and the city was pleased to this, but later they at-
> tacked and killed wealthy men, in order to seize their property, and re-
> spected citizens, who might become focuses of opposition. Clearly the
> distinction between the two types of victim depends largely on the
> viewpoint of the beholder.[1]

The dating of the *Gorgias* is thus crucial to Plato's reframing of the problem of justice, and his definitions of what is virtuous or honorable, and
what should rightly bring shame to virtuous men. The injustices committed against the two types of victims Sealey mentions above evidences a
flaw in the logic that oriented the system of justice in Athens in the
fourth century BCE. The courts can be used to bring about justice or to
harm people unjustly. The ruling definitions of these terms—justice, virtue, shame—will determine the distinction in the court's effects.

The *Gorgias* is a pivotal dialogue. W. R. M. Lamb reads it as Plato's
"manifesto."[2] The dialogue may indeed be intended to attract the cultured
student to the Academy, as Lamb suggests is evident in Plato's style,
content (rhetoric "so flourishing and influential in forensic and political
debate") and choice of interlocutor (Gorgias), a sophist "famed all over
Greece for his ingenious wit and jingling eloquence."[3] However, in the
following reading of the dialogue, I am challenging Lamb's claim that
this is its main intent. I argue that its main objective is far greater than
the subject of rhetoric and the question of professional ethics in public
speaking. I argue that the primary task of this dialogue is to struggle with
the heroic *ethos*, and to expose the faulty foundations of its notion of justice as distribution of honors and shame. If Plato can get the definition of
shame right here, then justice too is reconfigured, and Socrates is rescued
after all from the ill fate the court has assigned him, the shame of corrupting the youth and disrespecting the gods of Athens.

The dramatic date is crucial to its exploration of the clever words of
oratory and shame in matters of justice. A single year from the dramatic
date, Athens fell to Sparta and ended the Peloponnesian War. This resulted in a brief period of governance by a Spartan-appointed oligarchy,
whom the people named the "Thirty Tyrants." These aristocrats mounted

a reign of terror that shamed Athens in the eyes of the ancient world. They exiled hundreds of democrats, executed thousands more, and expropriated property from thousands of innocent citizens and foreigners, particularly heinous crime for the Greeks, as a contravention of the ancient law of hospitality. Socrates tells in the *Apology* of his confrontation with the Thirty, when they ordered him and four other men to arrest a certain man, Leon of Salamis, for execution.[4] Socrates refused, though the others submitted, placing his life in jeopardy. He would have been executed then, had the oligarchy not very soon afterward been disbanded.

Looking back upon these historical facts from his Academic armchair, Plato calls upon them as a fitting framework for the questions he is about to pose about justice and shame in this dialogue. The events of the dialogue are contextualized by the audience's certain knowledge that the dear old philosopher featured here will soon be executed, not by cruel tyrants with a reputation for injustice and shamelessness, but by freedom-loving democrats. When the democrats seize control of the state, after the fall of the Thirty, their methods will prove as unscrupulous as the acts of any tyrant; they will exile their opponents, execute innocents, and commit other shameless acts, in the name of freedom and democracy, a practice continued to this day in the "free world."

Through the lens of the *Gorgias*, the behavior of tyrants will appear indistinguishable from that of the Athenian democrats, and the reasoning the unscrupulous characters of the dialogue will call upon to justify tyrannical behaviors, Plato will expose as the commonest sort of reasoning. Socrates' examination of a morally-descending cast of characters will culminate with Callicles, whom Lamb names "the typical Athenian democrat."[5] The Thirty Tyrants tried to execute Socrates unjustly; the democrats will complete the task. The *Gorgias* will reveal to the reader how it is that two groups so radically different in their politics can be so similar in their worldly effects. The tyrants and the democrats will be shown to share a common *ethos*.

The dialogue opens. Socrates is accompanied by Chaerephon, the eager, eccentric fellow named by Socrates in the *Apology* as having delivered to him the Delphic oracle's proclamation that began his philosophical quest—the message that Socrates is the wisest man in Athens.[6] The two friends meet Callicles in the streets of Athens, and Callicles invites them to his house where Gorgias, the ageing orator, has just given a rhetorical display. Socrates questions Gorgias on the nature of his profession and the rules for the right use of his art.

   Gorgias, the aged professor, is clearly an honorable man, benevolent, gracious, and patient with the questions of Socrates and Chaerephon. He is accompanied by the young Polus, to whom the argument falls when Gorgias grows tired. The vehement attack that constitutes the younger protégé's oratory style foreshadows the direction that the art is assuming as the mentors grow old and die off.[7] It also foreshadows the direction that Athens will take as the noble old folk retire and become replaced by the more arrogant youths, who have learned well the lessons of crafty argument unfettered by considerations of truth and justice. Finally, Callicles, the radical democrat, will enter the discussion when Polus' defense of his art capsizes on the rocks of Socratic argument and sinks in self-contradiction. The ascending shamelessness of the cast of interlocutors exposes the descending moral direction that Athens will soon take under democratic rule.

   Socrates wants the famous Gorgias to explore with him the nature of the art of oratory. The tired old man wants to pass the conversation to his young protégé Polus. But Socrates objects, protesting Polus' unfitness for dialogue: "Polus has had more practice in what is called rhetoric than in discussion" (448e). Polus had already disappointed Socrates, when he had embarked on a flourishing eulogy on rhetoric, rather than fulfilling Chaerephon's request for a definition.

   Gorgias agrees to discuss rhetoric with Socrates and they come to the agreement that rhetoric helps men be able to speak, and helps them to understand the things about which they speak (449e–450e). But many arts have their effect in speech; rhetoric must be distinguished from things such as numeration, draught-playing, or geometry, if its distinctness is to be understood. Gorgias declares the distinction to reside in rhetoric's concerning itself with "the greatest of human affairs . . . and the best" (541d). After Socrates recalls that many practitioners—the doctor, the trainer, and the money-getter—make similar high claims about their arts, Gorgias obliges Socrates with a clarification: his art deals with the greatest good, because it brings freedom to people in general, and dominion to individuals in their cities (452d). Rhetoric has effects in the law courts, the council-chamber, the commons of the Assembly, and in any public meeting, because it allows one the freedom to speak and the power to persuade the multitude.

   Rhetoric is not the sole kind of persuasion, however; even instructors of numeration must persuade their students. Socrates presses Gorgias for a clearer distinction of *his* art. He asks him to declare what kind of things his art of persuasion seeks to persuade people. They decide that rhetoric "is a producer of persuasion for belief, not for instruction in the matter of right or wrong" (455a). So the rhetorician, as it turns out, is in the good company of such advisers as Themistocles and Pericles, in not concerning himself with instructing in right or wrong, but persuading better than the professionals in all matters and on all subjects.

Gorgias is emboldened; he continues a flourishing oration on his art, which includes a certain professional ethics in the definition. The art must be used rightly; one must use its power fairly. Gorgias insists that if a man takes training in rhetoric and then fails to use it rightly, the culprit may rightly be hated, expelled, and even put to death. On the other hand, he will not allow that the teacher be blamed for the student's misuse of the art. The orator takes no responsibility when his art does not produce good effects (457a–c); rhetoric is always a good thing, even when its practitioners go astray.

Since Gorgias has admitted that an orator can speak about any professional subject better than the professional can, the conclusion is reached that the orator need have no knowledge of the truth of the matters of which he speaks to be successful in his persuading. Socrates inquires whether the orator "is in the same relation to what is just and unjust, base and noble, good and bad" (459d). Can the orator also appear in the eyes of his audience to know something about these subjects too, whether or not he has actual knowledge? Gorgias affirms that the orator's skill permits him the appearance of knowing what he does not actually know, even in crucial matters of right and wrong. Rhetoric may be used to persuade an audience in directions that are questionable, even to the rhetorician, as to their moral worth. This admission allows for two corollary sub-challenges: an orator may make unjust and ignoble use of his art and an orator may take on pupils of questionable moral character and may well equip these students with dangerous powers to do harm to others.

Gorgias' eloquent eulogy of his art has now run up against several ethical roadblocks. Our famous teacher of rhetoric, whose skills are sought across Greece, has just been forced by the argument to admit that orators teach what they do not know, that they may well teach what is unjust, ignoble and bad, and they teach it to anyone who happens to come by for instruction. Socrates notes a contradiction in the eulogy: "You were saying this that rhetoric could never be an unjust thing, since the speeches it makes [are] always about justice; but . . . a little later you told us that the orator might make even an unjust use of his rhetoric" (461a).

Polus now intervenes in the dialogue to defend his teacher, and he attempts to rescue him from the twists of the argument by raising the theme of shame, showing shame to be a limiting characteristic in his teacher: "Gorgias was ashamed not to admit your point that the rhetorician knows what is just and noble and good" (461b). Gorgias' shame will not allow him to tell an untruth, even to win an argument. Clearly this is a poor rhetorician (by some accounts) but a good man. His shame held him back from claiming knowledge beyond his ken, and accounts for his running amuck in the argument.

Polus will take over the argument from his teacher, because, we may assume, he is not limited by the moral conventions that restrict the old professor. Polus feels no shame. His shamelessness is immediately demonstrated by an immodesty and arrogance that would surely have shamed his teacher. Socrates affirms, "You claim, I understand, that you yourself know all that Gorgias knows, do you not?" Polus crows, "I do" (462a).

So the dialogue continues, with Polus replacing Gorgias in the argument, just as his kind (of shameless youth) very soon will come to replace his teacher's kind (benevolent elders who are sensitive to matters of honor, admit what they do not know, and are limited by feelings of shame). In the law courts, the commons of the Assembly, the council-chamber, and the public forums, a new kind of man is cropping just in time for Socrates' trial, a very few years later. Plato is showing why Socrates received the foul treatment that he did at the hands of his citizen-fellows in the trumped-up charges seen in the *Apology* and the death sentence seen enacted in the *Phaedo*.

Socrates goes on seeking a definition of rhetoric. His *diairesis* separates false from true arts, and leads to the assertion that, as cookery and self-adornment are false arts that insinuate themselves as medicine and gymnastics, so rhetoric and sophistry pretend themselves to be equivalent to the true arts of justice and legislation. Rhetoric is not a true art, after all. Genuine arts have as their goal the true good of their object, just as medicine or gymnastics "bestow their care for the best advantage" of the patient (464c). An imposter art composes a "habitude or knack" or "flattery." Socrates describes rhetoric as "a shrewd, gallant spirit which has a natural bent for clever dealing with mankind . . . I sum up its substance in the name *flattery*" (463b). Flattery "cares nothing for what is the best, but dangles what is most pleasant for the moment as a bait for folly" (464d).

Gorgias thought he would rescue the argument after the ashamed Gorgias let it get away from him. But flattery, pleasantries, and folly? Rhetoric has fallen substantially from its perch as the "greatest good" to a false thing, quite base and frivolous. Polus is getting desperate. He needs to redeem the seriousness of his art, so he challenges Socrates to consider whether orators have not the truest good, and great power in their cities. Socrates responds by challenging what is popularly understood by the term "power." Here Plato is launching a new conception of power that will show Socrates to be most powerful and his accusers powerless. Socrates responds with the shocking denigration "the orators have the smallest power of all who are in the city" (466b).

Polus' retort to this insult grants the audience another telling glimpse into the moral differences that separate Polus, the young orator, from his benevolent old teacher, Gorgias. the distinction again foreshadows the moral turn that Athens is taking as it moves into the democracy, the turn that will in a few years sacrifice justice and Socrates. Polus crows shamelessly (466c), "Are [orators] not like the despots, in putting to death anyone they please, and depriving anyone of his property, and expelling him from their cities as they see fit?" In a brief few years from the dramatic date of this dialogue, Athens will behave in just the ways that Polus has now boasted. Thirty Tyrants ill commit just these crimes against citizen and foreigner in their fair city. Soon thereafter, Athens will see a young upstart orator, as shameless as Polus, bring false accusations against the old philosopher whom Polus is now addressing, persuading the city that justice resides in executing the old man.

Polus' shameless admission stops short the smooth flow of the dialectic and the friendly investigation of ideas. His words are so radical and scandalous that Socrates is moved to exclaim "Hush, Polus!" Polus admits to Socrates, before his illustrious teacher Gorgias and the entire public audience at the house of Callicles, that when the powerful harm others—whether justly or unjustly—they are enviable. Polus says aloud what others may be thinking but would never admit. He can say these scandalous things aloud because he does not know shame. His shamelessness reveals the lack of knowledge that sets him apart from the old professor. Polus lacks the social knowledge of propriety and prohibition that would cause him to feel appropriate shame when saying (and presumably doing) unseemly, ignoble, base and unjust things.

Socrates' "Hush" calls for silence. It reminds Polus—and the reader—of the many ears that are listening, the many listeners present. Socrates' "Hush" is recommending shame to Polus as an appropriate response to what he has just said. The pain of shame has to do with how we present ourselves to others, and how we are perceived by them. Socrates' "Hush" warns Polus that his peers will think less of him when they hear what he is currently saying. Polus must silence himself to preserve the audience's false sense of his (Polus's) worth. The "Hush" confirms a positive aspect of the heroic *ethos* that warns through embarrassment and humiliation against committing unseemly acts and stating unseemly opinions. It warns Polus, and reminds us, of the destructive (and constructive) power of peer opinion.

On the other hand, according to the heroic *ethos*, a sense of shame goes well beyond the problem of how others perceive us, to the question of our inner worth as human beings. The hero's shame is an indicator of his own diminished value, when he acts inappropriately. Heroic shame is indeed other-related; Achilles feels a very real sense of diminution in the eyes of his countrymen, when Agamemnon treats him disrespectfully. The immoral act (seizing Achilles' war-bride Briseis) belongs to Agamemnon. However, it is telling that the shame belongs to Achilles. There is more to Achilles' shame than simply the pain that comes with realizing that others will look at what has occurred and think the less of him. He too thinks the less of himself; he feels truly disempowered and socially demoted, by suffering the disrespect of Agamemnon.

The hero's tendency to claim for himself the shame that rightly inheres in the act and belongs to the agent of wrongdoing is another flaw that inheres in the heroic ethos. The shame of the hero immediately translates into the reality of power relations. Poor treatment from one's peers is taken as actual evidence of lesser worth. The powerful peer, even in his misbehavior, does not lose his social status; indeed he seems to gain social stature if his act of wrongdoing is an act of power.

Agamemnon crows to Achilles that he is teaching him and others a lesson, by doing him this injustice. Social learning happens through the exemplars of a society. It happens through the epic tales that tell the stories of the culture, sing the praises of their heroes, and chart the rise and fall of their histories. Social learning happens through the modeling that great leaders do, and the explanations they give for their actions. Agamemnon is the powerful king, and the leading general of a vast army and a great people. Thus his words and actions have great weight with his people, and with future generations of his culture. So there is great moral weight in the king's explanation for his unjust action against Achilles: "Thus you may learn well how much greater I am than you, and another may shrink from likening his to my power and contending against me."[8]

The hero in this story has learned his moral lesson well. Achilles shows his social learning because he feels shamed by the injustice done to him. He thus becomes morally entwined in the punishment he endures for an injustice that he has not committed. Worse than Orestes and worse than Prometheus, Achilles cooperates in his own undoing, by granting to his potent peer the authority over his social status and his emotional well-being. Shame, in the heroic view, is a direct attunement to power relations, where power is universally understood in very specific terms—as the power to influence others, for good or for ill. Achilles has been influenced for ill, and his vulnerability to influence causes him the extreme pain of shame.

Polus does not suffer from Achilles' sensitivity to other people's opinions of him. He does not feel shame, though Socrates' sharp exclamation indicates that he ought to have readily felt it. Socrates, as a kindly grandfather, is guiding Polus toward a moral lesson. His guiding confirms that Polus *needs teaching*. It bears out that Polus is missing some crucial aspect of moral learning. If Polus's social education had been completed successfully, if he had already learned his moral lessons well, he would have felt what Socrates was feeling *for him*, expressed in the warning "Hush!" Polus would have felt a stinging sense of shame, had he the moral sensitivity to recognize the shamelessness of his words. The ability to experience shame thus indicates that social learning has already taken place, that the society's prohibitions on certain misbehaviors and mis-speaking have already been internalized. If one has been properly schooled, one does not need the teaching of others. One is empowered by the learning itself to monitor one's deeds and words, and to punish one's own misconduct. Shame is an internal punishment that is self-inflicted.

Polus has shamelessly admitted before an audience what he ought to have kept hidden. This falsely suggests that shame is simply other-related, so that, like Gyges (an old legend retold at *Republic* 359d ff.), one may do as one wishes, as long as others cannot see. But Socrates immediately clarifies that the shame he recommends speaks to the inner Polus and not to the outer audience. In the moralizing tone of prescriptive language, Socrates makes his moral lesson clear for the muddle-headed learner: "we ought not to envy either the unenviable or the wretched, but pity them" (469a). Wretchedness, pitiable—Socrates is telling Polus that his passions are out of whack; he is feeling one passion (pride, triumph) when he ought rightly to be feeling another altogether different passion (shame).

In pointing to Polus' inner responses as the problem, Socrates is shifting the discussion of shame from the other-related heroic *ethos* to an inner-related *ethos* of the soul's attunement. Proper learning, when it has been successfully accomplished, is about the appropriately passionate inner self. Shame is a painful feeling that intervenes to direct appropriate responses. In the best cases, it intervenes before the misconduct occurs; in the second-best case, it delivers the pain of humiliation, to check the misconduct in its tracks, immediately that one oversteps the bounds of propriety.

Socrates' "Hush" had suggested otherwise, but now we see that Socrates is not concerned with what others think. Later in the dialogue, he will unequivocally confirm: "Do not call upon me to take the votes of the company now . . the many I dismiss . . . to the multitude I have not a word to say" (474ab). But what of powerful kings? Should we allow the powerful to determine for us, as Achilles does, what is right and just? Is power such that it cancels out the moral lessons we learn as children about justice and fairness and propriety? Socrates must redefine power to help us think through this question.

The despot in his argument, and Polus and his radically democratic cronies, mistakenly understand power to reside in the ability to do any amount of harm to others. Plato must undermine the definition of power that lets fine old teachers be killed by lesser men. He has Socrates prove to Polus that power does not consist in behaving as a despot and whimsically harming others. He takes Polus through a line of argument, which reveals that people act according to what they believe to be good; they walk because they think it good; they stand when they conceive it to be better. People want to do what is best and want to avoid what it is worse. Polus agrees (468cd). If power consists in accomplishing what one wants, and one always wants what is good, then doing harm to others, reasons Socrates, frustrates people's power to get what they truly want. Harming people—whether justly or unjustly—is never ever enviable. Socrates employs an analogy to make his point:

> Suppose that in a crowded market I should hide a dagger under my arm and then say to you, "Polus, I have acquired by a wonderful chance, the power of a despot; for if I should think fit that one of those people whom you see there should die this instant, a dead man he will be, just as I think fit; or if I think fit that one of them shall have his head broken, broken it will be immediately; or to have his cloak torn to pieces, torn it will be; : so great is my power in this city" Then suppose that on your disbelieving this, I showed you my dagger; I expect when you saw it you would say: "Socrates, at this rate everyone would have great power, for any house you thought fit might be set ablaze on these methods, and the Athenian arsenals also, and the men-of-war, and the rest of the shipping, both public and private." But surely this is not

what it is to have great power—merely doing what one thinks fit. (469de)

Doing wrong involves no great power, then, since it does not bring about what is desired, the good. The only great power resides in the ability to bring about what is good. The wrongdoer is not powerful; he is wretched and unhappy. "Then to my thinking," concludes Socrates, "the orators and the despots alike have least power in their cities" (466d) unless the punishments they dish out bring about some good.

Socrates continues his teaching to Polus on the matter of honor and shame, punishment and justice. He presses Polus to consider these bad consequences of which they have been speaking (seizure of property, prison, or death), and to determine when these, the despot's punishments, are simply bad or whether sometimes they may be good. What is the boundary, the limit, or measure, that separates good from bad use of these evil effects? "Then when do you say it is better to do these things? Tell me where you draw the line," Socrates presses Polus (470b). Polus accepts Socrates' answer: "It is better when these things are done justly, and worse when unjustly" (470c).

Then the two explore the question of whether the wrongdoer is made happy by submitting himself for punishment. Polus believes that the unjust man will be happier to get off without penalty, but Socrates argues that the unjust man is wretched in any case, and he will be the more wretched if he escapes his punishment. Punishment brings requital from gods and men, Socrates argues (472e), echoing Euthyphro (*Euthyphro* 4c), though he had challenged this claim in the earlier dialogue.

Polus suggests that they call an audience vote to decide the question, but Socrates' argument for the desirability of punishment is not grounded in public opinion; his *ethos* is not other-related. What matters is whether punishment is just or not. The just is the good and brings about good effects. The unjust is the bad all around. Just punishment to a wrongdoer relieves the unhappy state, the pain of shame, which plagues (only) the well-schooled soul that recognizes its error. Paying debts for moral errors lifts the pain from the soul and removes the stain of dishonor. Happiness is clear conscience. "A man must keep a close watch over himself so as to avoid wrongdoing since it would bring a great deal of evil upon him," affirms Socrates (480a).

The "line" or boundary that Socrates was seeking, in order to distinguish right punishments from wrongful, is the same line that separates the fair from the foul in all things, "like bodies and colors and figures and sounds and observances" (474d). The line is a measure or a standard, such that "the 'fairness' of [things] cannot lie beyond those limits of being either beneficial or pleasant or both" (474e). Where punishments are just, justice being always fair, the punishments are fair and beneficial. Where punishments are unjust, then they are foul. "Who pays the penalty suffers what is good," states Socrates (*Agatha ara paschei ho dikēn didous*), and is "relieved from the greatest evil" (*Ar oun tou megístou apalláttetai*) (477a).

Since of the three things that punishment touches—property, body, and soul—soul is the most precious, its corruption is far more tragic than loss of property or bodily harm. Thus the soul's relief from corruption, through punishments, is of greatest benefit to the wrongdoer. Punishment is a "good" when it is justly administered. "The justice of the court reforms us and makes us juster, and acts as a medicine for vice" (478de). And since the vice-free soul is happiest, one ought not solely accept punishment happily and readily, but Socrates recommends the wrongdoer "go of his own freewill where he may soonest pay the penalty, to the judge as if to his doctor, with the earnest intent that the disease of his injustice shall not become chronic and cause a deep incurable ulcer in his soul" (480ab).

Socrates' axiom that punishment is an unequivocal good clarifies a point that had been left unclear in the earlier dialogue, the *Euthyphro*. Since the dialogue had culminated in exposing Euthyphro's wisdom in the area of his claimed expertise (piety) as false arrogance, the reader is left with the impression that Euthyphro's prosecution plans witness his arrogance, rather than his true insight into rightful use of the courts. We are left with the distinct impression that Euthyphro is indeed doing something "maniacal" in prosecuting his father for murder. However, in the *Gorgias*, Plato has us rethink this conclusion. Socrates' affirmation of punishment as a blessing that brings about happiness forces us to consider the correctness of Euthyphro's decision. Perhaps, though unwittingly, he is making right use of the courts after all. Socrates affirms:

> If [a wrongdoer's] crimes have deserved a flogging, he must submit to the rod; if fetters, to their grip; if a fine, to its payment; if banishment, to be banished; or if death, to die; *himself to be the first accuser either of himself or his relations*, and to employ his rhetoric for the purpose of so exposing their iniquities that they may be relieved of that greatest evil, injustice. (480d; emphasis mine.)

Thus the court system of Athens and punishment *per se* find redemption, in a new definition of power, which is sovereignty of soul. A just soul (freed from injustice) is a happy soul, whereas the despots/orators, who are dishing out unjust punishments to innocent victims (such as Socrates), are burdened with their foul deeds, and so are most wretched and unhappy. Two famous Socratic paradoxes have been presented here: *it is better to suffer than to do evil* and *the unjust man of absolute liberty is less happy than the just.* These paradoxes have far-reaching consequences for Plato's critique of the democracy that executed Socrates: together they prove that Socrates, wherever he may be, is both better and happier than his accusers, while a dark penalty of wretchedness and misery is prophesied for the democracy, the state that values absolute liberty above the lives of good men.

Socrates closes his discussion with Polus with a further critique of current punishment practices in Athens. He warns Polus that under no circumstances should punishment of any culprit, "whether an enemy or anyone else," be undertaken by the one who has been wronged (*mē autos adikētai hupo tou ekthrou—touto men gar eulabēteon*). This admonition hearkens back to the pre-Solonic form of justice, when the responsibility for social justice fell to the victims, who had to prosecute their offenders personally. The admonition on the surface, then, ratifies current juridical procedures at Athens.

However, seen from another perspective—that social offense is always a wrong against the whole community since crime offends the peace and harmony of the whole—the admonition challenges the system that punishes any criminal at all. Moreover, since Socrates mentions friend and foe in his admonition, one may extrapolate further that Socrates may have been reproaching Athens for its hostility against other cities, since all acts of war constitute punitive measures against enemies for perceived injuries.

In Athens, a charge against a defendant could only be initiated by a male citizen. Socrates' admonition affirms the responsibility of male citizens to serve the needs of their social subordinates by lodging charges on their behalf, but warns them not to use the courts as arenas for increasing their personal influence. By condemning the use of the courts for personal actions, Plato is challenging the very purpose for which, according to ancient legend, the courts were created—to give vent to the anger of offended individuals that would otherwise turn excessive and spawn vigilantism.

To appreciate the novelty of the Platonic reformulation of ideas about justice and punishment, it is important to understand Plato's conception of the human soul. For Plato, the soul cannot be truly harmed by external acts or agents. A soul can only be harmed from within, by doing—rather than suffering—bad action. Doing injustice scars the soul and the soul being far more valuable than the body, injustice must be avoided at any cost by attempting always to do right. Thus the care of the soul falls to the individual agent and amounts to rigorous self-examination, constantly probing one's own acts and intentions to catch oneself before the harm is done. A strong sense of shame can help with this, warning one before the error is made. If the warning comes too late and the wrong is already done, then punishment can be called upon to correct the situation. Punishment, in this view, becomes a crucial aspect of the care of soul, something that should be welcomed as an opportunity for purifying the soul after it has gone astray and committed an injustice.

Ideally then, social learning prepares the individual to avoid such errors in advance, sending shame to warn the agent in advance. But where the early-warning signals have failed to save the soul from wrongdoing, punishment is a corrective, just as medicine corrects health and stops the course of bodily disease. Plato insists that injustice is only dangerous for the agent, not for the sufferer. Thus, Plato has just inverted the logic of jurisprudence and the function of punishment from their current meanings in the popular understanding of fifth century Athens.

Plato's objective is no less than the complete undermining of current Athenian juridical procedure as grounded in a politics of honor and shame. The role of the courts is no longer to redistribute social status in response to the outcries of angry victim-citizens, who feel themselves to have been shamed and dishonored by offenses from their peers. The courts no longer exist to serve the fragile egos of heroes and filter (through reasonable procedure and formalized language) the needs of offended victims, disposed to reactionary excess. Punishment no longer exists to satisfy heroic pride. In Plato's revolutionary reconfiguration of justice, the court system and its arsenal of punishments exist for the sake of the offender, and not for the sake of the offended.

Plato rejects the old meanings by rejecting the prevailing language that captured these ancient purposes. Where the language of myth and tragedy had configured punishment as social demotion or "giving justice" (*didonai dikēn*) and the act of punishing as the re-seizure of social place or "taking justice" (*lambanein dikēn*), Plato instead speaks of *doing injury* (*kakos poiein*) and the object of injury becomes inconsequential—"whether an enemy or anyone else" (480e). Plato shifts the very language of justice and punishment by introducing the substantive *kolasis* and the transitive verb *koladsein* (which always takes an object). For Plato, the outrage of the offended has no currency in the language of justice and punishment, and neither does his sense of "being shamed" by mistreatment. For Plato, the sole concern of the courts and their punishments is the good of the wrongdoer, to teach him the social learning he has previously missed, to relieve his wretchedness and cure the stain of injustice, and render him capable of feeling the shame that will in future help him toward sounder choices.

Callicles enters and takes over the discussion (at 481), seeing it through to its end. He is scandalized by what he has just heard from Socrates and exclaims that Socrates must be joking. Callicles rails at Socrates in an *ad hominem* argument that lasts for four full Stephanos pages, beginning with a long tirade about shame and convention. Gorgias, he recalls, had felt shame at admitting that he would be willing to instruct a man with no knowledge of justice but only a desire to learn rhetoric.[9] Polus, too, claims Callicles, was too ashamed to admit that he thought suffering wrong is fouler than doing wrong.

Their mistake, and Socrates', argues Callicles, is their vulnerability to shame. Callicles is even less limited in his conduct by this negative passion. He continues the argument with Socrates. Their error, he posits, was to think nature (*physis*) and culture (*nomos*) in tune, when the two are actually opposed to each other. A man may be schooled to feel shame, argues Callicles, for what is culturally unacceptable, but in nature the powerful are unashamed of whatever they do from sheer might. The argument is that culture invents unnatural regulations. Shame is a tool of convention, an instrument of political *techne*, designed to keep people in their social places. Shame, like the codes of propriety and honor which it regulates, is nothing more than a social construction. Shame simply indicates the individual's attunement to the power relations of the society. It illuminates an individual's slavishness. It reveals culture's power to control, not only the bodily acts of the citizens, but their entire souls, their ideas about right and wrong, their sense of moral worth, and the social places to which they are assigned.

According to Callicles' definition, shame is the marker of a citizen's internalized submission to political force. His claim is a radical one, and sounds convincing even millennia later, framed as it is in the seductive language of freedom. The radical democrat's premise launches a challenge at a fundamental level concerning citizen liberty. A citizen is free from political coercion to the extent that she is shameless: the individual's shamelessness marks her refusal of the hegemony of her culture's dicta. Crime might be the only evidence of the citizen's political skepticism, her cynicism, her cultural critique, her individual conscience, indeed her philosophical life.

Callicles' challenge encoded in his definition of shame is seductive in its imagery. But its substance illuminates Plato's greatest objection to democracy. In the *Republic* Book VIII, Socrates traces the spiraling decline of the three kinds of states—rule by one, rule by many, and rule by the people—from their best forms (monarchy, aristocracy, democracy) to their worst forms (oligarchy, democracy, tyranny). Again referencing the analogy of bodily illness, Socrates tracks the advent of democracy from oligarchic greed. In their intemperance and licentiousness, the insatiable few sap the nobles of their wealth and reduce them to poverty, by purchasing the support of "the drones and paupers" of the society, so that the state soon becomes at "war with itself" (8.556e). Socrates continues:

> A democracy, I suppose, comes into being when the poor, winning the victory, put to death some of the other party, drive out others and grant the rest of the citizens an equal share in both citizenship and offices—and for the most part these offices are assigned by lot. (8.557a)

Democracy is born "by force of arms or by terrorism" (8.557a). This city *appears* more beautiful than all others for its being "a garment of many colors, embroidered with all kinds of hues . . . decked and diversified with all kinds of character" (8.557c), but because it is "chock full of liberty and freedom of speech," the people reject their responsibilities, both with regard to the laws and to their political obligations. The citizens feel disdain for all the "solemn pronouncements" of convention and law that threaten their absolute freedom. They spend their time feasting and pursuing pleasures, until the society breaks down, neglecting the proper education of the youths. Ultimately, as in oligarchy, the corrupt sense of the good becomes the cause of the state's downfall: "is it not the excess and greed of [absolute liberty] and the neglect of all other things that revolutionizes this constitution too and prepares the way for the necessity of dictatorship?" (8.562c).

Callicles, the radical democrat, exemplifies the worldview of current Athenian leaders. He is incapable of shame because he has lost the illusion that any of a society's rules serve any good beyond politico-cultural coercion. His excessive love of absolute liberty causes him to see oppression in the least measures of social learning that might train the conscience in appropriate feelings of shame, which militate in the society against actions of extreme impropriety. For Callicles, social learning evidences coercion, and illuminates the power of all societies and all governments to manipulate the individual's sense of right and wrong to suit its evolving needs. Callicles is raising a fundamental challenge to ethics *per se*. But his objection (of the constructed nature of laws and conventions) exemplifies the extreme views that Plato has cited as propelling the dissolution of democracy into tyranny. Callicles' rejection of Socrates' redefinitions of justice, shame, and punishment foreshadow the fall of Athens into licentiousness and brutality, and ultimately dictatorship.

The problem is that Callicles has reached his conclusion of the coerciveness of social convention by studying Socrates' discussion with Gorgias and Polus, and tracing the rise and fall of shame across the earlier dialectic. So Callicles is challenging Socrates too with being a coercive interlocutor, wielding shame as a weapon to win his arguments. The suggestion is that shame is a weapon as powerful and as comfortable in the hands of the philosopher, as in the hands of the tyrant. Is philosophical inquiry nothing more than a heroic *agon* that shames and honors people into agreeing with the philosopher's conclusions?

Callicles can level this challenge to Socrates, and to philosophy *per se*, only because he misunderstands Socrates' definition of shame. Socrates does agree that shame witnesses social learning. But, for Socrates, feelings of shame represent conflict *within* the individual soul, a painful *self*-relation. According to this definition, one cannot be shamed *by another*, but one is *ashamed of oneself*. Socrates' shame is the result of a self-examination in which one comes up short in relation to one's self-expectations of moral worth. Callicles' argument and his challenge to Socrates rely on a definition of shame that is other-related; It is the archaic form of shame as in *being shamed by others* that is a cultural ruse and a political weapon wielded by those in power.

The differences that distinguish the two definitions of shame are instructive for understanding how our heroic *ethos* goes wrong. Shame may indeed be a useful tool for cultivating the self-regulation and self-discipline that bring a sense of moral worth and the happiness of a life thoughtfully lived. On the other hand, shame is something that unscrupulous people wield to get their way with others. Plato seems to be intimating that shame is no simple virtue, and that shame may have good uses in self-application but cannot be *put to good use* by others against us. Shame, it seems, only works when no one works it; it is effective only when the moral work (of social learning) has already taken effect.

The ability to feel shame can be a mark of moral distinction, a sign of decency and high ideals (what Socrates would name "nobility"), a disposition of soul that leads one to live a certain kind of life. But the epic heroes tended to confuse being ashamed with being shamed. This distinction helps us to better solve the riddle of the philosopher's dialectic of shame. The shame that Gorgias and Polus experienced was instructive of their inner souls, their moral tempers. Gorgias felt the shame that evidences social learning; he was sorry to admit that he sometimes does things of which he thinks better, under self-scrutiny. He wishes he could avoid teaching students who have no interest in matters of justice, but because of "the habit of mind in people which would make them indignant if refused," he becomes coerced into doing what he knows he ought not do (482d). In other words, Gorgias shows a doubly sensitive moral compass: sometimes he does shameful things so as not to shame others.

Polus, on the other hand, feels the kind of shame that fears being made to look ridiculous. Though he shamelessly claims to know all that Gorgias knows, Polus's shame is not of Gorgias' higher type that evidences internalized learning in virtue, but his shame evidences simple egoism.

Callicles, the radical democrat, is incapable of either kind of shame. His love of absolute liberty will not permit him to see rules of propriety as anything but limits on his freedom. His flaunting of all laws and conventions as political coercion displays the greatest weakness of democracy as a political form and foretells a gloomy, tyrannical future for an Athens in the hands of the extreme democrats.

I have said at the outset of this rethinking of the *Gorgias* that Plato, in attempting to can get right the definition of shame here, seeks to reconfigure justice. He presses the new formulation of shame to move our thinking about how to respond appropriately to injustice. In place of the *dikephoros* (avenging) justice bequeathed from the archaic world Plato presses us toward an enlightened judicial response of a *therapeuma* (healing service) justice. By pulling off this definitional shift, Plato has achieved a double victory. He has not only raised justice to the level of ethics, but he has rescued the beloved Socrates from the ethical misrepresentation to which the indictment had condemned him.

However, ironically, if we accept Plato's redefinition of shame, then Socrates no longer requires saving. He has not been shamed, even by the vile convictions leveled against him (corrupting the youth of Athens and challenging the gods), because the court's misjudgment is their failing, and not the failing of Socrates. The charges thus have no ethical implication for the state of Socrates' soul. Being convicted and executed brought Socrates no shame. His moral learning was already so highly advanced that his conscience, which he named his *daimonion*, always warned him *before* he acted shamefully and thus he did not need the courts or Plato's dialogues to save him. His sense of shame saved him before any moral fall.

Notes

1. Raphael Sealey, *A History of the Greek City States 700 to 338 B.C.* (Berkeley: University of California Press, 1976), 381.

2. Plato, *Lysis, Symposium, Gorgias*, W. R. M. Lamb, trans. (Cambridge, MA: Harvard Loeb Editions, 1996), 249–250.

3. Ibid., 250.

4. Plato, *Apology* 32c.

5. Ibid., 252.

6. Plato, *Apology* 21a.

7. The younger orator Polus, who replaces Gorgias, recalls the young Polemarchus, who takes over the argument, when his old father Cephalus retires to his religious duties. Polus' entrance too mirrors the fierce entrance of Thrasymachus in the *Republic*. Both claim that previous speakers have been too "ashamed" to tell the whole truth, however dark; they do not share the sense of shame that would quiet their uglier opinions.

8. Homer. *Iliad*, 1.185-186.

9. Callicles shows that Gorgias' actions are governed by a sense of shame that is other-related; he explains that Gorgias would accept students lacking knowledge of justice because he is sensitive to people's habit of becoming indignant if refused what they want.

Chapter 7
Plato's Revolutionary Penology

In Plato's *Statesman*, the enlightened ruler, or true statesman, does not punish. He maintains no arsenal of penalties to keep his citizens in order. His governance method, the best rule administered in accordance with the "science of right judgment," is his personal and painstaking guardianship over each and every citizen. As a kindly shepherd, he guides each stumbling individual along the path of her life, advising and steering her toward the good in her every decision and action. As a doctor remains at the bedside of the patient, directing the treatment and overseeing the healing at every phase of the illness, so the statesman administers over the citizens' growth in virtue, so that they never fall into bad habits in the first place, and so never require the curative of punishment. The image of the shepherd signals the most extreme remove of the science of governance from the coercive, dictatorial governance style, such as that which the tyrant imposes. The statesman rules according to a care-based ethic, which places the individual citizen at the center of the state's concern. The statesman's governing method stands out against a power- or wealth-based politics, which serves the interests of the ruler or the class of wealthy and powerful citizens, by exploiting the socially inferior.

Plato has already given us a glimpse of this care-based model in the *Apology*, when he has Socrates explain his divinely ordained mission (and the work of philosophy) in the city. Here, Socrates tells that he has worked tirelessly all his life in the public places of the city, questioning one citizen after another, for the sake of caring for their souls. He admits to neglecting his personal affairs, forgetting his family and sons, to perform his divinely ordained task to fullest responsibility.

In the earliest Platonic dialogues (the *Euthyphro, Apology, Crito,* and *Phaedo*) as Plato presents the final weeks and days of Socrates' life, the problem of justice in the city and the question of right methods of teaching virtue to citizens are topics Plato is constantly exploring, as he considers the path that his own life will take—politics, philosophy, or some poetic art. Thus it is not surprising that he pictures Socrates challenging, from a number of angles, the juridical structures and accepted methods for dealing with social offenders. From the dramatically first dialogue, the *Euthyphro*, Plato launches his challenge to citizens who have the arrogance to challenge "fathers" of their city. In the *Apology*, he offers a more fitting model, an enlightened alternative approach, for dealing with simple annoyances, such as Socrates had proven to be to his powerful fellows.

> Either I have not been a bad influence, or it is unintentional . . . if I un-intentionally have been a bad influence, the correct procedure in cases of such involuntary misdemeanors is not to summon the culprit before this court, but to take him aside privately for instruction and reproof, because obviously if my eyes are opened, I shall stop doing what I do not intend to do. But you deliberately avoided my company in the past and refused to enlighten me, and now you bring me before this court, which is the place appointed for those who need punishment, not for those who need enlightenment. (26a)

This is the first dialogue in which Plato initiates the distinction between voluntary, intentional harmdoing and involuntary or unintentional harmdoing. It is also the (dramatically) first instance of the launching of the notion of an ethic of care in dealing with social deviance. The model of the city as parent and the citizen as child suggests a reciprocal relationship of responsibility. The child owes obedience to the parent; the parent owes right teaching, patience, and noble, just example to the child.

In a moral community, Socrates extends the argument, not merely the city/parent, as a whole albeit abstract entity, but every individual citizen has the responsibility to teach those who unintentionally go astray.[1] As a child is guided by a loving parent, so the city and its elders and indeed any citizen in the (moral) know has a duty to every other citizen to help them to do the right thing and to cultivate virtue. This is clearly Plato's way of affirming once again the moral work in which Socrates engaged himself as a citizen. This is precisely the service he is claiming in the *Apology* to be doing for his fellow citizens.

[S]o far from pleading on my behalf, as might be supposed, I am really pleading on yours, to save you from misusing the gift of god by condemning me. . . . God has attached me to this city to perform the office of [a gadfly] and all day long I never cease to settle here, there, and everywhere, rousing, persuading, reproving every one of you . . . like a father or an elder brother [seeing] each one of you privately, and urging you to set your thoughts on goodness. (30d-31b)

When Plato stages Socrates counseling his fellow citizens that they ought to have reproved him privately for his unintentional offense, Plato is suggesting ironically that the good citizens of Athens ought to have followed Socrates' own example, the very practice for which he was prosecuted and executed. Contrary too to Plato's guiding rule of the *Republic* that people specialize and "mind their own business," here he affirms that fellow citizens ought to interfere, as brothers and sisters, in each other's business, and help each other along toward greater moral awareness.

The correct method for righting social wrongs is to take the culprit gently aside and guide him toward better moral understanding. In the case of involuntary wrongdoing, this is best done privately, with the care and guidance modeled after the loving and concerned parent. Plato affirms this view again in the *Protagoras*. He has wise old Father Parmenides instruct the young Socrates in the best way to raise virtuous citizens. The children of the wealthy are most fortunate because they can start their education at an early age and continue it the longest.

When they have finished with teachers, the state compels them to learn the laws and use them as a pattern for their life, lest left to themselves they should drift aimlessly. You know how when children are not yet good at writing, the writing master traces outlines with the pencil before giving them the slate, and makes them follow the lines as a guide in their own writing; well, similarly the state sets up the laws, which are inventions of good lawgivers of ancient times, and compels the citizens to rule and be ruled in accordance with them. Whoever strays outside the lines, it punishes, and the name given to this punishment both among yourselves and in many other places is correction, intimating that the penalty corrects or guides. (326c-e)

Again in the ideal state of the *Republic*, amongst the guardian class, the role of parenting the young is a communal duty shared by all adult citizens, male and female. Just as in the ideal state of the *Statesman*, shepherding and setting a good example are the rules for educating in the direction of the good. Force and cruel, coercive punishments are unnecessary, since gymnastics and appropriate music attune the body and soul rightly to be begin with, and then the constant tending of the adult guardians keeps the children on the right path.

However, ideal states are far from the imperfect ones that we know, and in Plato's time as in our present era, no such worthy leaders as the learned statesmen and the valiant guardians are available to run our affairs and model justice for us. So in our flawed and often corrupt states, laws must step in to take over the role of responsible leaders, directing even them toward the good, drawing the clearest "lines" for all to see, and setting boundaries to behaviors.

Getting the boundaries right, then, becomes a crucial task. In the last work of Plato's corpus (*Laws* 9.860e ff.), written during his most conservative period of old age, Plato addresses the reality, rather than the ideal, in addressing the problem of justice in human communities. Yet much of his penology remains constant with his earliest ideas. He still maintains the same firm insistence on a corrective response, rather than a merely punitive, in dealing with wrongdoing, that he posited in his earliest dialogues. The *dikephoros* (avenging) justice of the archaic world Plato consistently advised be abandoned in favor of a *therapeuma* (healing service) justice. In the *Laws*, he has the Athenian Stranger instruct Clinias and Megillus on the matter of this distinction:

> Now we should not regard all these cases of causation of damage as *wrongs*, and so come to the conclusion that the *wrong* done in such acts may be of two kinds, voluntary, or again, involuntary—involuntary *damage*, as a form of damage, is as common and serious as voluntary. . . . What I maintain, Clinias and Megillus, is not that when one man causes hurt to another unintentionally and of no set purpose, he does him wrong, but an involuntary wrong—I shall not regard such causing of detriment, serious or trifling, as a *wrong* at all. (9.861e-862a)

The act that causes the damage may not be considered a "wrong" at all, then, if the actor did not intend the damage. Nevertheless, Plato insists, innocence of intention and legal innocence does not exculpate the agent from responsibility for the damages.

> There are thus two considerations [the legislator] must keep in view, the wrong committed and the detriment occasioned. He must do all he can by his laws to make damage good, to recover the lost, rebuild the dilapidated, replace the slaughtered or wounded by the sound. He must aim throughout in his legislation at reconciling the minds of the authors

and sufferers of detriment by award or compensation, and converting
their differences into friendship. (9.862bc)

Plato confirms here one of the original purposes of the Athenian court
system, appeasing victims and restoring losses so that social harmony
may be resumed. Plato does not forget the victim and the outrage of
harmed parties that can tear a city apart. But the overriding message is
that the court system and its arsenal of punishments are not for the sake
of victims, and also not for the sake of inadvertent wrongdoers, but for a
different sort of offender altogether—the calculated, deliberate, willful
criminal who knows the right but chooses the wrong. Voluntary harmdoing signals "malady of the soul" and legislators "must cure them whenever they are able" (*Laws* 9.862c). The law steps in to "both teach and
constrain" the voluntary harmdoer.

What kinds of punishments are fitting to visit upon a voluntary perpetrator in order to "both teach and constrain" him? Plato catalogues the
arsenal:

> If we can but bring a man to this—hatred of iniquity and love of right
> or even acquiescence in right—by acts we do or words we utter,
> through pleasure or through pain, through honor bestowed or disgrace
> inflicted, in a word whatever the means we take, thus and only thus is
> the work of a perfect law effected. (9.862d)

Plato recommends everything from kindness to cruelty be tried to effect
the desired result of healing the perpetrator's soul. For some harmdoers,
uttering sound advice and showing them kindly the right road will be
enough to cure them of their recent vices. For others, more cruel methods
might be needed. For a rare few, the response will be a most final curative.

> But should our legislator find one whose disease is past cure, what will
> be his sentence or law for such a case? He will judge, I take it, that
> longer life is no boon to the sinner himself in such a case, and his de-
> cease will bring a double blessing on his neighbors; it will be a lesson
> to them to keep themselves from wrong, and will rid society of an evil
> man. (9.862r-863a)

Is it simply that in Plato's old age, he loses his patience with "sinners"
and advocates in favor of anything that works to squash social deviance?

Certainly Plato shows himself willing to reach farther and farther into
the penal arsenal for more and more serious punishments to cure more

and more serious offenders of their impulses toward harmdoing. Has he lost sight of the perpetrator and the metaphor of correction and healing, then, in his old age, and become fixated on the protection of victims and property? Another explanation offers itself if we consider Plato's views on the afterlife. Plato is heavily influenced by the Pythagorean School that echoes Eastern ideas on the transmigration of souls. For Plato, as for Empedocles and Pythagoras before him, all souls are on a journey propelled by their moral histories toward their deserved fates. In the Phaedrus, we have Plato's formulation of the launching of the journey, in the myth of the Feast of Being.

Here (246a ff) Socrates once again tells us a story, rather than relating to us a truth, which "would be a long tale to tell, and most assuredly a god alone could tell it." He introduces the soul imaged as a charioteer and two horses, the one of noble stock, beautiful and fine-formed, the other a lowborn and twisted creature. The soul is covered with "wings," the bodily part which shares in the nature of the divine, "which is fair, wise, and good and possessed of all other such excellences" (246e). The human souls hurry after a magnificent parade of gods and daimons, following in the train of the Mighty Zeus. The divine pageant steps up a steep ascent and off the summit of the world and the revolving heavens carry them around, revealing to them the beautiful regions thereabout. There "true being dwells," tells Plato, "the veritable knowledge of being that veritably is" (literally, "being being'ly being"). The souls of the gods feed upon the excellence there displayed and return to their homes satisfied and blissful.

But what has happened to the sorry human souls? They were scrambling up the steep rise that leads to the edge of the Heavens, when last we saw them. They were trying their best to follow in the train of the god that they most love. But sadly, they have been waylaid on the sharp slope by a characteristic that inheres in their being but does not plague the divine choir—phthonos. Pthonos is a quality that contains all the negative characteristics we see in our capitalistic culture—greed, envy, avarice, competitiveness, and acquisitiveness. Because it so burdens the human souls, they push and shove and fight and trample each other, each trying to reach the crest of the hill before the others. In the scuffle, their wings are crushed and broken (they lose their divine aspect? they lose their lofty aspirations? they lose sight of higher things?) and then, as fluttering feathers, they drop from their lofty perch into earthly bodies below. Where do they fall? Plato has Socrates explain the justice of their places:

Hear now the ordinance of Necessity. Whatsoever soul has followed in the train of a god, and discerned something of truth shall be kept from sorrow until a new revolution shall begin. . . .The soul that hath seen the most of being shall enter into the human babe that shall grow into a seeker after wisdom or beauty, a follower of the Muses or a lover; the next having seen less, shall dwell in a king that abides by the law, or a warrior and ruler; the third in a statesman, a man of business or a trader; the fourth in an athlete, or physical trainer, or physician; the fifth shall have the life of a prophet or a mystery priest; to the sixth that of a poet or other imitative artist shall be fittingly given; the seventh shall live in an artisan and farmer; the eighth in a Sophist or demagogue; the ninth in a tyrant. (248de)

The souls fall into all sorts of human identities that Plato sorts according to their occupations, or more accurately, their loves, showing that human being draw themselves toward the fulfillment of their fates. Even the worst and farthest fall, to the ninth realm of human existence, does not readily sound so bad. A tyrant is only a single level if being away from a Sophist, such as the noble Gorgias or the less noble Polus.

However, if we shift to the *Republic's* more detailed treatment of the life of the tyrant (9.576 ff), we see a very sorry life; friendless, fearful, maddened by his passions, enslaved by his desires, the tyrant is the most miserable human being of all. Socrates does the math; the tyrant is seven hundred and twenty nine times more miserable than the legitimate and just king whose throne he usurps (9.587e).

Callicles (whom we met in the *Gorgias*) and Thrasymachus (of the *Republic* 1.336b ff.) are examples of such sorry men who believe that might is right. They argue that in *physis* (nature) the strongest rule, and so do they in the human world, if we were but honest enough to admit the truth. Custom and law (*nomoi*) intercede to trick fools into believing that justice is the highest virtue. The idea that men holding such harsh views and promoting the use of injustice will ultimately fall from heaven into a lonely hegemony in their states seems small punishment for the crimes they will admittedly commit in good conscience. If we can trust Polus' testimony, tyrants can be counted upon for "putting to death anyone they please, and depriving anyone of his property, and expelling him from their cities as they see fit?" (*Gorgias* 466c). But at the close of the *Republic*, in the Myth of Er (10.614b ff), Plato has Socrates give a fuller description of the just desserts awaiting such men after death.

Er is a bold warrior who was slain in battle and remained dead for twelve long days. Just as he lay upon the funeral pyre, he revived and told his friends what he had seen in the world beyond. He reported seeing the openings up to heaven and into the earth and he saw great processions of souls passing to and fro, from heaven and from Tartarus, and he witnessed the judgment that determined their path.

The righteous journeyed to the right and upward, the unjust took the road to the left and down. The souls returning from the heavens "related their delights and visions of beauty beyond words" that their heavenly journey had afforded them. Those returning from Tartarus however "recalled how many and how dreadful things they had suffered and seen in their journey beneath the earth," that had last over a thousand years. Those who had severely wronged others paid a penalty tenfold for each offense, measures in periods of a hundred years each, "so that the punishment might be ten times the crime." Worse, those from Tartarus explained that some of their fellow sufferers, the tyrants, were not allowed to leave when their time was up. The mouth would not allow them passage. When they would try to escape, "savage men of fiery aspect . . . laid hold on them and bore them away . . . flung down and flayed them and dragged them by the wayside, carding them on thorns [and finally] hurled [them] into Tartarus" (615e).

From the outset of his corpus, Plato begins to design a new approach to punishment, a revolutionary penology that focuses upon justice and punishment as centered on a process of healing the morally diseased. Contrary to the focus in the courts of Athens in Plato's day, Plato insists that the justice system, the courts and their arsenals of punishments are not about victims and their outrage. Socrates had taught him well that a bad man cannot harm a good one. A perpetrator, whatever his crime, cannot have truly harmed a victim, because loss of property or even bodily injury, though undoubtedly inconvenient and painful, cannot touch the most precious part of the human being, the soul. Only *doing* harm—injustice—not *suffering* it, can do true harm, and *that* a person does to herself.

So first (and last) Plato distinguishes between the intentional wrongdoer and the involuntary or unintentional agent, whom he insists may have harmed someone, but who has nevertheless done no "wrong." If we follow Socrates' advice of the *Apology*, a trial will not be necessary for this case, but rather the good citizens must take him in hand, take the ignorant fellow aside and correct him in his misunderstanding of right conduct. If the clear "lines" drawn by the law have not been adequately learned or internalized, it is a simple matter of getting out the pencils again and helping the pupil to correct his vision of the boundaries and his skills at keeping inside them. The state intercedes in unintentional harmdoing only in the matter of overseeing recompense, because harms must always be put right, for the sake of the harmony of the community. With Plato, it is the voluntary harmdoer who becomes the primary focus of the judicial machinery of the state.

The trial remains an elaborate process of testimony to get at the truth of the matter. But when wrongdoing has been proven and can be determined unequivocally to be intentional, the victim can be dismissed, and the court's attention may be turned directly on the perpetrator. Since injustice inheres in the soul of the agent, there exists true "malady of soul," and so the state, ever the good parent, must rush to correct the culprit and heal his disease. The citizen-child must be taken in hand and curatives must be applied. What are the appropriate curatives? They will be punishments, from pleasure and gentle words of advice to harsher bodily punishments and even the death penalty. The state parent will administer curatives as harsh as is required to turn the culprit from his unjust ways or put an end to his misery.

Notes

1. See also *Protagoras* 326d ff.

Part Three
From Punitive Science to Public Spectacle

Chapter 8
The Science of Penal Measure

We have seen in Part One that an excessive "will to punish" was an ever-present danger of the Greek aristocratic world, since their notion of justice was peer-dependent and anchored to notions of honor and shame. The function of justice was to manipulate the social status of conflicted parties so as to reinforce the parameters of noble conduct that was expected within the group and was crucial to the maintenance of social order among the powerful princes.

The individuals within this society enjoyed a robust sense of self, grounded in a clan identity, attended by a rich bank of familial mythology that included legends of ancestral glories. The broad existential grounding that underpinned aristocratic identity made for a strength of character that rendered affronts from social inferiors, such as those launched by Thersites or even the young Paris, all but inconsequential. As Nietzsche rightly points out, a strong man can afford "the noblest luxury" of letting those who harm him go unpunished. "What are my parasites to me? . . . May they live and prosper. I am strong enough for that!"[1] In the cult of the hero, moral outrage was reserved for social equals, males of equal social status. When the princes revenged the affront of a Paris, they direct their *dikephoros* (avenging) justice at Hektor, not the trifling Paris.

By the time of the democracy in Athens, the old aristocratic families were being replaced by a new merchant class, a new breed of men unashamed of handling money and seeking profit. Of common birth, the *nouveau riche* were without family name and had no illustrious past to live up to, so their values tended to be more base and immediate—wealth and power. By the classical era, the old aristocratic ways grounded in aretaic values of honor, glory, and excellence were being replaced love of money and shameless greed. As Plato describes in his Seventh Epistle, under this new breed of men, all hell is breaking loose.

The democrats inherit the aristocratic model of justice as vengeance but unrestricted by the aristocratic code, their will to punish is more base and shameless, lacking the noble generosity of which Nietzsche speaks, which Athena exemplifies (in Aeschylus' *Oresteia*) and which Plato philosophically urges. The base-minded capitalists at the helm of the polis lacked the appropriate social learning that had restrained a higher breed of men in centuries past through a deeply instilled sense of shame.

In the wake of the reign of the Thirty Tyrants, the democrats, newly returned to power and furious with their treatment during the conservative reign of the Spartan puppets, are unashamed to vent their petty resentments on the weak and old, such as Socrates. They are unashamed to take advantage of the socially inferior, as a means of confirming their elevated social place, inside the social boundaries that so recently softened to allow their upward movement.

The irony, captured by Aeschylus' *Prometheus Bound*, is that people (even divine kings) can be shameless when greedy for legitimacy and status, and yet in rigorous moral communities (such as aristocratic society), shamelessness is precisely what prohibits one's ascent up the social ladder and undermines one's claim to political legitimacy. This is because an honor-bound society is not really about glory; rather, its fundamental orienting value is excellence. Shame is the guardian at the gates of excellence, patrolling the moral borders *from within* the hearts and minds of the already converted.

Later, under the democracy, the orienting value of excellence came to be replaced by mere wealth and power, so the inner restraints that had caused good men to restrict their behavior were replaced by the mere external restraints encoded in law. The guardian of shame patrolling the boundary between honorable and dishonorable behaviors was replaced by the far weaker guardian of guilt before the law.

The shift from shame to guilt, as a guardian of citizen behavior, represents a dual degradation in social values. First, the law is a poor substitute for a code of excellence, since the latter, whatever its hypermasculine excesses, aspired to the highest ideals in thought, speech, and deed, in public and in private life. Laws do not pretend to aspire to excellence, but encode only the barest, most minimal rules of propriety, without which a civilized human community would cease to exist. Do not murder or take advantage of young girls, respect the property of others, tell the truth in a court of law—these are rules crucial to societal harmony and sound business practice, but the citizens who keep *only* these rules will hardly be excellent neighbors. Morality asks something more from us than simply to observe the law.

The second way in which the move from shame to guilt is a moral degradation is that excellence calls us to our best whether others are watching or not, but guilt occurs only once a court has declared that a law has been contravened. In short, guilt is the state of being *found* guilty, not the state of having committed a foul act. In this degraded moral universe, my conscience remains clear until the very moment that I have been *found out* as noncompliant.

Under a code of excellence, however, the mere thinking of a cowardly thought or pondering a treacherous deed would awaken the relentless guardian and inspire the sting of shame, regardless of whether anyone witnessed the dishonorable notion. A good example of the hyperethic of excellence, enforced by the guardian of shame, comes to us in the tale of the prince Leontius, son of Aglaion, which Socrates recounts in Plato's *Republic* (4.439e ff). Leontius is coming back from the Piraeus one day, when under the outer side of the northern wall, he comes across a field strewn with corpses, which had been tossed over the city walls after their public execution, as was the tradition in Athens, to show repugnance for the more vile breed of criminals. Suddenly aware of the bodies surrounding him, Leontius feels disgust and aversion, veils his head, and averts his eyes. However, ultimately, he is overcome by a base desire to look upon the decaying corpses. When he realizes his eyes have so betrayed his finer sensibilities, Leontius chastises his eyes, as though treacherous soldiers in the army of his noble nature. "There ye wretches. Take your fill of the fine spectacle!"

Laws are focused upon protecting the society by *repressing* the bad behavior of the deviant. The aristocrat's code of excellence is about *living up* to a history of greatness. An aristocrat must *live up* to the high standards set by his ancestral line and touted in family legends of valor and eminence. He must *live up* to the expectations of his peers, exemplifying the highest ideals of character, proving his worthiness of inclusion in the princely class. Shame is a valuable sentry that warns at the precipice of the impending fall into disgrace. In moral communities, it is not shame but its lack—shamelessness—that causes one to fall in social place. In the aristocratic worldview, shamelessness undermines social place, scars the dignity of the familial line, and leaves its dishonorable residue on generations of progeny.

Plato was an aristocrat who witnessed the moral decline of Athens, from its glory days fighting off the barbarian despots of Persia, through its moral degradation as shameless head of the Delian League that bullied, stole league funds, and slaughtered its reluctant neighbors, to its defeat and fall to Sparta at the close of the Peloponnesian War, and finally to its utter moral collapse under the rule of the Thirty Tyrants, who disgraced the city by their ruthless treatment of citizens and foreigners. Plato witnessed the Athenian shift from the aristocratic code of excellence to the democratics' meager constraint of legal compliance. He saw, in the case of Socrates, how the *dikephoros* justice of the Athenian courts could be used to serve private interests and vent petty men's will to punish.

Plato set out in the earliest dialogues to explore questions about the nature of justice and right punishment, and to discover their link with the morally motivating, but often excessive, forces of honor and shame. In the *Republic*'s extended meditation on the definition of justice, Plato refuses the traditional definitions—"to tell the truth and return what one has received" (1.331d) and "to do good to friends and evil to enemies" (1.332d). Instead, he reframes justice as a state of individual soul, where the passion for glory (and the outrage of disgrace) and the appetites (for base worldly things) find harmony and balance, yoked to a reason that loves excellence for its own sake.

The upshot of the search for a definition of justice in the *Republic* is that justice is found to compose an excellence of soul; indeed it is identified as *the* excellence of the human soul—"the specific virtue of man" (1.335c) and again, "the definitive excellence of man" (1.353e). If justice is definitive of human excellence, then it follows that injustice is a malady or disease of the soul. A corollary of this discovery is that "when [men] are harmed, it is in respect of the distinctive excellence or virtue of man that they become worse" (1.335c). That is, injustice in the soul is the way that harm is achieved, and that kind of harm is one done to oneself by choosing unwise acts, not a harm that is undergone at the hands of enemies.

By having Socrates lead his interlocutors to a new definition of justice, Plato is leading us as well to new insights about the purpose of the machinery of justice in the state. If injustice is a disease of the soul, then curing citizen deviance and bringing about harmonious and stable human community will require curing the souls of offenders. Plato reconfigures the purpose of the courts and their arsenal of punishments so that they serve the wrongdoer, as a doctor serves her patient, healing the disease that ails him. Justice and punishment become targeted upon the offending individual's salvation, rather than balancing the social register, placating outraged tempers, or compensating offended victims.

Plato signals his shift in the focus of justice and punishment by a dramatic shift in language. He abandons the language of "giving justice" (*didonai dikēn*) and "taking justice" (*lambanein dikēn*), in favor of the language of "doing injury" (*kakos poiein*), literally "making bad," which takes the offender as its object. For Plato, the object of injury (the offended party) becomes inconsequential—"whether an enemy or anyone else" (*Gorgias* 480e). Punishment is no longer an "evil" (contrary to Thomas Aquinas' claim), but instead becomes a good, a curative, to help the culprit to remove the stain of injustice from his soul, to cure his unhappy heart, and cleanse himself of the polluting effects of his acts of injustice.

Plato sets out to restructure the definition and language of justice and punishment in Athens, about the time he begins writing the *Gorgias*, in the fortieth year of his life. At this time, he is opening the Academy, where he hopes to teach the youth of Athens and other disciples that flock to his school a better method for helping citizens toward excellence than the current institutional understandings and practices seem to be doing. His revolutionary reconfiguration of justice and punishment is short-lived in its effects on subsequent philosophers and on the machinery of justice in Athens. But in other ways, his effects are far-reaching, as we shall see in the next chapter.

Plato's most famous student, Aristotle, was faithful to a great deal of the master's philosophy, but when it comes to Plato's revolutionary penology, he was a recalcitrant pupil, a traitor to the master's penal revolution. Aristotle was born in 384 or 385 BCE. in Stageira. His father, Nichomachus, a master of the medical sciences of his time, served in the court at Pella, as the physician to the king of Macedonia, Amyntas. Aristotle was but seventeen when he joined Plato's Academy. As J. A. K. Thomson states, in his Introduction to Aristotle's *Ethics*, "Young Aristotle must have felt a little like a Rhodes scholar going up to Oxford."[2]

We can be certain, from Diogenes Laertius' description of him in the "Life of Aristotle," that, as a non-Athenian, he would have been regarded by many as a simple "*barbaros*" foreigner. He may have been the most eminent of Plato's pupils, but Diogenes' description of him, ridiculing his figure and bearing, is decidedly uncomplimentary. He reports that Aristotle "had a lisping voice . . . very thin legs, they say, and small eyes; [and] he used to indulge in conspicuous dress, and rings, and used to dress his hair carefully."[3] For the Greeks, convinced of the unity of virtues (thus the coexistence of physical beauty, intelligence, and moral merit in all worthy men), Diogenes' derogatory description of Aristotle says more than might at first be heard by modern ears; it challenges not only the philosopher's bodily presence, but his wit and his moral character as well.

Aristotle remained a dedicated disciple of Plato for more than twenty years, before finding his own way and dissenting more emphatically to the master's teachings. Aristotle too saw much political strife and misuse of the juridical machinery of states. In 338 or 337, when Plato died, Aristotle left Athens for Assos in Asia Minor and, after the torture and execution of his protector and friend, Hermeias, went to Mytilene on the island of Lesbos, where he met up with his friend from the Academy, Theophrastus, a native Lesbian. About three years later, he left Lesbos for the court of Philip of Macedon, to serve as tutor to the young Alexander the Great, who ascended to the throne when Philip was assassinated in 336. The following year, Aristotle left the court and returned to Athens to open his own school, the Lyceum, which flourished for some twelve or thirteen years, until a new wave of anti-Macedonian resentment drove him from Athens to Chalcis, where at the age of sixty-two years, he died.

Thus we can see that Aristotle lived through those "interesting" political times deplored in Plato's *Seventh Letter*, and witnessed plenty of evidence to suggest that the machinery of justice often simply served the interests of the rich and powerful, more than it served the "excellence" of justice. His response to the troubled realities of his times was to approach the chaos of human realities under the rubric of scientific order. Aristotle was a rigorously systematic thinker, an analytical genius, the founder of the sciences, as the study of the natural world, and the creator of formal scientific research methodology, that is, the tireless collection of material or evidence, and its analysis and classification according to categories of genus and species.

In his analyses of "measures" of "prosecution and defense" in the *Rhetoric*, Aristotle demonstrates unfaithfulness to Platonic innovations in the realm of justice and punishment. He approaches the question of right justice and punishment in terms of appropriate "measure" by considering the emotions that are implicated in offense and retribution. Aristotle shifts the terms of the discussion, so that the right measures to be used in justice and punishment are consistent with the "measure" to which he turns in the whole of his ethical philosophy; the correct measure will always lie on the "golden mean." So for punishment to be just, it must be applied according to standards of moderation.

Aristotle arrives at this conceptual destination through an analysis of anger. In the *Rhetoric*, he notes that anger is interwoven with the passion of revenge. Aristotle states:

> Anger may be defined as a desire accompanied by pain, for a conspicuous revenge for a conspicuous slight at the hands of men who have no call to slight oneself or one's friends. (1378a)

In insisting on the "conspicuous" nature of both the original offence and the avenging passion or act, and in reverting to the language of vengeance in analyzing matters of "prosecution and defense" Aristotle echoes the excessive "will to punish" that I have located as the moral flaw in the ethos of the archaic princes, suggesting that this problem persists long after the age of kings and well into the classical period.

If excess remains an active problem, long after the courts and jury trials have been fashioned precisely to give purgative outlet to the outraged victims of crime, then Aristotle is shrewd in pointing his readers towards an ethic of moderation. But in focusing upon moderation, to manage the excessive will to punish in outraged victims, Aristotle has reverted to a logic of punishment that is far less generous than that of Plato, and indeed less generous than Athena, in Aeschylus' mythological account of the first Athenian trial. His concern for sticking to a middle road, between the excess of an avenging anger and the deficiency of a punishment that may not quite satisfy the victim outrage, leaves him saddled with the utter necessity of some form of punishment, and never a generous pardon, that "errs on the side of generosity."

Aristotle's treatment of justice in the *Rhetoric* treads a careful path between the victim and the perpetrator, arriving ultimately at the doorstep of the legitimate authority who dishes out the punishment. Aristotle raises the concern that unbridled desires may undermine the work of justice, when the punishing authority is overcome by unhealthy desires, which are evoked in the act of punishing. He admits (at *Rhetoric* 1378b) a certain "joy" in punishing that can undo the ethic of right measure and drive the punisher toward penal excess.

Plato had shifted the language of punishment to reconfigure it as a curative good, rather than penal evil. He had removed the spotlight of justice from the outraged victim and turned it square upon the offender, as a person of moral disease who needs the aid of his community and their machinery of justice to regain the soundness of his soul. Plato's innovative theory of restorative justice represents a revolution in the prevailing ideas about justice and punishment, just as his generous arsenal of punishments, where pleasure and honor join with pain and disgrace in a "whatever works" practical philosophy of curative reckoning (*Laws* 9.862d) are strikingly enlightened; indeed his approach to punishment is strikingly akin to the modern model applied in Conflict Transformation and Mediation theory, whose primary therapy is to expand the arena of available options until an alternative comes to light that can satisfy all conflict parties.

But the penal revolution seems to have been left behind at the Academy. Aristotle moves toward a rigorous penal science, but the logic of justice and punishment are consistent with the archaic logic, which locates the perfect measure of punitive pain in relation to the heinousness of the crime and the outrage it has elicited in its victim and the community, abandoning the measure of right punishment to cure the disease of injustice inhering in the soul of the condemned.

The revolutionary penal philosophy of Plato, with its focus on restoring the moral health of the soul sickened by injustice, is one aspect of the Platonic corpus that has not received its due tribute of "footnotes" over the centuries. On the other hand, it is Plato's theory of morally evolving souls, suffering their way toward a purification and salvation, that comes to be adopted and transformed into the Christian theory of history that punishes the souls of sinners and infidels. The theory that punishment is good for a soul is wielded as a persuasive weapon of church power and territorial expansion, justifying a plethora of violences against peoples, thought to be less spiritually advanced than their white European brothers in Christ.

In the Christian world, the authority of Aristotle was absolute, and that authority increased as the Middle Ages reached their height. Aristotle's astronomy, the science in which he went farthest astray from the truth, underpinned the Christian worldview. Thomson explains: "Astronomy depends on mathematics, and he had not so good a head for mathematics as he had for other disciplines."[4] Aristotle pictured the world as a solid, immobile ball, at the center of a spherical universe, a structure of crystalline spheres like the layers of an onion, wherein the sun, moon, and stars followed their orbits, encircling the earth.

The Aristotelian cosmology, which completely enthralled the Middle Ages, allowed for a view of the natural world as prone to change, chaotic with generation and decay, in diametrical contrast to the perfect heavens with their stable, ordered motions, a fitting abode for the god. The heavenly spheres provided a stable pattern for the human world that reigned well into the 1500s in Europe, guaranteeing social stability and immobility, within a rich network of rigorously hierarchical, lifelong, unwavering social relations, rooted in the land, determined by birth, maintained by timeworn tradition, and overseen by the god, his church, and the divinely empowered monarch. Everything had its proper place, determined by birth, sorted by grace and divine right, in a world that made perfect sense. Nature held secrets beyond human ken, and god gifted knowledge discriminately, so, throughout the Middle Ages, faith guided human knowledge and theology was queen of the sciences.

Notes

1. Friedrich Nietzsche, *On the Genealogy of Morals*, Walter Kaufman, trans. (New York: Vintage Books, 1967), 72.

2. Aristotle, *The Ethics of Aristotle*, J. A. K. Thomson, trans. and introd. (New York: Penguin, 1958), Introduction, 9.

3. Ibid.

4. Ibid., 16.

Chapter 9
A Christian Penology

Whatever disparagement contemporary Athenians may have launched at the *barbaros* Aristotle, the Christian world would recompense many times over, with a reverence and a faithfulness that was singularly focused. The Christian fathers would follow Aristotle, rather than Plato, throughout the Middle Ages and into modernity. So convinced were they of the Stagirite's preeminence in all things philosophical, they would refer to him simply as "the Philosopher," as though all other thinkers paled by comparison with him.

Aristotle's approach to justice will reinstate the aristocratic (*dikephoros*) configuration of justice as vengeance, in the feudal world. On the other hand, Plato's theory of punishment as curative (*therapeuma*) ritual will find its way by a back door into the Christian theory of history and have far-reaching and palpable effects in the Christian worldview, in determining the methods of global evangelism and territorial expansion that Christians will undertake by the rise of the capitalist era to secure their empires and spread the word of their god.

The idea that punishment and suffering are goods that cleanse evil from the soul of sinners will have a great effect upon Christian strategies of social control, both within their own congregations and in dealing with "infidels" and "pagans" at home and abroad. Plato's theory will set the stage for a Christian theory of history that will be called upon by popes and clergy, Christian kings, conquistadors, crusaders, colonials, and evangelical zealots to justify their cruelty and repression of indigenous peoples the world over, on the unfortunate corollary to the Platonic model of *therapeuma* justice, whereby the suffering of punishment is configured as a benefit to the soul.

Augustine of Hippo

St. Augustine of Hippo (354 to 430 BCE), heavily influenced by Plotinus and the NeoPlatonic School of Philosophy, gives us an early glimpse of the direction Christian theory will take, in regard of justice and punishment of its "sinners." In his *Confessions*, we find echoes of Plato in the configuration of punishment as a good, but Plato's generous approach to punishment as an expression of parental care toward the offspring citizen, will be transformed, under the deterministic theory of the unfolding will of god, into a justification for all suffering that befalls a person in her life. Any person who is suffering, in this perfectly administered universe, has brought her misery upon herself, and at every moment is simply receiving the rightful wages for her sins.

In Chapter Three of the *Confessions*, "Free Will and the Problem of Evil," Augustine states:

> The will's free decision is the cause of our doing evil, and your just judgment is the cause of our suffering evil . . . I was absolutely certain when I willed a thing or refused to will it that it was I alone who willed or refused to will. Already I was beginning to see that therein lay the cause of my sin. I saw that what I did against my will was something done to me, rather than something I actually did. I concluded that it was not my fault but my punishment, but I quickly confessed that I was not punished unjustly, for I thought of you as being just. (3.5)

In a conceptual move reminiscent of the Furies' relentless and merciless pursuit of the hapless Orestes, all suffering is configured, in Augustine's worldview, as the enactment, as well as the evidence, of the perfect justice of the god. We don't need to understand that justice or *rationally* agree with its forms or effects, because god's reason is so far beyond human capacity that we must simply accept the rightness of god's justice as dished out in our worldly fates, on faith in the god's perfection.

In the *Confessions*, Augustine is chronicling his own struggles against vice and his ultimate victory in self-overcoming. Augustine follows Plato and Aristotle in locating the underlying source of the problem of evil in the passions, the failure of the charioteer of reason (free will, in Augustine's terminology) to hold back the unruly desires of the body and curb the fiery enthusiasm of the heart. When he suffers or undergoes anything unpleasant—"something done to me"—Augustine interprets these sufferings as rightful punishments, just desserts, better understood, in this utterly just universe, as dished out by a perfect god through the agency of another human being or other natural force. He sees himself as entirely deserving of all the pain and misery he receives from the least holy of sources, because god is in the background of the great human drama, ensuring the perfect justness of each event.

Augustine struggled with Manichaeanism in his early intellectual life, and imagined a wicked force, a devil, as interfering in god's world and creating the things he found "evil." But as he comes to better grasp the logic of omnipotence and appreciate the fullness of the power of the god, he recognizes that an alien force would compose a limit on god's power, so dismisses the idea of a devil, wreaking havoc among god's creation. Through the course of the *Confessions*, Augustine abandons Manichaeanism and lands in the NeoPlatonic camp, which figures all of creation as good, as a Great Chain of Being, where the perfect fullness of the whole of creation makes for the richest spectrum of existents of greater and lesser degrees of goodness.

> We see the face of the earth, adorned with earthly creatures, and man, made to your Image and likeness, and by this, your own image and likeness, that is, by the power of reason and intelligence, set over all non-rational animals. (Book 13. Ch. 32)

All things are good, but some are more good and some less so. As for us human beings, we are much like the sea god Glaucus, in Plato's tale in the *Republic*:

> [The soul's condition] resembles that of the sea god Glaucus whose first nature can hardly be made out by those who catch glimpses of him, because the original members of his body are broken off and mutilated and crushed and in every way marred by the waves and other parts have attached themselves to him, accretions of shells and seaweed and rocks, so that he is more like any wild creature than what he was by nature. (10. 611cd)

Augustine is unrelenting in the rigor of his self-condemnation for the youthful failure of his will against his decadent passions, which scars his soul and removes him farther and farther from the company of his god. This rigor in condemnation of sin, seen as primarily lodged in the body and the passions by an obstreperous free will (that exculpates god of the sins of his faulty creations), is extrapolated universally across the spectrum of a sinful human world. It is carried along in the history of Christian philosophy in a view of the human world as deeply flawed in its very nature by wayward passions and perverse will. Human suffering is the way god exacts due recompense for the moral failure of his imperfect creations. The god, for all his power, does not seem to enjoy access to the broad arsenal of punishments that Plato recommends.

Thomas Aquinas

In his deliberations on punishment, St. Thomas Aquinas, a priest of the Dominican Order (1225 to 1274 CE), uses the (Latin) language of *vindicatio* (punishing, guaranteeing, defending, avenging), *vindico* (to punish, threaten, force, or lay claim to), and *vindicta* (the name for the manumission staff, which was used by church authorities to deliver punishment or mercy). In his *Summa Theologica* Question 108, "On Vengeance," he asks a series of questions about punishment: *Is it lawful? Is it a special virtue? How should it be taken and on whom?*

Aquinas gives us the definition of punishment which remains the most commonly accepted definition to this day: *the infliction of a penal evil upon one who has sinned* (Art. 1, Obj. 5), though secular audiences may substitute for "sin" the language of "offense" or "crime." His method, in the *Summa*, is to review the authoritative literature to see what the tradition has declared on each of the questions of punishment, in turn. He finds that *Deuteronomy* and *Romans* declare definitively that vengeance belongs to god, and so punishment, he notes, is unjust in the hands of human beings (*Deut.* 32:35, *Romans* 12:19). Indeed the tradition suggests that "bearing with" the wicked renders the bearer a good person. In Article 1, Objection 3, he turns to Augustine and affirms the latter's assertion that the "New Law" of Jesus Christ is "not a law of fear, but of love" (*Contra Adamant*, xvii).

However, following his anthology of objections against punishment, he begins to demolish each claim in turn, in his "Replies" to the Objections. He decides that a legitimate authority, receiving his power and authority from god, is legitimated to punish in god's stead. Wrongs committed upon an individual Christian may be "borne with" and bring great benefit to the individual, but wrongs committed against god, the church, or the neighbour ought rightly be punished. Though the new law is one grounded in brotherly love, those sinners who are not persuaded to good behavior by the law of love, Aquinas declares, responding to Augustine, may rightly be persuaded by punishment. Furthermore, and most telling for explaining centuries of church-sponsored cruelties, Aquinas affirms in his Reply to Objection 3 that the church owes its forgiving love only to its own fold, and even then only to the deserving among that fold. He states:

> The law of the Gospel is the law of love, and therefore those who do good out of love, and who alone properly belong to the Gospel, ought not to be terrorized by means of punishment, but only those who are not moved by love to do good, and who, though they belong to the Church outwardly, do not belong to it in merit.

Worse, in the Reply to Objection 5, Aquinas affirms that, while an individual ought to "bear with" the evil of others, it is not only right and lawful, but it is the *duty* of authorities to punish, and punish may well be directed, not simply toward individual sinners, but toward entire populations when "a wrong done to a person reflects on God and the Church." Aquinas does afford that generosity *might* prevail and that only the principal evildoers *might* be severely punished, as an example of fear to the rest of the sinners.

Then arguing from "the Philosopher" in *Ethics* 2.1, Aquinas declares punishment a "special virtue." He states:

> Just as repayment of a legal debt belongs to commutative justice, and as repayment of a moral debt, arising from the bestowal of a particular favor, belongs to the virtue of gratitude, so too the punishment of sins, so far as it is the concern of public justice, is an act of commutative justice; while so far as it is concerned in defending the rights of the individual by whom a wrong is resisted, it belongs to the virtue of revenge.

In the Reply to Objection 3, Aquinas again echoes Aristotle:

> Two vices are opposed to vengeance: one by way of excess, namely, the sin of cruelty or brutality, which exceeds the measure in punishing: while the other is a vice by way of deficiency and consists in being remiss in punishing, wherefore it is written (Proverbs 13:24): "He that spareth the rod hateth his son." But the virtue of vengeance consists in observing the due measure of vengeance with regard to all the circumstances.

Here Aquinas reminds us of the "golden mean" of right punishment, between excess and deficiency. The "avenger" must act from the will to educate, and not from the dangerous emotions that had concerned Aristotle in the *Rhetoric*, such as anger and hatred.

In the next article (3), Aquinas addresses the question of how, and on whom, punishment should rightly "be taken." The verdict is on the arsenal of appropriate punishments ranges from death to mercy. He explains:

> Vengeance for sin should be taken by depriving a man of what he loves most. Now the things which man loves most are life, bodily safety, his own freedom, and external goods such as riches, his country and his good name.

On the question of who may rightly be punished, Aquinas answers "all sinners." Concerned that if groups of sinners should be punished, then perhaps an innocent soul might be spent in vain—"there is fear lest the wheat be uprooted together with [the cockle]"—he assures us that, far from the good being harmed by wrongful punishment, much good can come of punishment. Indeed, "sometimes the wicked can be uprooted by death, not only without danger, but even with great profit, to the good."

After a careful review of the authoritative literature, from the Bible to the Church fathers to "the Philosopher" (Aristotle), Aquinas reaches a number of significant conclusions, that continue to have great weight in the Christian view of justice and punishment. First, Aquinas gives us our prevailing definition of punishment. Second, the term "vindication" indicates the many faces of the "evil" of punishment. With one blow, vengeance punishes the evildoer, guarantees and defends the social harmony (and the status quo of power relations), and avenges the victim who has been wronged.

Thus, for Aquinas, punishment is decidedly a virtue, a good that may be used unsparingly. But it is the *imposing* of punishment that has become a virtue, rather than an unpleasant duty for the sake of the offender, as in Plato's curative penology. Punishment is still about cleansing the sinner's soul, but only obliquely is this an objective of punishment. Rather, punishment has become about the expression of legitimacy: the punisher is the one authorized by god to carry out the god's justice. The punisher is the one who accrues salvatory credit from his participation in the "evil" act. This assertion will no doubt come in handy, along with the promise that "the wicked can be uprooted . . . with great profit," in justifying colonial abuse and church profiteering.

The Latin words Aquinas uses in speaking of punishment (*vindicatio*, *vindico*, *vindicta*) tell a great deal about his (and in general, Christian) ideas about punishment and justice. These terms, which mean "guaranteeing," "defending," and "avenging" turn penal attention once again upon the victim of crime. *Vindicatio* takes an object, and the object of *vindicatio* is the victim. Punishing an offender is about guaranteeing justice *for the victim*, defending *the victim* against social offenders, and avenging the wrong done *to the victim*. Clearly, Aquinas, following Aristotle, rejects the Platonic logic of justice and punishment, and exemplifies instead the pre-Solonic notion of punishment as "vengeance" upon social deviants for the harm they have caused to their victims. Aquinas' warning, again following Aristotle's, that punishers, performing their virtuous task with zeal, might over-punish out of the joy of punishing witnesses Aquinas' astute awareness of a Christian problem for which there is abundant evidence in the history of the church, the problem of the all too enthusiastic indulgence of Christian authorities in the "virtue" of punishing.

We have seen that, in the archaic Greek world, the worst plague in the communities of hot-tempered princes was the problem of containing their righteous indignation when a peer failed to treat him or his family with the respect that was his rightful due. The passionate princes, according to tragedy and myth, often suffered from an overblown and obsessive "will to punish" which could lead to cycles of vengeance murders that could continue over many generations.

The Athenian court system sought to overcome the vigilantism that spurred the cycles of violence, year after year and generation after generation, by instituting a trial, a complex "hearing" process, which both gave vent to the outrage of the victim and channeled that outrage through the formal language of court justice. Since the hearing took place before a jury of interested peers who shared the same code of ethical behavior as the victim and the defendant, the community's *nomoi* were reaffirmed with every fresh trial. And since the "best practices" for trials was constantly confirmed in myth and tragedy in the model of the wise and just Athena's first trial, there existed, at least in theory, a shared understanding of punishment as a re-balancing of the social register to reflect an elevation of victims from the disgrace of the previous disrespect, and a demotion of the perpetrator for his disgraceful behaviors toward a peer. The trial too aspired to reflect the shared value of "erring on the side of generosity" in punishing one's peers, which helped to defuse the loser's resentment for the shame cast upon him for his crime.

The Athenian trial by jury clearly represents an improvement over the vigilante justice of the archaic age, witnessed in Homer's *Iliad*. Nevertheless, the trial system continued to reflect the *nomoi* of a people whose idea of justice had not evolved a great deal beyond that vigilante stage. Justice remained focused upon the victim and the trial amounted to

the exacting of vengeance, until the populace, represented in the jury, felt
convinced that the debt had been duly paid to the victim.

Plato's painstaking studies of justice and punishment had reconfigured justice as an internal state of soul, not a transaction in the social
world between victim and offender. This reconfiguration permits him to
position punishment as a curative to diseased souls. Turning penal attention away from the victim and onto the soul-sick perpetrator, Plato is
able to enhance the "best practices" of Athena's court, rethinking the
juridical response of the parent/city to its unintentionally offending citi-
zen/children, along the model of social teaching. Punishment makes
sense only for intentional offenders, and in dealing with this group of
culprits, Plato outdoes even Athena's generosity by designing an arsenal
of punishments (now configured as curative "goods" for the soul) that
includes, besides unpleasant consequences, persuasive speech and honors
and other pleasurable rewards for social learning.

> If we can but bring a man to this—hatred of iniquity and love of right
> or even acquiescence in right—by acts we do or words we utter,
> through pleasure or through pain, through honor bestowed or disgrace
> inflicted, in a word whatever the means we take, thus and only thus is
> the work of a perfect law effected. (*Laws* 9.862d)

Plato's punitive responses to intentional crime are solely focused upon
bringing the offender to a love of the good and a hatred of injustice. His
insistence upon education as the core of the justice process and his generous array of punishment options make for a pragmatic "whatever
works" philosophy that is a model from which societies today might still
find great benefit.

Aquinas' affirmation that whole populations may rightly be punished
leaves the Christian logic of punishment at the far end from the Platonic,
on the spectrum of penal generosity. Many hard-line defenders of punishment, Aquinas among them, might object that Plato's arsenal of punishments has expanded to such a breadth that many of his penal options
cease to be "punishments" at all, not "evil" enough to have deterrent effect. But, as the history of punishment in the Western world attests to the
fact that punishment has never had any deterrent effect upon offenders or
potential offenders.[1]

We have seen that, through the Middle Ages, Christian philosophers
maintained an unwavering devotion to Aristotle and that this singularity
of allegiance eclipsed the most generous aspects of Plato's revolutionary
penology, by which he strove to turn the eye of justice solely upon the

perpetrator and reconfigure the purpose of punishment as the task of curing the unjust soul's malady. Yet his idea of the work of justice as re-education and soul-healing found ready acceptance within a Christian theory of history that all too often evidenced an obsessive and zealous "will to punish" its sinners and infidels, on the Platonic argument that punishment was good for the sinner.

We see in St. Augustine that the Platonic distinction between intentional and unintentional misconduct has been abandoned. Furthermore, the notion of misconduct as a result of the parent/city's failure to fulfill its didactic duty toward its citizens, sin is reinterpreted by Augustine as the deliberately willful act of a freely decadent soul, rebellious to God and the church. Sin seen thus calls for a fervent dispensation of a harsh punishment that adequately avenges this dual affront (to god and church). Due recompense may be delivered by the heavy hand of a church authority, or, as Augustine suggests, it may well be exacted upon the sinner through the agency of another human being, though, rightly understood, all suffering, according to Augustine's account, truly originates in the righteous will of god.

Aquinas' choice of language (*vindicatio*) and his careful review and analysis of the history of accepted scholarship on the various questions surrounding rightful punishment demonstrate that the Christian doctrine returned to the pre-Solonic era's retributive model of justice, the eye-for-an-eye "due recompense" for sin that exacts wages for transgression in equal (or harsher) measure to the seriousness of the crime. And crime being always a willful act of rebellion against god and the church, it is entirely comprehensible that delivery of punishments might reach such a degree of fervor that Aquinas would rightly be concerned about its capacity to elicit in the punisher the sickened joy, against which Aristotle had warned.

Did the Christians find their consciences as the Middle Ages waned, when penal practices softened into less spectral festivals of horrific cruelty and retired into secret chambers? This is highly unlikely. Even today, Christians are quite comfortable with violence. Radical Christians are quite often the first in their countries and communities to rally behind wars, they tend to be the most fervent supporters of the death penalty, and they generally place an enthusiastic trust in corporal punishments in their homes and schools, despite expert testimony about its futility and dangers.

Notes

1. Georg Rusche and Otto Kirchheimer, *Punishment and Social Structure* (New York: Columbia University Press, 1939), 23.

Chapter 10
From Karitas to Penal Spectacle

Every system of justice and punishments purports to be serving the highest ideals of educating its social deviants to better practices of life conduct, more conducive to societal good, but the specific forms assumed by
these institutions have their roots in the interests of the dominant class of
the society in which they are instituted. Since the dominant social class
prevails in economic as well as political arenas of citizen life, it is impossible to understand a society's "penal temper" without appreciating the
productive relationship at play among economic and political arrangements, historical preconditions, and present circumstances of life within
the society. Crime and punishment *per se* do not exist, but only specific
acts and practices, designated as "criminal" and "just" by the society.
Politico-social responses to citizen acts, seen as criminal, become encoded in the formal architecture of law, upheld in court justice processes,
and validated through the penalties the courts exact. Thus a people's penal temper is determined by patterns of social and political power, but
cannot be fully interpreted without reference to the arrangements and
relationships of exchange—the specific economic circumstances—that
function within the society.

In the archaic age of Greece, old, powerful, landed families, which
traced their ancestry back to heroes and gods, comprised the dominant
social class. For over eight hundred years, justice amounted to observing
and respecting due prerogative toward peers. What was understood to
comprise injustice was a word or deed of effrontery that treated a peer as
though he were a social inferior, to whom less respect was due. Thus the
process of justice and the practices of punishment, from the archaic age
through to the Athenian democracy, were designed precisely to recali-

brate the social register among the wellborn (and later, the *nouveau riche*), to socially disgrace and demote the offender to exact revenge for his having disgraced a victim peer.

The problem was that the hot-tempered high-born warrior class were often carried away to extremes of punishment under the force of their righteous indignation, when they felt dishonored and disgraced. Although shame acted as a potent social force working internally to monitor conduct within the limits of the accepted codes of behavior, boundless outrage often carried the powerful to shameless lengths in their pursuit of revenge against their enemies. Vengeance could be so harsh and unmeasured that cycles of violence would rebound, generation after generation, between families who may have long forgotten the substance of the original affront.

The political and social organization of the age of the great princes of Greece, which we witness in the Homeric epics, was dying out by the seventh century BCE, when the city-state of Athens was well established. Athens began as an aristocracy, ruled by nine supreme officials named archons, who held the office annually and then automatically joined the ranks of the prestigious Areopagus Council. The challenge during that early period of the state was always to avert the tyranny, threatened at regular intervals by powerful wealthy individuals who, lacking noble birth, were excluded from power and were always happy to exploit the discontent of other wealthy men and the impoverished masses to seize the reins of the state.

However, from the seventh century, as the political hegemony of the old aristocratic families began to slowly give way to competing social forces, Athenian power slowly extended from the confines of aristocratic families—the *eupatridae* or wellborn—to include the new wealthy citizens, the class of merchants and traders, and ultimately (or at least in theory) all the citizens of Athens.[1] As the political center of gravity shifted in the polis, so too did the interpretation of justice, to reflect the interests of the changing power nodes. Laws were put in place to reflect the changing ideas and interests of the powerful.

Solon, appointed chief archon and special mediator between the masses and the notables in 594 BCE, instituted constitutional changes directly reflecting the swinging pendulum of power. The exclusive power of the *eupatridae* was decisively undercut by Solon's *seisachtheia* or "shaking off of burdens," by which all existing debts were cancelled and debt slavery was abolished. The export of agricultural products was prohibited as well, to ensure adequate food for Athens' own citizens. But most importantly, Solon undercut the old tribal bases of power by several important political reforms. He redefined the four classes of the state according to annual production of corn, oil, and wine, he opened the archonship (and consequently the Areopagus) to the two upper classes, and to the lower classes, he opened minor offices and membership in the *Boule*, or Assembly of 500, which assumed some of the functions previously reserved only for the aristocratic council. These changes rendered Athens a broader-based oligarchy, with many democratic compensations to placate the poorer citizens. Most notably, three points in Solon's constitution served the demos: the prohibition of loans on the security of the debtor's person (debt slavery); the right of any citizen to press redress on behalf of anyone being wronged; and the institution of jury-court appeals. A curious feature, reported by Aristotle, regarding Athenian laws under Solon's recrafting of the constitution, is that the laws were purposely kept quite indefinitely worded, to leave plenty of leeway for interpretation, so that matters of dispute could readily be brought before the courts for a communal reconsideration that kept pace with the fluctuating temper of the changing times.[2]

Solon went to great lengths to accommodate all classes in his reconstruction of the structure of power in Athens, recognizing the importance of fitting laws, broad-based courts, and flexible punishment practices to the general social order. But for the philosopher Plato, witnessing the political tug of war and the rampant corruption that maintained long after Solon's rule, Solon had not gone far enough toward managing the fragile passions and shameless greed of the powerful and reconfiguring justice to cure the general soul sickness of the Athenian citizenry.

Plato pressed philosophical ideas about justice and punishment in a new, more generous direction, shifting the vengeance (*dikephoros*) language of "giving and taking" of justice to the *therapeuma* language of "curing" the malady of sickened souls. He was convinced that justice had to transfer its focus from the outraged offended party, with his fevered will to punishment, to the impoverished soul of the harmdoer, whose deeds reflected an infection with the sickness of injustice. Any means should be employed, Plato argued, from gentle persuasion and noble example to the firmer influence of harsher penalties, but always according to the "loving parent" paradigm, which seeks to correct the behavior of a faltering child.

Aristotle did not follow in Plato's penal revolution, but returned to the language of "give and take" but he did respond to the problem of the excessive will to punish by turning the discourse of justice and punishment toward a consideration of appropriate measure, recommending a "golden mean" of punishment, between the insufficiently lenient and the excessively cruel. Aristotle also showed his appreciation for the problem of *dikephoros* justice and its tendency toward extreme penalties, when he warned of an ever-present danger in punishment not previously raised in discussions of penology: a certain "joy" that accompanies engagement in the act of punishing.

For the Christian world, the word of "the Philosopher" (Aristotle) was sacrosanct. Aristotelian cosmology was confirmed in Augustine's two-world view that split the cosmos into the heavenly city of god and the earthly city of sinners. The natural world, unstable and chaotic with its cycles of generation and decay, stood in stark contrast to the perfect heavens with their predictable, ordered motions. The heavenly spheres provided a stable model for emulation in human affairs, showing that the "right" way to live was in fixed, lifelong, stable relationships of patronage and servitude, rooted in the nature (the land), determined by birth, maintained by timeworn tradition, and overseen by the god's representatives on earth—the church and the divine monarch.

For the Medieval Christians, everything had its proper place, determined in advance by grace and expressed in the fortunes of birth and the providence of worldly affairs. "Evil" describes a state of soul, in the tradition of Plato and Augustine, and sin relentlessly exacts its wages, in the worldly fortunes of individuals and in a merciless afterlife, resonating the tragic vision of Aeschylus and the rigorous and often excessive moral accounting of the archaic princes. However, the ancients' rigorous exclusion of the lower classes (*hoi polloi* or "many") from designations of the good (*aristos* means a "nobleman" but also designates the generic attribution of "good" and "noble") was carried into the medieval era, in curiously reformulated ways. Under the influence of the NeoPlatonic holistic worldview of a Great Chain of Being, the feudal era understood every lowly creature to have its important and vital place in the whole of things.

The holistic perfection of the Great Chain of Being permitted the individual to know her place in the great scheme of things and granted unique value to each individual part of each level of existence, as necessary to the completeness and overall perfection of the whole. Thus the serf, however lowly his estate, was conceived of, by the upper classes, as necessary and even noble in his own humble way. Though the conceptual universe continued to be split in two, between the heavenly "City of God" and the fallen "Earthly City," the social universe was, in the social imaginary of medieval Europeans, configured by the old Indo-European tripartite division, depicted in Plato's *Republic* and evidenced in monarchies from time immemorial. The division of society, the ideology runs, is paralleled in the human body. The head (king and priests) rules heart (military) with wisdom, the heart fights courageously to defend, and the belly and other lowly regions (peasants) provide the manual labor to feed the whole.

The holistic organic model seems a healthy and balanced one, but it was often misused, and called upon to justify social repression and exploitation of the laboring masses. One example of its misuse is by the Roman consul Menenius Agrippa in his speech to the rebellious plebes on the Aventine Hill. In subduing the exploited masses, as they rebelled against Rome, Menencius drew upon the tripartite ideology, but he argued that the poor, so sadly resourceless, under-contributed to the balanced "equalities" that make up the balanced whole. The stomach simply feeds off the better parts of the organism, who do the more important work of the governing and protecting, he argued.

In the feudal era, there was a general sense of the balanced nature of the organic unity of their world, and a general agreement of the "rightness" of the social arrangements of European economies. The social order of the early Middle ages in Europe was taken as a natural and god-given order that benefited all social levels. A theory of interwoven integrity granted to the least lofty of social places a dignity of its own. Alaine de Botton describes "an unusually strong appreciation of the value of the poorest class . . . [and a belief] that the peasantry was no less vital and hence no less worthy of dignity than the nobility or the clergy."[3]

The feudal manor system composed a paternalistic arrangement. The lowest class of field workers was thought of as an extension of the lord's own family. That is to say, the social arrangements rested on a general assumption that the peasants were like children, simple and dependent, thus owing gratitude and loyalty to the parents, while the lords had the duty to care for the lowly as parents should care for their offspring. De Botton cites a spectrum of artistic and literary forms from the early Middle ages that depict peasants as valued members of their communities.[4] Indeed often the poor serfs were cited as the *most valuable* of all social classes, without whom the nobles and the clergy could not survive. Aelfric, the Abbot of Eynsham, the Bishop Gerard of Cambrai, and Hans Rosenplüt of Nuremberg name but a few of the poets across medieval Europe who paid homage to the "noble ploughman" who "feeds all the world."[5]

In the medieval worldview, all along the Great Chain of Being, nature reflected the goodness of the god, concealing divine secrets and enjoying a specific measure of the god's grace, and thus was every creature worthy of contemplation and study. The field worker had his particular expertise, living close to god's good earth, just as the patron enjoyed his special proficiency in managing the estate. The church fathers and monarchs taught that god granted knowledge as he granted economic fortune and power—entirely discriminately, according to faith and by grace. Birth determined from the start of one's life what the god, in his infinite wisdom, knew to be most fitting for the most functional arrangements of society.

Theology was the unchallenged queen of the sciences, and god "spoke" only through the church, so the church fathers enjoyed an undisputed monopoly on truth. However, the sublime mysteries of nature, hidden in oak and stream, were also hunted down in pagan schools by other means than grace—magic, alchemy, astrology, and many other occult practices. Private faith in the village wizard and the witch astrologer paralleled (and often complemented) the more public faith in the efficacy of prayer and other rites and rituals in the religious setting.

The paradigmatic description of the Christian worldview during the Middle ages is expressed by Dante (1265 to 1321 CE) in the *Divine Comedy*, written at the high point of the Medieval era (c. 1308).[6] James Franklin states, "There could hardly be a more medieval figure than Dante, nor a more perfect expression of the medieval world view than the *Divine Comedy*."[7]

Dante's opening words of this epic work announce the overriding problem of human existence on earth: "I woke to find myself in a dark wood, where the right road was wholly lost and gone." Straight off, Dante acquaints us with the wages of our necessarily faulty steps along the morally bewildering path of life: he plunges us into twenty-four circles of Hell to witness the varying wages of sin. Dorothy Leigh Sayers summarizes Dante's journey through the *Divine Comedy*:

> Down through twenty-four great circles of Hell we go, through the world and out again under the Southern stars; up the two terraces and the seven cornices of Mount Purgatory, high over the sea, high over the clouds to the Earthly Paradise at its summit; up again, whirled from sphere to sphere of the singing Heavens, beyond the planets, beyond the stars, beyond the Primum Mobile, into the Empyrean, there to behold God as He is—the ultimate, the ineffable, yet in a manner beyond all understanding, "marked with our image."[8]

Each of the nine circles of Hell, with seventeen distinct rings, is reserved for a particular brand of sin. Dante's Hell was inhabited by a range of individuals who had been successful in worldly terms—poets, generals, bishops, emperors, merchants and even popes are shown, stripped of their privilege and enduring the least imaginable sufferings as punishments for having contravened god's laws. In the fourth ring of the ninth circle, Dante, accompanied by Virgil, witnesses the screams of traitors being ravaged in the jaws of the three-headed giant Lucifer. The great and the lowly meet with an agonizing justice here. The first ring of the seventh circle finds Alexander the Great and Attila the Hun struggling to stay afloat a river of boiling blood, as centaurs fire arrows to force them back under the bubbling froth.

Certainly the ten spheres of Heaven, representing the provinces of reward to the possessors of specific virtues, offer a counterbalancing image to the many hellish realms of ingenious tortures and brutal miseries. However, the place of prominence is most decidedly afforded the latter realm. It is difficult to avoid locating the seeds of a cruel and brutal penal temper in the pages of this classic work, though the cruel tortures Dante details grant us less of a view of the penal temper of his own era (early 1300s) than that of the later Middle ages. The pivotal place of the descriptions of Hell in this work foreshadow the central role that punishments will come to play in maintaining order in the later Middle ages, as the church extends its power across the globe, and as economic times become increasingly difficult. When the rigid hierarchies of power and static networks of intricately interdependent social relations of the feudal era begin to unravel and disintegrate, and give way to a new breed of wealthy citizen, the bourgeois entrepreneur, and new capitalist forces of production enter the Mercantile Period, attitudes toward the poor, definitions of crime, and the cruelty of punishments move in new directions, in keeping with the changing times.

In the early Middle ages, relations between the landlords and their serfs were for all practical purposes the equivalent of a precisely defined legal relationship. There was not much room for a system of state punishment, in the absence of strong centralized power. The strictly determined social conditions tended to avert social upheaval in the first place. When local problems did occur, the nobles were expected to mediate and put things aright, as parents intervene among squabbling children to guide them toward just relations. Rusche and Kirchheimer, in their classic study, *Punishment and Social Structure*, describe:

Tradition, a well-balanced system of social dependence, and the religious acknowledgement of the established order of things were sufficient and efficient safeguards [for preserving the peace]. The main emphasis of criminal law lay on the maintenance of public order between equals in status and wealth.[9]

The main crimes in this society of wealthy and secure landowners had little to do with property rights, since property was rarely in question, anything of any value belonging almost exclusively to the property-owning class. Rather, what was deemed crime involved offences that challenged the stable social order by crossing the boundaries of decency or religious prohibition. Cases of severely harming or killing a neighbor, perhaps in the passion of the moment or in a state of intoxication, composed serious crimes against the communal peace, because these offenses could easily spark a blood feud or instigate anarchy. Therefore such severe crimes among the estate family obliged a grim punitive response from the lord of the estate. Alternatively, the parties might engage in private arbitration to settle the dispute.

The most minor offences could trigger very hostile responses from the entire entourage of the victim's family, servants, and allies, if not settled forthwith. If a public court were chosen to deal with a crime, then the trial followed the traditional process: a solemn gathering of free men determined culpability and pronounced the penalty. Justice remained configured after the archaic Greek logic of *dikephoros* justice, understood as "due recompense" or giving punishment to take retribution for the social offense. Justice remained fixated on the offended party because the fear of private vengeance vendettas remained the primary concern of the society. Reminiscent of the archaic age of Greece, the principal preoccupation of criminal law in the early Middle ages across Europe was with preserving the balance of social order among powerful families. Crime was regarded as an act of war upon a neighbor.

Another telling aspect of justice in the middle ages was the fact that penances and other punishments almost always took the form of a monetary fine. Fines were generally carefully graduated to fit the social status of the offender but also reflected the seriousness of the crime, according to the social status of the offender relative to the social status of the victim. But offenders from the lower classes had enormous difficulty making good the least of penance requirements. Therefore, over time corporal punishment came to replace penance as the punishment most regularly exacted upon the poorer citizens. This practice soon became universally applied, but it does not seem to have presented a favorable alternative for the impoverished. Often corporal punishment meant not only an immediate beating or flogging. It could also entail the more extended torture of suffering in prison, and as Rusche and Kirchheimer affirm in the following passage, that might well mean a term of incarceration that could be open-ended:

> This development can be traced in every European country. A Sion statute of 1338 provided a fine of twenty livres in assault cases; if the offender could not pay he was to receive corporal punishment by being thrown into prison and fed on bread and water until the citizens interceded or the bishop pardoned him.[10]

Fines appear to represent the more humane form of penalty exacted in the middle ages. However, it did not take long before shrewd and powerful public and church leaders came to recognize the enormous potentiality for profit involved in the collection of penance from wealthy offenders and the forfeiture of chattel from felons in general. Once this realization was made and justice showed its potential for enhancing wealth, hegemony over justice and punishment was contested at many levels of the social ladder. As in every great business venture, profit depends on organization; the business of justice had to be organized rationally, formalized and bureaucratized to maximize its potential for profit-making. The sizable revenue that justice represented was the main reason that the machinery and technology of justice proliferated over time and shifted its venue from the private and communal domain in the hands of the feudal lords and church fathers, into the jurisdiction of increasingly centralized authorities of the state, whether the royalty in England and France or the princes in Germany. Rusche and Kirchheimer explain:

> In Tuscany and upper Germany, in England and France, the attempt to extract revenue from the administration of criminal justice was one of the principal factors in transforming criminal law from a mere arbitration between private interests, with the representative of public authority simply in the position of arbitrator, to a decisive part of the public law.[11]

At this point, however, the serfs, having little money for penance and no property to confiscate, remained looked upon from above with charity and benevolence, as providing the backbone of the manual labor that "fed the world." They remained somewhat protected from penal abuse under the moral net of *karitas* and within the clear and time-honored paternalism defining relations between them and their landlords.

By the fifteenth century, however, social circumstances across Europe shifted dramatically. Populations, decimated by the Black Death of the mid-fourteenth century, were steadily becoming replenished, just at the moment when European empires were expanding their territories across the globe and acquiring foreign markets for their products. Agriculture, long a localized concern, became recognized as an enormously profitable enterprise, with global potential. This realization was the single most important factor in bringing about the close of the feudal era, grounded in relations of interdependence and mutual respect and responsibility among the social classes.

With the birth of globalized agri-business, the value of land across Europe rose sharply. Sharecroppers were thrown off their plots and common lands were enclosed to make room for the enormous agricultural and pasturage enterprises that were budding across England and the continent. Amongst the wealthy old stock, the increasing size of families made for mounting numbers of younger sons without the prospect of land inheritance. By the beginning of the sixteenth century, large sections of the population of Europe were pauperized and hordes of unemployed, downtrodden, property-less people drifted into the cities.

The results of this lifeworld collapse are entirely predictable. Vagrants filled the streets and turned to whatever activities they could to feed themselves. Property crimes, prostitution, and mendicancy spiraled. Vagrants formed criminal gangs that terrorized the cities and plagued the countrysides, while others joined bands of mercenaries, and attached themselves to rising princelings, vying for a share of the wealth and power. For the poor across Europe, times were hard, life grew cheap, and the noble ploughman became the ignoble thief and the despicable vagrant.

The cities responded to the changing circumstances by closing their doors to newcomers, just as the guilds closed their ranks to the waves of immigrating craftsmen and traders. As the stable networks of social life of the feudal period crumbled before a budding global capitalist world, so too did the dominant ideas, concerning what constituted crime, and what punishments composed fitting responses to those crimes, keep pace with the changing times. As petty crime among the homeless and poverty-stricken masses increasingly plagued the cities of Europe, the ruling powers clamped down with harsher and harsher responses. The laws evolved to target precisely the lower classes.

Dishonesty was considered not from the angle of the property stolen or damaged, but rather from the angle of the person stealing or damaging; he would be dealt with much more harshly if he happened to be homeless or of low social status. . . . When it was a question of damage done to property by members of the upper classes, legal opinion was not so severe.[12]

As the poor bled out onto the streets of Europe and legitimate opportunities for employment eroded steadily away, harsh laws were instituted across Europe to target the petty crimes that sustained their wretched lives.

Simultaneous to the collapsing conditions for the poor, the wealthy classes grew ever more resentful of the droves of hungry beggars clogging the streets and pressured public authorities for crack-downs. At the same time, the wealthy grew more shameless in their pursuit of gain. The conception of the feud, still very much alive, gave the upper classes a convenient cover-up for all forms of property seizure. Moreover, in the unlikely event that their mischief brought them to prosecution, they could count on preferential treatment in the courts.

It was the rising class of bourgeoisie across Europe, who began to add to the public outcry for legal and juridical reform against the criminal poor, the demand for an end to the preferential treatment that the wealthy enjoyed in the courts. The entrepreneurial class, rising across Europe in the middle ages, was a major force pressuring for institutional change in the state machinery of justice and punishment. They achieved the introduction of harsh, new laws to protect their growing property, harsher punishments to make the laws stick, and greater efficiency in the administration of those laws and punishments across the full breadth of the social register. They recognized the abuses of the wealthy scoundrels, who could purchase favorable verdicts from the magistrates or exemption from punishment. The bourgeoisie pressured the monarchs to abolish the royal pardon, often used to conceal upper class crime.

There is no doubt that what was considered criminal activity at this time had more to do with the class of the offender than with moral conceptions of right and wrong. "Legislation was openly directed against the lower classes," affirm Rusche and Kirchheimer.[13] The greater the numbers of the swelling ranks of the poor and the more miserable their conditions, the more the laws evolved to target their particular crimes, and the harsher the punishments exacted upon them to deter them from their ways. Before long, almost every crime of the poor was punishable by the death penalty. The vital question became what form the death sentence would take, what cruel and horrifying methods would be devised to teach the poor their lessons in virtue.

Once supplementary, corporal punishments now became the norm for addressing property crime among those lacking the means to buy their way out of crime. Where the death penalty and serious mutilations had previously been applied only in cases of most severe crime, now executions, exile, and physical punishments of increasing severity and public exposure became the rule rather than the exception. By the late middle ages, floggings, mutilations, brandings, and executions were freely dished out in efforts to exterminate the hordes of petty criminals that plagued the cities and the towns across Europe. Rusche and Kirchheimer afford us a glimpse at the severity of the problem:

> The data for England, which must be approximately correct, give us an idea of the situation prevailing throughout Europe. We are told that 72,000 major and minor thieves were hanged during the reign of Henry VIII, and that under Elizabeth vagabonds were strung up in rows, as many as three and four hundred at a time. And the population of England was then only about three million.[14]

In these sweeping attempts to clean the city streets and the countrysides of vagrants, little concern was evidenced for the guilt or innocence of the criminal, or the dangerousness or triviality of his crime. Often the sign of the defendant's guilt was already marked on his body from previous punishments; fingers, toes, and hands were removed, tongues were torn out, eyes were burned or poked out, ears were severed, castrations were performed. Criminals having undergone these tortures often died in the process. Where they survived, they were broken individuals, scarred with their criminal histories, and thus readily marked for further persecution and perhaps execution. Unlikely to find honest work, *if any were to be had*, they would be forced back into a life of crime until they met with their final punishment.

That final punishment was not only public but included extremes of barbarity difficult for us to imagine today. Michel Foucault chooses, as the opening words for his classic study of the genealogy of punishment, *Discipline and Punish: The Birth of the Prison*, a description of one of the final examples of the medieval spectacle of punishment:

> On 2 March 1757 Damiens the regicide was condemned to "make the *amende honorable* before the main door of the Church of Paris," where he was to be "taken and conveyed in a cart, wearing nothing but a shirt,

holding a torch of burning wax weighing two pounds"; then "in said cart, to the Place de Grève, where, on a scaffold that will be erected there, the flesh will be torn from his breasts, arms, thighs and calves with red-hot pincers, his right hand, holding the knife with which he committed the said parricide, burnt with sulphur, and on those places where the flesh will be torn away, poured molten lead, boiling oil, burning resin, wax and sulphur melted together and then his body drawn and quartered by four horses and his limbs and body consumed by fire, reduced to ashes and his ashes thrown to the winds."[15]

We can clearly see, from a gloss of the social, legal, and penal trends across the Middle ages in Europe, the crystallization of a string of inter-woven relationships among socio-economic phenomena: the fewer the jobs, the lower the wages, the higher the number of homeless poor and the rate of petty criminality; the greater the petty crime rate, the louder the outcry of the upper classes against petty offences against their prop-erty, the tougher the laws constructed to target these petty offences, the crueler and more final the punishments, the less the concern for guilt or innocence of the defendant, and the diminishing respect for the poor and hapless, and for human life in general. But one more important phe-nomenon must be added to this string: the increasingly *public* nature of punishments. The penal spectacle is born from the public thirst for vengeance (*dikephoros*) justice.

What forces lie at the base of the growing severity and public exhibi-tionism that configures the penal temper of Europe in the late Middle ages? Certainly, the growing greed of a burgeoning capitalist world hardened the minds and hearts of those preoccupied with amassing their private fortunes. Furthermore, as the paternalistic relations of feudalism gave way to the centralization of state power, the tendency grew for monarchs and princes of Europe to publicly display, by grand spectacles of cruelty, their divine right to rule.

Philosophical and religious influences too had their effects on penal tempers. Unmistakable is the resonance between the litany of punish-ments imposed upon the regicide Damiens and Dante's imaginative de-scriptions of the tortures of Hell, detailed some four and a half centuries earlier. The cruel forms and the public nature of the penal spectacles of the high middle ages suggests a logical connection between the Christian worldview and the generally deteriorating penal temper of the era. If cruel tortures are the stuff of redemption for sinners in god's retributive universe, then magistrates and kings can hardly be faulted for following the god's example. Aquinas' injunction, that whole populations may rightly be punished for the acts of the sinning few, helped to justify the miles upon miles of swinging vagabond corpses, strung up along the roadsides of medieval cities. The saint's warning, echoing Aristotle, against the "joy" that can be incited by punishing, foretold the sadism that would increasingly infect all levels of society across the middle ages—from the church authorities in their pursuit of pagans and infidels, to the kings and princes and local magistrates in their spectacular public executions, to the masses' ever increasing thirst for cruel spectacle.

Many factors contributed to increasing inflame penal tempers across Europe in the later middle ages. The cruel punitive spectacle was not simply a legal or political trend; it served many functions in a chaotic world. It had become a purification ritual, a legalized outlet for resentment and frustration, and a public sport. A frustrated clergy, losing their grip on the souls of society, saw a divine justice in the Hellish tortures and executions. The wealthy resented the decay of public order and demanded retribution for the attacks against their property. The poor simply needed the spectacle as diversion from the difficulties of their miserable lives.

As the stable relationships of feudal times gave way to the wage labor relations of capitalism, as populations swelled and the poor were pushed off their plots and flooded into the towns, as diseases plagued the overcrowded cities, and natural disasters of fire and failed crops rendered food supplies precarious, outlaws, witches, Jews, gypsies, and foreigners came under increasingly brutal persecution. Lay populations, as much as legalized authorities, cried out for retribution for the chaos of the times. Aliens of all descriptions made convenient scapegoats for the indignation of the wealthy, the puritanical outrage of the acquisitive bourgeoisie, as well as the general wretchedness of the lower classes, wallowing in an atmosphere of oppression, desperation, and hopelessness, alongside obscene extremes of wealth.

Notes

1. For a complication of this neat evolution, see Jacques Rancière, *Disagreements: Politics and Philosophy*, Julie Rose, trans. (Minneapolis: University of Minnesota Press, 1999).

2. Aristotle, *Constitution of Athens*, 9A.

3. Alain de Botton, *Status Anxiety* (New York: Vintage Books, 2004), 48.

4. Ibid.

5. Ibid., 48-51.

6. James Franklin, *The Science of Conjecture: Evidence and Truth Before Pascal* (Baltimore, MD: Johns Hopkins University Press, 2001), 52.

7. Ibid.

8. Dante, *The Divine Comedy: Hell* (Dorothy L. Sayers, trans. and introd. (New York: Penguin Books, 1982), Introduction, 9.

9. Rusche and Kirchheimer, *Punishment and Social Structure*, 9.

10. Ibid., 9-10.

11. Ibid., 10-11.

12. Ibid., 15.

13. Ibid., 18.

14. Ibid., 19.

15. Michel Foucault, *Discipline and Punish: The Birth of the Prison*, Alan Sheridan, trans. (New York: Vintage Books, 1995), 3.

Part Four
A Modern Penology of Shame

Chapter 11
The Business of Punishment

Michel Foucault opens his brilliant genealogical study of punishment practices in the West, *Discipline and Punish: The Birth of the Prison*, with the declaration of a "sudden"—over the span of less than a hundred years—shift in the "economy of punishment" in Europe and the United States, at the turn of the nineteenth century. Foucault sketches a history of penal forms from protracted and horrific public spectacles of tortures, mutilations, executions, and dismemberments, to public processions of convict chain-gangs, paraded across the breadth of Europe with shaven heads and infamous dress, to inconspicuous, black cell-carts slipping down alleys and silently disappearing into prisons to deliver bloodless punishments hidden from public view. This complete conversion in the way that European states administered punishments to their deviants, Foucault explains as paralleling an inversion in public sensibilities regarding the shame associated with penal violence.

Where public mutilations and executions had provided a day of festival, a respite from the general misery of a cruel and exploitative age, a display of the power of the monarch and clergy, and a preview of the torments of afterlife tortures promised by Christian mythology, people's delight in public cruelties turns suddenly to shame. Suddenly, Foucault posits, over less than a century, the public perception of shame *in crime* had shifted to a shame *in punishing*. Shame was lifted from the criminal and transferred to the executioner, and by association, attached to the powers behind the executioner, the governing powers of church and state. The victims of penal tortures had become the objects of public pity. The punishers had become the cruel henchman of prodigal sons.

The apportioning of blame is redistributed; in punishment-as-spectacle a confused horror spread from the scaffold; it enveloped both executioner and condemned; and although it was always ready to invert the shame inflicted on the victim into pity or glory, it often turned the legal violence of the executioner into shame.[1]

Punishment retired to the secret confines of prisons and private execution rooms, argues Foucault, because people have come to recognize that punishing is more shameful than crime, so such activities must be tucked away neatly from public view, "under the seal of secrecy."[2]

Foucault ascribes the dramatic shift in penology to a reconfiguration of the logic of shame in public sentiments, as well as in the juridical orientation, of Western states at the turn of the nineteenth century.

Now the scandal and the light are to be distributed differently; it is the conviction itself that marks the offender with the unequivocally negative sign; the publicity has shifted to the trial; the execution itself is like an additional shame that justice is ashamed to impose on the condemned man.[3]

But why this change? Why "suddenly" at this moment at the turn of the nineteenth century? Foucault explains that public sensibilities, under the influence of Enlightenment ideals, such as the dignity and equality of man (sic.), have driven punishment from the scaffold into the dungeons, the labor camps, and the fields. Like the good Leontius ascending from the Piraeus, the public has become ashamed of the desires after which their eyes had thirsted. But instead of chastising their eyes, as Leontius did, they projected their shame in their penal tastes onto the executioner, and from him to the legitimating authority that fed those savage tastes, in legislating the cruel and bloody spectacle. Because shame indicates moral failure, the challenge to the edifice of power presented by the people's shame was a moral challenge. Moral arguments always question not only the rightfulness of an act, but the rightfulness of the actor. It challenges legitimacy to rule.

In naming the public spectacle shameful, its audience was challenging the system of justice and the entire hierarchy of state power that stands behind the henchman. Everyone has grown shame-full, with the exception of the criminal, who has become the object of public pity and the victim of a barbaric system. Straightway (over less than a hundred years, according to Foucault's theory), detested criminal is transformed into pitiable victim of an unjust system. The moral debt to the convict is made good through the application of healing therapies. The "army of experts" set right the historical wrong of penal violence, illuminated by the public shame.

Punishment in the modern era, according to Foucault's genealogy, moves from spectacular cruelties administered upon the convicts' flesh before a public audience (that observers may learn from the offender's mistakes and recognize the awesome power of the crown, clergy, and magistrate) to discreet hidden technologies of re-education—"disciplines"—to reorient the deviant's soul. A "slackening of the hold on the body" marks the shift in the penal temper of Western states from "punishment" to "discipline." The methods of punishment imposed upon the convicted, as justice systems enter the modern era, are milder, more humane, more rationalistic forms, which increasingly target the soul, rather than the body. There is no escaping the fact that the new penal methods, which ran from imprisonment and other forms of confinement, to forced labor, deportation and penal servitude in distant colonies, and galley labor, involved convicts' bodies in the punitive process, since bodies are directly affected by the rationing of food, sleep, and exercise, sexual deprivation, corporal punishment, solitary confinement, and arduous labors of prison life. But the connection between punishment and the flesh became incidental, rather than directly significant.

> The body now serves as an instrument or intermediary . . . to deprive the individual of a liberty that is regarded both as a right and a property. The Body, according to this penality, is caught up in a system of constraints and privations, obligations and prohibitions. Physical pain, the pain of the body itself is no longer the constituent element of the penalty. From being an art of unbearable sensations punishment has become an economy of suspended rights.[4]

The new economy of punishment requires the proliferation of a system of experts and technologies; a "whole army of technicians"—wardens, doctors, chaplains, psychiatrists, psychologists, educationalists—takes over from the executioner in a complete and total overhaul of penal tradition. Even in the case of the death sentence, these "experts" intercede to place themselves between the criminal and the executioner as agents of the former's welfare, guaranteeing the condemned a painless, bloodless, instantaneous, and highly private demise.[5]

Foucault still admits a "trace of torture" in modern mechanisms of criminal justice, but penal torment has in the modern era retreated into private cells, ships' holds, and plantations in faraway lands, and its methods and procedures have morphed into subtle forms that "discipline" the soul, rather than "punish"—pain and scar—the body.[6] Tortures have seeped down into the innermost reaches of the criminal's being with the object, not of scarring the flesh so that all may see the felon's shame, but of changing *who the felon is*, in his deepest nature and character. If Foucault is correct in his generous genealogy, Plato has won out against the vengeful princes after all, and the machineries of justice across Europe and the New World have overcome the excesses of punitive vengeance in favor of the higher form of curative punishments.

Foucault's genealogy of punishment represents an ingenious study and his treatment of the shift in the economy of penal practice in modernity has located, in the element of shame, a key factor in the logic of punishment per se, and an important explanatory element in the force of shifting penal practices. However, I will offer an alternative account of the revolution in penal forms to the one Foucault gives. I will argue that, while shame plays a central role in determining the penology adopted in modern Western states, its role is different from the role assigned to it by Foucault. I contend that Foucault's explanation for the dramatic shift in penal practices, as the Western world enters the modern era, is overly generous, and credits the citizens and power nodes of Western states with an ethical epiphany that they did not then, and have not yet, accomplished. If people have grown less enthusiastic about public tortures of their social offenders, that cooling of zeal has its explanation in far more pragmatic, rationalistic forces associated with the spread of a globalizing capitalism, rather than with a revolution in public ethical sensibilities.

Certainly, the populations of Europe may well have grown ashamed of the excessive "joy" that public spectacles of bloody mutilations and executions had come to elicit in them, and certainly too the French and American Revolutions shifted the terms of judicial discourse from "sin" and "indecency" and "regicide" to universal "rights" and "liberties," a shift in the conceptual universe that opened the door to new theories of justice, and with these, new perceptions of punishment. However, the concealment of penal practices, behind broad prison walls, deep in ship galleys, and far away in the plantation fields of distant colonies, as well as the new reluctance to execute social offenders, except for the most heinous of crimes, was not, I contend, the result of a sudden awakening of moral sensibilities in enlightened Westerners, but has another, far more practical explanation. The fact is that the moral force of shame has a tendency to serve power, rather than to challenge it, in this historical era as in every other. Shame works in far more complex ways and is a far more conservative force than Foucault allows.

What convinces me that Foucault gets wrong the economy of punishment and the logic of shame in his nonetheless ingenious genealogical study? Primarily the problem resides with Foucault's claim of the relative rapidity of the revolution in penal policy. What looks to him as a "sudden" revolution in Western penal practices at the turn of the nineteenth century was much more gradual and organic than Foucault appreciates, and the roots of this revolution can be definitively located hundreds of years earlier than he asserts. The mistaken dating of the penal reforms makes the latter appear as a "sudden" revolution in penal tempers that arises with the ideas of that later time, the era of Enlightenment ideals. But Enlightenment ideals, regardless of their rhetoric of universal rights and human dignity, consistently served power, justified the territorial expansion of empires, and provided metaphysical underpinnings to rationalize enslavement and slaughter. It is difficult to see the slowly but steadily growing forest of changing ideology, underway for many centuries, for the sudden late-born crop of high-sounding philosophical ideas.

Significant forces had been pressing European societies in the direction of the changes in justice and penology that Foucault describes, since the thirteenth century's displacements and enclosures had begun to throw hordes of poor peasants onto the streets of Europe. The forces of change began to take their full toll across the late medieval period, peaking in the sixteenth century. With the breakdown of the stable social relationships that had held the feudal world intact, masses of vagrants, beggars, and petty criminals arrived on the public scene, just at the critical moment when a new capitalist age was dawning bright and gazing across the seas to enormous profits in a global marketplace.

Attitudes toward the poor had been undergoing significant changes throughout this entire period, inverting the logic of shame that had granted dignity to the condition of poverty and compelled *karitas* from the wealthy. The hardworking "noble ploughman" and the unfortunate beggar of the early Middle ages had inspired pity or admiration in their wealthy patrons and the church clergy. As Marjorie Rowling tells in her classic study of *Life in Medieval Times*:

> Everyone owed services and obligations of some sort to those below and above them . . . . [W]ithout the work done by serfs on the manorial estates the whole fabric of medieval agriculture, on which monasticism and feudalism were built, would have collapsed.[7]

The richly interwoven tapestry of human life during the feudal period, along with the influence of church teachings on poverty, granted positive moral connotation to the condition of poverty in the lower classes. Jesus had been a humble carpenter, and there was no shame attached to his station. Indeed if shame was to be found, it was attached, not to the condition of poverty, but to its causes, neglectful patrons or clergy.

Conditions changed across the late medieval era as feudal relations broke down, jettisoning hordes of homeless poor onto the streets of the cities across Europe. As one worldview died, another rose to prominence. The ideology of the rising bourgeoisie, as Max Weber has rightly asserted in his class sociological study *The Protestant Ethic and the Spirit of Capitalism*, was grounded in the "Protestant Ethic."[8] Just as the conditions of the poor slipped to depths of misery unparalleled in centuries, the Protestant religions came into their own, preaching *against* the "good works" of almsgiving. For the wealthy Protestant entrepreneurs, worldly success was the surest indicator of god's grace to the virtuous, where virtue was understood as intelligence, industriousness, and economic asceticism—that is, the accumulation of capital. If one found oneself without prospects in life, one could assume that the god had spoken: you were unworthy of success, morally and intellectually faulty.

The Protestant Ethic gave religious justification to economic inequalities and rendered the strata of social class as moral justice. As the justice of social place became clearer in the public mind, negative moral connotations were increasingly attached to impoverishment, and the poor came to be progressively more blameworthy for their condition. Morally decadent, dishonest, foul, untrustworthy, lazy, and repugnant, the poor were utterly deserving of the miseries they suffered. They were nothing more than a social disease, which needed to be contained in dungeons or wiped out on the gallows. Almsgiving only exacerbated the problem, because the lazy poor would only work if they had no other means to secure their survival. The growing hegemony of the bourgeois class in economic affairs meant the mounting general acceptance of their social ideology: that the poor were in their lowly condition because they deserved to be.

Blaming the poor for their condition was a primary corollary of the bourgeois worldview: if entrepreneurs were self-made men who applied their industriousness, intelligence, and pecuniary asceticism to great reward, then those who failed economically must fail through a lack of these desirable qualities. That is, the poor are not poor because god so ordered the world that the simplest creature had its proper place, intrinsic value, special function, and dignity within the whole; the poor fail because rigorous economic times sift the wheat from the chaff, expose the morally faulty, and kick them to the curb.

Perceptions of what constitutes criminality and what forms of punishment adequately meet the crimes were entirely comprehensible in terms of the Protestant ethic that configured the worldview of the dominant class of the era. The lawmakers of Europe responded to the growing pressure from the rising middle class of entrepreneurs, with enthusiastic crackdowns, targeting the swelling populations of vagrant poor. The focus of law shifted abruptly to the protection of property and to the elimination of the petty crimes that sustained the homeless poor—prostitution, mendicancy, and theft. Almost every crime became punishable by the death penalty, usually exacted in drawn-out public spectacles of horrific tortures and brutal dismemberments.

However, by the end of the sixteenth century, the bourgeois ideology that figured the poor as simply lazy and stupid and fit for little but the gallows unfolded into its fullest capitalist spirit: the lost souls of the poor could be saved from themselves by their forced conscription in the virtue-builder of hard work—and at great profit! The entrepreneurial mind, always scouting fresh sources of revenue, chanced upon the great revelation of the age—that the impoverished classes provided an abundant supply of cheap labor for ready exploitation. Vagrants, prostitutes, and beggars, now turned into criminals, could be penalized for profit, under the wise direction of the entrepreneur.

The shift away from spectacular public executions and toward incarceration, deportation, galley servitude, and hard labor was the direct result, not of a sudden dawning of humanitarian sensibility on the part of the public spectator, nor of the mounting shame attached to the monarch and the executioner at the turn of the nineteenth century. The revolution in the economy of crime and punishment is explicable by reference to specific economic developments of a globalizing capitalism and the ideological influences of a rising middle class of Protestant bourgeoisie, over the course of the sixteenth century. These influences slowly took hold and gradually revealed the potential profitability of a ready store of human resources, utterly vulnerable and disposable to the labor pool.

Military recruiters under Frederick II of Prussia first pointed the way, when the labor shortage of the mid-sixteenth century caused rising labor costs that placed workers in a strong position to bargain for better working conditions. This rendered wage labor in fields and factories more attractive than dangerous mercenary work, so the bands of mercenary soldiers, who had previously been counted upon to swell the ranks of the military, suddenly retired to the fields and troops grew scant.

With the Thirty Years War (1618 to 1648) well underway, something had to be done to counter this phenomenon. "Press gangs" made their appearance. Officers began seizing passers-by and "pressing" them into military service. Soon "orphans, bastards, beggars, and paupers who were looked after in infirmaries" were forcefully recruited into the military.[9] Ultimately, the army turned from infirmaries to the courts to satisfy their need for fresh military recruits. Judges and jailers were consulted about the fitness of their populations for military service. The verdict was positive! Before long in many European countries, armies came to be looked upon as penal organizations, enlisting their chain gangs, not only from their own prisons, but from the prisons of foreign countries as well. It was only a matter of time before the shrewd entrepreneurial minds of the sixteenth century began to exploit this avenue of cheap labor for their cheap labor needs.

Foucault's idea that a new and general sense of shame, suddenly shifted from criminal to executioner to ruling powers, was responsible for the cessation of public and brutal punishments and the shift to more concealed and subtle "disciplinary" punitive methodologies is overly generous to the people who held power in early modernity. The penal shift occurred much more slowly, keeping pace with the mounting influence of the stark utilitarian and moralistic ideology of the entrepreneurs, industrialists, and monarchs that held sway in the early capitalist period. Shame did not protect the criminalized impoverished; on the contrary, shame was instrumental in rendering them responsible for their miserable condition and deserving of exploitation.

The era of cruel public punishments that arose across the middle ages parallels the over-abundance of human life and the lack of opportunities for their gainful employment. As the number of available working bodies increased, the price for wage labor plummeted, jobs grew scarce, and people turned to crime, as people always do in hard economic times. When the pendulum swung back in the opposite direction, after the middle of the sixteenth century, the populations of Europe dwindled again and created a severe shortage of unskilled, manual laborers, and wages began to rise again.

Normally, this situation could be expected to increase the value placed upon human life and improve prevailing attitudes toward the poor, as well as raise the rates of wage labor. But capitalism could not plow forward with its new globalizing enterprises, if wages continued to soar.

And since the Protestant Ethic configured the poor not only as undeserving of better conditions, but as morally ill-served by charity and welfare efforts, as well as by higher wages, the challenge became how to secure the labor of the poor, against their obstinate and indolent wills, without permitting a rise in labor costs which would tempt them to work as few hours as ensured their survival.

The legislators and the machinery of justice leapt to the challenge and rounded up the vagrant and the beggar. The gallows were exchanged for the prison and the prison was transformed into a manufactory. Or the prisoner was chained out of sight in the ship's galley and transported to the colonies to labor in the plantations and build a New World. The penal revolution, from spectacular public tortures and bloody executions to more discreet, more humane, and less public penalties, such as hard labor and imprisonment, which Foucault dates at the turn of the nineteenth century, was well entrenched by the late sixteenth century.

In their classic comparative macro-sociological study of punishment, Rusche and Kirchheimer confirm the earlier dates for the penal revolution. They assert that "the related problems of labor and poverty underwent complete change during the sixteenth century"[10] and that the new penal practices had their origin in the "houses of correction" that arose as early as 1555 in London and swept across every country of Europe by 1576.[11]

The earlier dating is also supported by the timing of significant events in the evolution of Protestant thought. Martin Luther (1483-1546) wrote his famed "Ninety-Five Theses on Power and the Efficacy of Indulgences," exposing the abuses of Roman Catholic clergy, including the practice of selling "indulgences," that is, extracting large sums of money from wealthy parishioners as a means of buying freedom from God's punishments for their sins. This work, published in 1517, is considered to have launched the Protestant Reformation in Europe. John Calvin (1509-1564) was preaching that "God helps them what helps themselves" at about the time when houses of correction were cropping up all over Europe to take the lazy poor in hand. These houses absorbed vagrants, beggars, prostitutes, thieves, and "idlers," but also took in "ne'er-do-well children and spendthrift dependents" for a handsome fee.[12] Houses of correction were publicly designated as places "where those who were unwilling were forced to make their everyday practice conform to the needs of industry," a description expressly capturing the Protestant attitude toward work and their prejudice toward the economically unsuccessful and socially dependent.[13] It is hardly surprising that the development of correction houses reached its peak in Holland, which, at the end of the sixteenth century, was "the most highly developed capitalist system in Europe."[14]

Notes

1. Michel Foucault, *Discipline and Punish: The Birth of the Prison*, Alan Sheridan, trans. (New York: Random House, 1995), 9.

2. Ibid., 10.

3. Ibid., 9.

4. Ibid., 11.

5. Ibid.

6. Ibid., 16.

7. Marjorie Rowling, *Life in Medieval Times* (New York: Paragon Books, 1979), 42.

8. Max Weber, *The Protestant Ethic and the Spirit of Capitalism*, Peter Baehr and Gordon C. Wells, trans. and ed. (New York: Penguin Books, 2002).

9. Rusche and Kirchheimer, *Punishment and Social Structure*, 216, note 22.

10. Ibid., 35.

11. Ibid., 41.

12. Ibid., 43.

13. Ibid., 42.

14. Ibid.

Chapter 12
Modernity's Shameful Penology

I have attempted to illuminate over the preceding chapters the way that definitions of crime and forms of punishment in any given historical period in the West reflect the socio-economic conditions of the age, and especially the interests of the dominant class. The poor, struggling at the base of the social ladder, become more and less vulnerable and thus more and less exploitable, with the fluctuating economic conditions of the time, according to the ebb and flow of population rates and the consequential abundance or penury of cheap labor. Prevailing ideas regarding what acts are criminal and what punishments are fitting to those crimes, for the most part, follow the needs of the market and the interests of the powerful. Justice, then, is a form of domestic politics whereby the powerful discipline their subordinates into serving their (the powerful's) interests, in the name of society's welfare.

What has largely slipped the attention of scholars is the extent to which the social force of shame is a political force as well. Across the history of the Western world, a "politics of punishment" has been in force, whose primary weapon is the agonizing affect of shame. Shame is the sentinel at the boundaries of social class that defends the "social order," mythologized as the "common good." Shame patrols the portal of the Areopagus, guards the borders of the manor and the castle, and walks the beat all up and down Wall Street, to keep the poor in the fields, the factories, and the prison workhouses and the princes, the lords, and the CEOs on their lofty perches of power. Shame has played a pivotal role in keeping people in their social places. But it has also been a determining force in the social construction of ideas about justice, crime, and punishment in Western societies. In this chapter, I will expose the power of this critical force for guiding public attitudes about justice and crime and for determining methods of punishment imposed upon social offenders, but I will demonstrate as well the power of shame for motivating people to crime.

During the archaic age of Greece, the aristocratic class understood, as well as negotiated, their social place in the community of peers, according to a specific vision of virtue, the virtue of a warrior ethos— bravery in battle, loyalty to friends, and viciousness to enemies. The *aristoi* were by definition "the good" in a society where justice was seen as embedded in the cosmos. The best are best *in their nature* and that nature is indicated by their birth into the best and wealthiest families. In this worldview, the ubiquity of cosmic justice dictates that the best rise to the top *naturally* and, as the good, they are the happiest, whereas the ignorant are rightly lowly in kind, in social position, and in rational capacity to judge their unhappy state.

The opinion of those below the aristocrats—the *hoi polloi*—counted for less than nothing to the wellborn. But the opinion of their peers held such great weight that social place within the group was determined by the respect afforded them by the others. Thus an individual was socially promoted and demoted on the social ladder on the basis of the honor or shame accorded him by his peers. Peer opinion and peer treatment was so important in determining social place that if another treated an individual badly, social demotion was realized thereby. Public opinion could fluctuate with the honorableness of the individual's conduct, but it might well only follow the dictates of capricious popular opinion. The aretaic ethos found its theater in noble contest with peers and against enemies, and heroic deeds (or ignoble) had their effects in the glory (or shame) attributed the individual on the stage of public opinion. But even where conduct was admirable, the respect of the peer group could not be guaranteed, so the matter of social place was always a source of sore concern among the aristocrats.

If a prince were to be treated badly by a peer, as Achilles was maltreated by Agamemnon in Homer's *Iliad*, the social demotion was very real, as was the shame felt by the demoted, witnessed in the moving scene when the great hero stands at the seashore, wailing in agony to his mother. The only way to recapture honor and regain social place was for the offended to wreak a due measure of harm upon the offender. This resulted in cycles of avenging violence that endured across generations, as pictured in the three books of Aeschylus' *Oresteia*.

The *Oresteia* offers the mythological explanation for the creation of a formal system of justice in Athens. The trial by jury initiated in the polis of Athens introduced a process that attempted to interrupt the cycles of violence at their source, by offering a public stage where crimes (*atimoi* as "deprivations of honor") could be brought for renegotiation before the community of peers, who shared the same code of conduct as both the offender and the offended. Thus the community's traditional *nomoi* concerning social justice could be applied and simultaneously confirmed, but their fresh application in the present circumstances also permitted them an opportunity to evolve, to keep pace with changing historical circumstances.

The trial took the form of a "process" of public hearings, which could last as long as a full day. The process allowed a healthy venting of the righteous indignation (*aitiai*) of the offended one, as well as an exposure of the mitigating circumstances that had driven the defendant to his offensive actions. After the tradition of Athena, the objective was simply to put right the social wrong and return the offended one to his rightful social place, by demoting the offender, if found guilty of dishonoring a peer. But the ideal of Athenian justice was colored by a spirit of generosity, and often punishments would be foregone if the work of pacification had been achieved without further manipulation of the social register and without further episodes of harmdoing.

The arsenal of punishments reflected the nature of justice as redistribution of social place. They ranged from minor penalties, such as prohibition from public places, to various forms of shaming in public places (such as stocks and flogging), to elimination from the city altogether through exile. In the case of more heinous crimes, public execution was the just response. The dishonoring was greatest when the executed bodies, rather than being respectfully buried, were thrown over the city walls and left to rot in the sun or to be eaten by birds and dogs.

By the fifth century in Athens, at a population of 350,000 persons, the economy was propped up by a generous body of slave labor. It is difficult to state for certain the number of slaves that supported this society, but given that the majority of citizens owned at least one slave, and even poor peasants are said to have had several, the lowest estimate of 20,000 slaves seems a conservative estimate. By this time, the old aristocratic families, whose claim to power had been based on birth and (old) wealth, were losing social ground to a rising middle class of *nouveau riche* merchants, artisans, and traders, both Athenians and foreigners, who had begun flowing into Athens, as her power as a world leader and a pivotal hub of culture and trade grew.

Thus a great diversity of human talent shared the dangers, hopes, and interests of an evolving international economy. The rising middle class challenged old ideas about the rightness of a fixed social order, grounded in old money and the chances of birth. The citizens most *naturally* fit for leadership could now be seen as those with the most at stake in the changing economy. In the organic harmonious Greek universe, where the best are seen to *naturally* rise to the top, the middle class, rising from lowly birth to wealth and power, could readily make the argument that they had risen much farther than those born into power and wealth in aristocratic families, thereby grounding their claim to greater fitness for power. Pericles' funeral oration locates the greatness of Athens at this period, not in the illustrious histories of old wealthy families, but in the free participation of worthy citizens in civic duties, such as law-making, and in their *self*-submission to the laws.

Thus by the fifth century in Athens, social place had been opened up to include in the ranks of power any who were economically successful. Where shame had previously been attached to lowly birth and peer opinion, it began to lodged itself in the souls of individuals, who failed to show up for their civic duties or to willingly submit to the laws. In theory, the democracy opened its doors not only to the middle classes but also to those of lower birth. But in practical effects, the poor had little positive influence on the workings of power except when charmed by the slippery speeches of persuasive demagogues, who courted their votes for their own political aggrandizement.

The philosophers, Plato and Aristotle, recognized the dangers of extending power to the lowest ranks of society. Since slavery was altogether "natural," so too was ignobility in the ignorant masses. Merit, not noble birth nor mere citizen status, recommends one for participation in city affairs. The problem for the philosophers became how, under the democracy, to keep the poor in the fields, and out of the marketplace (where they will crave pretty things they cannot afford) and the council chambers (where they will be swayed by the seductive words of demagogues that can lead the state toward tyranny).

Ancient values maintained into the feudal world: a highly stable, intricately interwoven social network of obligations and responsibilities, held together by Christian ideals of servitude and *karitas*, and a metaphysics of divine power and free will. What was seen as criminal in this social context was the failure to uphold one's obligations to those above and below, the failure to behave in ways that maintained the social order and reflected the decency of one's house. On the manor where the serf was embraced as part of the lord's extended family, as in the town where the indigent poor were understood as wards of the church and opportunities to exercise *karitas*, the general attitude of the upper classes toward the poor was paternalistic.

The peasants, though their social place was lowly and their lot arduous and unenviable, were not only respected; they were often glorified in the song, poetry, and art of the period. They were typically deemed righteous, long-suffering "feeders of the world" and a secure place was reserved for them in heaven. Almsgiving to the indigent poor—the widow, the orphan, and the alien—was advocated by the church, both as a source of god's blessing and a duty that god had assigned to those he had blessed with prosperity. Shame, in the context of this highly structured and stable world, was attached to the failure to fulfill one's obligations toward the needy others, or the commission of acts of indecency that would reflect badly upon the entire household.

When crime did occur, the logic of paternalism dictated that the lords, by nature men of reason and arms, assume responsibility for the moral education of their serfs and servants, by nature less morally capable. The punishments should parallel the firm but fair corrections, applied by a loving parent. Executions of citizen sinners would make little sense, except in the most heinous of crimes, since killing off the labor supply would hurt the manor, and could upset the order of society. However, between the thirteenth and sixteenth centuries, the rigid social bonds of the feudal world slackened and broke down under the mercantile forces of a burgeoning capitalism. Hordes of poor flocked to the streets of the cities and turned to any activity that could grant them subsistence—begging, petty thievery, and prostitution, as well as other more organized crimes against property and wealth. The definitions of crime evolved in ready response. Property became the focus of the law. Offences against property and prestigious person were met with cruel punishments, generally administered in horrific public spectacles, to wipe out the social disease of crime and to serve as a deterrence to others.

There was practical method in the penal madness of the late Middle Ages. As populations increased, the price of labor decreased, and a lower and lower value was placed on human life. There was no place in the new economy for bands of vagrants on street corners and in forests. So their very existence became a crime. "The hard struggle for existence molded the penal system in such a way as to make it one of the means of preventing too great an increase in population," tell Rusche and Kirchheimer.[1] But this means that the depopulation strategy was necessarily "selective," the penalties behaving as an "artificial earthquake or famine in destroying those whom the upper class considered unfit for society."[2]

Where low class human material was in excess and the means to support them in shortage, public attitudes toward the poor fell to a level unimaginable during the earlier feudal paternalism and under the ideal of Christian *karitas*. But market forces were not the sole determinant of public perceptions of the poor. Prevailing attitudes were increasingly driven by the Protestant Ethic that valued the workers only for their labor, rather than for their fundamental humanity. The poor were to blame for their poverty, reasoned the wealthy, hardworking, rationalistic bourgeoisie. The vagrants, petty thieves, widows, orphans, and aliens were poor because they were lazy, dishonest, and stupid. Like animals, they were good only for their unskilled labor, which should never be bought at greater than subsistence pay rates or laziness would prevail, since the poor would only ever choose to work as little as it took for subsistence.

As capitalism gained its grip across Europe and spread across the globe to distant colonies, shame increasingly became attached, not only to unemployment, vagrancy, petty thievery, and illicit occupations such as prostitution, but to the condition of poverty itself. In a world where hardworking entrepreneurs were amassing their fortunes to prove themselves god's chosen, the poor could only prove their redundancy by their hungry bellies, dirty faces, and squalid living conditions.

One would expect the negative attitudes toward the poor to reverse, starting in the middle of the sixteenth century, when populations across Europe began to drop again, as the result of plagues and wars. Certainly a revolution occurred in the logic of crime and punishment at this time. Contra Foucault, I have argued that the market forces of a globalizing capitalism caused the shift from horrific public penal spectacles to more subtle modern forms of penal tortures—confinement in the house of correction or the prison, galley servitude, and deportation to, and penal servitude in, the colonies. Though we do witness wages rising in the second half of the sixteenth century, as labor needs increase and the labor pool dwindles, we do not see a corresponding re-valuation of the poor or a disconnection of the attribution of shame from the socially lowly, between 1650 and 1800. This is because the bourgeoisie hit upon a more cost-effective solution to the labor shortage problem, a solution that only continued to make sense as long as the poor could be blamed for their poverty.

The power of the Protestant Ethic over public perceptions of the poor and the allegiances between monarchs and the entrepreneurs, who had grown enormously powerful due to their tight grip on capital and technology, set the scene for a new economy of punishment. The burgeoning industrialism required cheap labor, in order to continue the accumulation of the capital that would support capitalist expansion across the globe. Since free laborers were in an advantaged position to bargain for higher wages and better working conditions, both of which ate into investment capital, the crafty bourgeoisie, unsentimental and utilitarian, followed the example of the "press gangs" raised by the Prussian army during the Thirty Years War (1618 to 1648). They turned to jailers and magistrates for a solution to the labor shortage problem, and began to restock their labor pools from the largest and most vulnerable class of their societies, the poor.

Foucault claims that punishment forms become more reformative and more restorative as Enlightenment ideals took over the public consciousness and the world became more civilized. However, I have contended that punishments shifted from the gallows and stocks of the town square to the prison cells, the colonies, and the galleys, not so that social conditioning could be more effectively performed under the panopticon gaze of the guards, though this result was certainly desirable, being conducive to the disciplining of productive laborers, obedient citizens, and faithful consumers. The penal revolution occurred because in an age of globalizing capitalism and expanding empires, criminology and penology followed the forces of the market and the interests of the ruling classes. The new forms of punishment that replaced cruel public spectacles of the medieval period served the need for cheap labor. Cruelty transformed into labor in prison manufactories, galleys, or colonies.

To a large extent, the forms of justice and punishment invented in the early mercantile period (1650 through 1800) have maintained throughout the Western world into modernity, with some significant alterations. Galley servitude is a thing of the past. We have run out of colonies to which we might deport our undesirables for profit. Thankfully, the solitary confinement, advocated as the best soul-curative by the Quakers, is rarely used any longer, since its use overwhelmingly had the consequence of madness, rather than convict contrition. Even arduous labors are largely abandoned as criminal penalties, as the global poor flows, both legally and illegally, to fill the unskilled labor pools of big business, outsourced to the most economically miserable areas of the globe. You are unlikely to experience traditional torture, unless you fall into the network of secret foreign prisons overseen by the CIA. Executions have all but ceased across the globe, America being the only modern Western state still killing its citizens to teach them moral lessons, and, as might be expected, the star performer in this infamous category of performance goes to that conservative (and hyper-religious) stronghold, Texas.

The overwhelming modern choice for punishments is the prison. Contra Foucault, humanitarian ideals of the Enlightenment were not the motivating factor in the evolution of the prison to punishment of choice in modern states. Rusche and Kirchheimer assure us that the establishment of the prison systems of Europe was "bound up with the manufacturing houses of correction" and that "the principal objective [was] not the reformation of the inmates but the rational exploitation of labor."[3] Working prisons were highly profitable in their time, but from the late eighteenth century, the pendulum had swung again and there was plenty of labor to be had outside the prisons and at cheap rates. Workers began to organize and to demand the "right to work" which ultimately led to the end of the use of prisons as manufactories.[4]

Modern prisons indeed impose strict regimens of discipline to maintain order and to discipline the inmates into submission, if rarely into rehabilitation. Strict separation at night is almost universally accompanied by some form of organized labor in the daytime. For the most part, however, discipline is maintained by "constructive, rather than merely repressive measures, by encouraging the prisoner to maintain a standard, rather than by holding out physical punishments *in terrorem*."[5] Regular and regimented activity, elaborate, graduated systems of rewards and privileges, and the carrot of reduced sentences for good behavior are the primary disciplinary methods employed in the modern prison. If prisons are tortuous now, they are much more furtively so. Punishment is controlled in practice by purely administrative regulations, but there is little doubt that these regulations can be arbitrarily interpreted.[6] Though prisoners are in theory protected from cruelty and have access to a procedure of complaint, recourse for criminals to complain about abuse "is not sanctioned by clear legal norms."[7]

Prisons have become big business in many Western states, often outsourced to private enterprise. As in the corporate world, the system hierarchy tends to protect the individual functionary from public scrutiny. Many of the leaders are hired from the military and import a worldview from that domain that supports the idea of violence as an efficacious tool of social control. Administrators tend to support lower officials and all employees tend to adhere to a code of internal secrecy, akin to the "Blue Code of Silence" that reigns in some police cultures. Furthermore, the assessment methods that report on the professional effectiveness of guards tend to be quantitative rather than qualitative, measuring *how many times* rather than *how effectively* the guards have dealt with problems on their watch. Moreover, the criminal whistleblower faces the same problem as whistle-blowers in other spheres of public and private life: speaking truth to power can have very real and unpleasant effects for the person complaining about power nodes, who nevertheless remain in control of her fate. Complaining can damage one's standing, and, for a prisoner, this means one's right of appeal can be affected, not to mention the possibility of being further punished for making "unwarranted" complaints.

The disciplines of prison life are designed, as Foucault rightly argues, to produce obedient citizens, productive laborers, and faithful consumers. If rehabilitation is the goal of prisons at all, then it is rehabilitation to industrious working lives. "Rehabilitation means adaptation to an orderly life with regular work, and rests on the assumption that the mode of behavior learned in prison will enable the convict to readjust himself to the outside world after release."[8] However, it is highly unlikely that modern prisons will actually have this positive effect on its wards. The verdict concerning the modern Western prison's rehabilitative effects is bleak in most countries of the West, and especially in the United States, where the recidivism rate remains appalling. According to the U.S. Department of Justice's Bureau of Justice Statistics, two very extensive studies show that a whopping sixty-seven and a half percent of prisoners convicted of all sorts of crimes, from violent crime to crimes against the public order to property crimes, are rearrested and reconvicted within three years of their release.[9]

So what goes wrong in the rehabilitative process that leads to the failure of the system to cure the souls of citizens sickened by the disease of injustice? For one thing, there has existed a trend in U.S. prisons over the past forty years, away from the hiring of experts and the application of rehabilitation technologies and toward the simple containment of criminals. Experts tended to control penal policy until the 1960s, then from 1964 through 1968, crime and punishment entered political discourse in the United States and the public began to dictate policy-making. As crime escalated, the public cried out for more repressive measures against social deviants; they complained about wasting public monies on experts and pampering criminals with decent prison facilities. Harsher laws, tougher sentences, and unpleasant prison conditions, the masses insisted, will teach deviants, as well as potential offenders, what they fail to learn in their families and their communities.

However, one thing that the history of punishment (and the law of logic) demonstrates unequivocally is that harsher laws only produce more criminals. And as every psychologist knows, corporal punishment has no positive effects on the receiver. Harsher punishments increasingly dehumanize criminals and harden their moral sensibilities. Harsher prisons over the past four decades have cultivated criminality in the prison populations of the United States, while having no deterrent value whatsoever for those who are tempted to crime.

What Rusche and Kirchheimer concluded in 1939 is still true today: "A more lenient penal policy . . . goes hand in hand with an appreciable drop in the crime rate," while "repressive penal policy has not been followed by a significant decline in the crime rate."[10] This is because in every society the number of crimes against property and the social order tends to fluctuate with the economic conditions of the poor, so unless a society provides decent conditions of life for the least of its members, crime will keep steady pace with the economic difficulties faced by the poor. Rusche and Kirchheimer affirm:

> The penal system of any given society is not an isolated phenomenon, subject only to its own special laws. It is an integral part of the whole social system, and shares its aspirations and defects. The crime rate can really be influenced only if society is in a position to offer its members a certain measure of security and to guarantee a reasonable standard of living.[11]

The stark fact of expert testimony is that repression has never worked to cure criminality. Modern punishment methods in the West may be more humane than the public torture and execution spectacles of the past. But they continue to have a very poor record for curing social deviance. James McGuire's *What Works: Reducing Reoffending* considers the various methods, approaches, and therapies used in dealing with offenders today, hoping to locate what methods best serve to rehabilitate criminals.[12] What works to convince people that crime does not pay and to keep them and others from offending? McGuire's findings are generally disappointing: nothing seems to work. None of the methods currently employed in prisons seem to make a great deal of difference—

neither shock therapy, nor isolation, nor boot camp, nor vocational training.

Two seminal studies of prison culture, David Garland's *The Culture of Control* and Gresham Sykes' *The Society of Captives*, show that confinement of the legally challenged with entirely criminal company is a highly successful form of criminal apprenticeship.[13] Prisons dehumanize inmates, but they represent a very thriving site for teaching criminal skills. Prisons supply the conditions for forging elaborate networks of criminal cultures, they stoke the fires of resentment and rage, and they provide closed communities where deviance can be normalized. Prisons are bad for curing criminal souls but they are great for the proliferation of crime!

The death penalty offers a final solution to crime, but its advantages stop at the erasure of the individual deviant. No monies are saved, no deterrence factor in potential offenders can be noted; the crime rate does not drop with each execution. Annihilating the criminal does effectively lop off from the social body the problematic limb. But, as Foucault rightly notes, when he (wrongly) attributes penal reform to the influence of Enlightenment ideals, it is shameful for state authorities to perform the very acts they deem most heinous in their citizens. The use of the death penalty puts the United States in the dubious company of some of the most barbaric states in the world—Iran, Saudi Arabia, and China—all infamous for their human rights abuses. If states cannot figure out how to solve their problems without radical violence, how can they expect their citizens to do so?

Indeed the single only thing that has shown the least success in reducing recidivism is what Plato prescribed all along—education. McGuire's negative prognosis notwithstanding, a wealth of prison research over the last decade has unequivocally confirmed that "inmates who actively participate in education programs have significantly lower likelihoods of recidivating, [a fact supporting] the normalization concept."[14] Most of the incarcerated people in the United States are under the age of thirty; many are first-time offenders, serving mandatory sentences. Only forty-six percent of those incarcerated have a high school diploma or its equivalent.[15] This mass of young people can readily be recruited and trained in criminal trades, if other options are not provided for their busy minds. And since a great many of these young offenders cannot even read, crime represents the only means of supporting themselves, if education is denied them in prison. Studies affirm that with two years college education, an inmate's chances of recidivism can be reduced by a whopping eighty-five percent, from the national average of above sixty-seven percent to about ten percent.[16] Yet, since the early 1990s, the Pell Grants, which provided the funding for study while in prison, have been withdrawn from the access of criminals.

In 1970, the state and federal prison population of the United States was 190,000. By 2002, it had spiraled to two million prisoners. Each year in the United States, federal, state, and local governments spend sixty-two billion dollars supporting their criminal populations. This is an average cost of $22,650 per prisoner per year.[17] By way of comparison, America's neighbor to the north spends three billion per year on its 150,000 prisoners, an average cost of about $90,000 per male prisoner, and $150,000 to $250,000 per woman prisoner. Canada imprisons far fewer of its citizens (131 per 100,000 compared with 726 per 100,000 in the U.S., which has the highest incarceration rate in the world) and spends a great deal more each year to correct each one. But this investment has permanent pay-offs: Canada can boast the lowest recidivism rates in the world.

Left to fester in resentment in dehumanizing conditions, the prisoners of America do their time, and then tumble out onto the streets of their country, only to return to jail within a few short months or years. This makes perfect sense, since the vast majority of young offenders that end up in prison hail from the lowest social echelons of this "beacon of freedom and democracy." They are almost entirely uneducated, urban, African-American males from the poorest class, who have difficulty being gainfully employed outside the criminal sphere.

This critique of criminal justice realities is not meant to suggest that those who end up in prisons are simply innocent victims of their system. These offenders cause a great deal of harm in their societies by preying upon others. Streets are unsafe in many neighborhoods, drugs are dealt on street corners up the block from where children play, houses are burgled in broad daylight, and families are terrorized in their homes, and by individuals that fit the stereotype we see plastered across our television sets: young, poor, urban, illiterate, unemployed, (disproportionately) black males. "Street crime is mostly a black and poor young man's game," as Police Chief Anthony Bouza asserts in his 1993 book, *How to Stop Crime*.[18] The reality of street crime is reflected accurately in the media and by Hollywood. As Jeffrey Reiman states in his brilliant study of crime, *The Rich Get Richer and the Poor Get Prison*, "They [the 'Typical Criminals'] are the heart of a vicious, unorganized guerrilla army, threatening the lives, limbs, and possessions of the law-abiding members of society, necessitating recourse to the ultimate weapons of force and detention in our common defense."[19]

On the other hand, as Reiman goes on to demonstrate, the portrait of this Typical Criminal, who so gravely endangers society and for whom we feel so much fear and loathing whenever we see his face on the nightly news and in our favorite cop shows, emerges

> *not [from] merely objective readings taken at different stages in the criminal justice process: Each of them represents human decisions.* "Prison statistics" and "probation reports" reflect *decisions* of juries on who gets convicted and decisions of judges on who gets probation or prison and for how long. "Arrest records" reflect decisions about which crimes to investigate and which suspects to take into custody. All these decisions rest on the most fundamental decisions: the *decisions* of legislators as to which acts shall be labeled "crimes" in the first place. The reality of crime as the target of our criminal justice system and as perceived by the general populace is not a simple objective threat to which the system reacts: *It is a reality that takes shape as it is filtered through a system of human decisions running the full gamut of the criminal justice system*—from the lawmakers who determine what behavior shall be in the province of criminal justice to the law enforcers who decide which individuals will be brought within that province.[20]

By emphasizing the role of human decisions in creating the reality of crime that exists, Reiman is not merely blaming system officials for voluntarily constructing that reality. Rather system officials, from police to parole officers, to members of juries, to judges and legislators, make the decisions that they do because their views have always already been shaped by the social system in which they have grown. Crime in society takes on the reality that it does because the society is structured in such a way as to shape people to make certain decisions, rather than other alternative decisions. Their decisions are a reflection of the social phenomena that form the parameters of their lifeworld, not mere rational reactions to an objective reality that confronts them.

The system does not merely respond to realities *out there* in society, it has a weighty hand in creating the realities that arise. Those officials and policymakers, who make the decisions at every stage of the criminal justice process, help to determine the future of the young, poor, illiterate, urban, black male who shows up in arrest records and ultimately is schooled in criminality in under-funded, dehumanizing prisons. As dangerous as he may be by the time he exits the criminal justice system, his individual reality may have been otherwise, had his family raised him in a society where poverty was not a shame, blamed on laziness, stupidity, and moral decadence; where his schools were funded adequately enough that his teachers were qualified to teach him to read; where his first delinquent act was recognized as acting out the anxiety and depression that poverty breeds and met with the support services he needs;

The young, poor, illiterate, urban, black male might not have fulfilled the criminal reality that society expected of him, had it not been decided that the "crimes of the poor" that *he* performs should be targeted, rather than the most dangerous acts that threaten people's well-being— corporate crime, embezzlement, occupational safety violations, medical irresponsibility, and the ongoing corporate chemical warfare that increasingly assails the land upon which people build our houses, the air they breathe, and the water they drink. Our "typical criminal" might have accomplished a different reality, if it had not been decided that *he* should be arrested for those crimes. Once arrested, our typical culprit's future still might have been otherwise, if *he* had had access to a top-notch lawyer who could convince a jury to acquit him and a judge to expunge his record. Our poor, illiterate, urban, black youth might never have fulfilled the reality of criminal identity that society expects of him had they not fully expected that reality, that is, had the myth not been socially constructed from the outset that *he* is the type of individual that is *by nature* defective, cannot be *nurtured* by education and counseling, to a productive and law-abiding life, and needs to be contained by force.

Twenty percent of American youth suffer a mental health disorder before age 21, and one in ten children suffers severely enough that their daily life functioning is severely impaired.[21] Yet fewer than twenty percent of these young people receive the services they need, according to the U.S. Public Health Service. When adolescents "act out" their suffering in deviant behaviors, the juvenile justice system identifies their behavior as delinquent, rather than recognizing it as symptomatic of mental disorder, often attributable to their conditions of life. Conflict theorists argue that depression and anxiety go hand in hand with the alienation, isolation and moral compartmentalization that are a general and entirely predictable result of life in advanced capitalist, industrialized societies, as we rat-race toward material success at the expense of communal and individual integrity. The families on the bottom of the social ladder are the first hit by external pressures, the first arrested for their acts of defiance, the first prosecuted for their offenses, and the first punished for their crimes. A juvenile's fate can be decided very early on in his life, depending on the color of his skin, the budget of his elementary school, the neighborhood where he lives, and the size of his family's bank account.

Without education in prison, the criminals incarcerated today are unlikely to be more literate, more employable, or more motivated to adopt law-abiding ways, when they exit the prison system tomorrow, with a criminal record added to their resumes. The powers that control penal policy in modern societies may as well post at the portal of their prisons the dictum that Dante imagined announced on the portal to the gates of Hell: *Lasciate ogni speranza chi entrate*. Abandon all hope, ye who enter here.

Notes

1. Rusche and Kirchheimer, *Punishment and Social Structure* (New York: Columbia University Press, 1939), 20.

2. Ibid.

3. Ibid. 65.

4. Ibid., 93, 95. The French constitution of 1793 recognized the human right to work. Prison labor was abolished and foreign labor expelled from Paris in 1848.

5. Ibid., 155.

6. Ibid., 157.

7. Ibid.

8. Ibid., 159.

9. Patrick A. Langan and David J. Levin, "Recidivism of Prisoners Released in 1994," U.S. Department of Justice, Bureau of Justice Statistics (Washington, DC: 2002), NCJ 193427; Patrick A. Langan and David J. Levin, "National Recidivism Study of Released Prisoners: Recidivism of Prisoners Released in 1994," U.S. Department of Justice, Bureau of Justice Statistics (Washington, DC: June 2002), NCJ 193427. See also Steven Steurer, Linda Smith, and Alice Tracy, *Three-State Recidivism Study* (Lanham, MD: Correctional Educational Association, 2001).

10. Rusche and Kirchheimer, *Punishment and Social Structure*, 197, 203.

11. Ibid., 207.

12. James McGuire, *What Works: Reducing Reoffending* (John Wiley & Sons, 1999).

13. David Garland, *The Culture of Control* (Chicago: University of Chicago Press, 2001); Gresham M. Sykes, *The Society of Captives* (Princeton: Princeton University Press, 1999).

14. Miles D. Harer, "Prison Education Program Participation and Recidivism: A Test of the Normalization Hypothesis," Prepared for the Federal Bureau of Prisons, Office of Research and Evaluation Report, May 1995.

15. C. W. Harlow, "Education and Correctional Population," US Department of Justice, Bureau of Justice Statistics (Washington, DC: 2003), NCJ 195670.

16. Cindy Hendricks, James E. Hendricks, Suzie Kauffman, "Literacy, Criminal Activity, and Recidivism" available (June 26, 2010) at www.americanreadingforum.org/yearbooks/01_yearbook/html/12_Hendricks,ht m. See also Williams, D., "Project LEAD builds bridges," *Corrections Today*, Vol. 58, No. 5 (1996), 80-83, 91; F. Porporino and D. Robinson, "The correctional benefits of education: A follow-up of Canadian federal offenders participating in ABE," Journal of Correctional Education, Vol. 43, No. 2 (1992), 92-98.

17. PBS Special Report: "By the Numbers: American Prisons" Available June 1, 2007 at www.pbs.org/now/shows/322/america-prsions.html.

18. Anthony Bouza, *How to Stop Crime* (New York: Plenum, 1993), 57.

19. Jeffrey Reiman, *The Rich Get Richer and the Poor Get Prison* (Boston: Pearson, 2004), 59.

20. Ibid. Emphasis Reiman's.

21. Elizabeth Bonham, "Adolescent Mental Health and the Juvenile Justice System" *Pediatric Nursing* Vol. 32.6 (November-December 2006), 591-95.

Chapter 13
Shame, Social Injustice, and the Poor's Right to Crime

As the Western world has made its way from ancient to modern times, notions of honor and shame have played changing, but always critical, roles in the common mental worlds of their populations. These notions have consistently been entwined with the structure of the social order and prevailing ideas about how "civilized" people behave. Thus, across the West, notions of honor and shame have had implications for the chosen configurations of systems of justice and punishment, by affecting definitions of crime, processes of prosecution, and modes of punishment.

With the archaic princes of Greek as with the feudal barons of the medieval world, honor was attached to a "wellborn" class. But it did not follow from this social reality that shame was attached to the state of being lowborn. Rather, shame was a condition of being in poor standing among one's peers. Shame accrued from failing (or being seen to fail) to fulfill the noble ethos, failing to live up to a code of responsibility specifically attached to elevated social status. In the aristocratic worldview, it was generally understood that where much was given, much was expected. Part of the expectation of the wellborn was their care for the poor of their society. Abuse of the poor for the sake of profit, as in the institution of debt slavery, came to be seen as shameful in Athens. Similarly in the medieval era, shame was attached not to poverty, but to failure to respond with adequate *karitas* to the needs of the lowborn and the unfortunate.

However, as the Western world comes of age in the sixteenth century, it throws away its childish ideas about nobility of birth, the goodness of works (almsgiving to the poor), and the dignity of the hardworking peasant. Under the mushrooming sway of capitalism and the Protestant Ethic of the entrepreneurs, the condition of poverty comes to be reassessed and assigned a moral identity: the poor are poor because they lack the industriousness, the intelligence, the pecuniary frugality, and the honesty of the economically successful, qualities the rising bourgeois class identified in their own ranks as explanatory of their success and proof of their status as god's elect.

The Protestant Ethic has persisted into the twenty-first century, though it has grown subtle, secularized, and sublimated in the public consciousness, which overwhelmingly accepts the political and judicial world as rational, objective, and thus free of religious prejudice. The baseness and ignobility of the poor is no longer a matter for public expression, in an era that at least pays lip service to tolerance for difference. Nevertheless, shame is still attached to the condition of poverty, both by the wealthy and by the poor themselves. Shaming the poor for their condition fits well with the logic of the "American dream" and similar capitalist dreams across the world. If anyone who sincerely and intelligently applies herself can realize the dream, then poverty exists because some people lack the moral and intellectual qualities to succeed, rather than because those people are burdened by unlivable wages, employer greed, and uneven access to educational and employment opportunities and decent living conditions. The work of social justice can be postponed indefinitely, as long as we can blame the poor for their lowly condition.

The longstanding modern prejudice that distinguishes the poor as shameful and the economically successful as morally worthy and honorable is simply a ruse, invented by the powerful and wealthy to maintain their social hegemony, to justify the gross inequities of their society, and to keep wages minimal and profits high, while concealing the greed which drives the system. There is an abundance of evidence to show that when people are given the resources they need for success, they will rarely disappoint their dreams. But there is also ample proof that when people grow hopeless for achieving success by legal means within their system, they will turn to alternative methods of survival—cheating, stealing, and selling drugs and their flesh.

The kind of criminality that actually gets targeted, prosecuted, and punished in modern societies is the kind tied up with social injustice; petty crimes always bleed out the bottom of the social ladder, onto the streets, and into the prisons. Harmful acts that are criminal in nature occur at every level of the system, but the meanings that make their way into law to define criminality in the public consciousness are determined by prevailing prejudices—ideas about the "nature" of the poor and what inherent features explain, and confine them to, their lowly condition. Just as positive moral qualities were once seen to inhere in the nature of the *aristoi,* negative moral qualities are now seen to inhere in the nature of the poor, captured in bloodlines and races and family trees. If people are lowly in their "nature," then it makes little sense to manipulate the conditions of their "nurture" to give them access to jobs and power, where their decadence will simply undermine the integrity of the system. Institutions of justice, definitions of crime, and systems of penal retribution are not designed to bring about social justice and share the common wealth across the human landscape. They are designed for the sake of the continuance of the existing social order and to exclude from power those seen as unfit.

In *Status Anxiety,* Alaine de Botton explores the factors that contribute to the distribution of wealth in capitalist societies. His study rightly points out that wealth is as much a function of the vicissitudes of fortune as character:

> A multitude of external events and internal characteristics will go into making one person wealthy and another destitute, among them luck and circumstance, illness and fear, accident and late development, good timing and misfortune.[1]

Between external events and internal characteristics, De Botton places greatest emphasis on the external, quoting Michel de Montaigne's explanation for discrepancies in wealth and power: "chance [bestows] glory on us according to her fickle will [and often] chance march[es] ahead of merit."[2]

Whatever the ethos of our times, we are likely to believe that our prevailing institutional forms and the moral principles underpinning them are the hard-won triumphs of science, rationality, and a "history of progress" that culminates with us. That is to say, we are overwhelmingly likely to see our own institutions and the values that we hold dear as the crowning articulations of the genius of human endeavor and the highest products of human civilization.

Our faith in the rightness of current institutions is all the more pronounced in modern democracies, where the propaganda of "freedom and equality" is ubiquitous. The poorest individual is convinced that she has a fair shot at the American dream. Our faith is confirmed by the mere existence of the world's dictatorial and hierarchical regimes, deemed "backward" beside our economic progress. The rightness of our systems will be paraded before us as self-evident truths that belong to the very fabric of democratic existence, rather than as the local tastes of particular powerful and wealthy people, with a specific history and culture, and explicit practical and psychological interests to defend.

As long as we believe the self-perpetuating mythology of the naturalness and rightness of current ideas and practices, we will continue to pay homage to a starkly utilitarian worldview and a pathetically self-serving ethical vision. The Protestant Ethic, which blames the poor members of society for their poverty and condemns them to their just desserts of low wages, the ghetto, and the prison has simply dropped its religious garb, but its truths endure and configure for the worst our view of the poor, the unemployed, the criminal, and the lower classes in general. This means too that we continue to attach the powerful force of shame to people's economic conditions, rather than to our failure to respond to our neighbors' needs and create opportunities for everyone's success. The Protestant Ethic shields us from the reality that crime is a function of poverty and poverty is largely a function of the ill luck of birth (including the misfortune of being born with a darker complexion into a predominantly light-skinned society), exacerbated by a rigged system.

The Protestant Ethic endures because it has a prodigious force behind it, the power of shame. We may state that shame, like justice and crime, is a socio-economico-political phenomenon, not only because ideas about which things and people are shameful in a society have concrete effects on people's social, economic, and political circumstances in the present, but because these ideas arise in response to specific historical circumstances that entwine these three aspects of citizen life. These ideas (about what/who is honorable and what/who is shameful) are doggedly conservative, so they can only be properly understood through a comprehensive examination of the socio-politico-economic relationships that prevailed at the time and place of their original occurrence. Ideas about what is shameful arise in the context of the *public* realm and have their effects in general social relations and specific social behaviors, but the locus of the efficacy of these ideas lies deep within the *private* confines of the individual psyche, where social learning is internalized.

Since the primary site of social learning is the family and local community where a common mental world is shared, ideas about what is shameful and what is honorable are implanted in the primary existential site of the family parlor and then more broadly enforced at the communal hearth, beginning in the earliest days of citizen lives when minds are most pliable. The social learning that takes place in those most trusted venues of human experience carves its truths deep within the psyches of individuals, and configures the grounding logic of their inner mental life.

This is because the pedagogical tools by which social learning takes place in the home and community are the most powerful forces that exist—the forces of love and pain. Love causes its victims to prostrate themselves before its holy altar and to willingly absorb its truths into their hearts and souls. But far more intensely and profoundly does the pain of withholding love scar the learner and etch moral messages into her psyche. While the rod and the whip may scar the body, they are no match for the tortures of the psychological kind, the primary example being shaming (which can, but need not, be attached to corporal punishments to enjoy its fullest effects). Punishments and shame have their most profound consequences, where they are administered by the same authorities that feed and clothe us and kiss us goodnight. When those who dish out the love for good acts also dish out the pain for our failures, social learning is instilled far below the flesh. It lodges in the very core of our being, in the respect we have for ourselves, the meanings we attach to our lives, and the view we hold of the world and our place in it.

Social teaching is itself ironic, because a society's prevailing ideas about what is honorable and what is shameful, so religiously instilled in the home and in the local community, have their source in the grander political situation and thus fluctuate over time in response to historical changes. Ideas about what is shameful, like ideas about what acts are lawful and what political responses just, remain faithful to the interests of the ruling class or party, as is captured succinctly in the stark political realism of Thrasymachus, cited at the opening of the current study.

> And each form of government enacts the laws with a view to its own advantage, a democracy democratic laws and tyranny autocratic, and the others likewise, and by so legislating they proclaim that the just for their subjects is that which is for their—the rulers'—advantage and the man who deviates from this law they chastise as a lawbreaker and a wrongdoer. This then, my good sir, is what I understand as the identical principle of justice that obtains in all states—the advantage of the established government. (*Republic* 1.338e)

To extend Thrasymachus' political wisdom to the subject of honor and shame, we find that in societies where a military aristocracy reigns, honor attaches to the individual's status on the battlefield (which is tied up with wealth and bloodline) and is alterable by individual feats of strength and bravery in battle. The hyper-masculine ethos of the warrior configures aggression against enemies and plunder of their goods as honorable vocations. Cowardice in battle, failure to pay due obedience to commanders and respect to peers, and the love of wealth (indicated by a lack of liberality with others) are seen as shameful. But, apart from ignoble actions, even the "being seen" by others as having base values or ignoble qualities could result in loss of peer respect and demotion in social place.

Where a landed gentry governs, the idea of the inherited nobility of landed wealth maintains as the governing ideology. But since Christian values have bled into the warrior ethos in the Middle Ages, we saw that what is regarded as shameful is the upsetting of public order and the neglect of the obligations and responsibilities assigned your class. When *noblesse oblige* falters into benign neglect, shame descends as a cloud upon the entire household and spreads to besmirch the god's representatives on earth, whose duty it is to administer over their communities in matters of the soul, to promote *karitas* among the wealthy and bring god's just will to pass.

Where the bourgeois class predominates, success is seen as the result of hard work, intelligence, and economic asceticism. "God helps them what helps themselves," in this utilitarian ideology, so the wealth of the entrepreneurs is taken as proof of their status as god's elect. Their honor resides in their stinginess, because the god despises profligacy. So what is deemed shameful is the failure to achieve economic success, a failure that is attributable to laziness, dishonesty, and intellectual inferiority. The poor are seen as deserving of both their poverty and the shame attached to their miserable condition.

Shame

Shame attaches to differing acts and different people in different times and places. But what is this debilitating force that robs people of their social place and draws the contempt of their fellows? Shame is a feeling, an emotion that arises deep in the soul. We have seen from Plato's *Gorgias* that shame is a reliable indicator of social learning. To employ Platonic terms, shame "animates *logos*" or turns the soul in the direction of the good. Thus shame is an affective force, a self-relation that connects the soul to a vision of excellence that it loves and a code of ideals it values. Shame evidences moral education already accomplished. On the other hand, if one has not had the benefit of moral learning, one has no occasion to feel shame. One cannot be held to ideals and codes of conduct one has not internalized.

Thus arises the paradox of shame: only a just soul can feel shame for its moral failures. That is, shame only works when the work of social learning has already been completed. Shame reveals the unworthiness of an act in him who is morally worthy of better behavior. The ashamed person has already learned her social lessons, her soul has been "turned" toward a vision of the good, so she recognizes the gap between her unworthy act and the ideals to which she aspires. She recognizes that she has lost the "Hellenic harmony" that aligns her deeds with her highest standards.

A second paradox of shame arises from the first: if shame is a function of social learning and learning is a function of teaching, then the errant individual cannot be blamed (or cannot be solely blamed), if the parent and society have failed in their teaching. Socrates makes precisely this point in the *Gorgias* when he presses the famous orator about his responsibilities with regard to the behavior of his errant students. Gorgias has the appropriate learning that permits him to feel ashamed when Socrates raises this question, but Polus, Gorgias' student, evidencing Gorgias' failure as a teacher, shames himself in his discourse with Socrates, by paying homage to tyrannical values.

Socrates further affirms the responsibility of the teacher for the student's moral learning, when in the *Apology* he urges his prosecutors that, if they truly believed him to be going astray, they ought to have taken him aside as a parent would a wayward child and taught him the lessons he needed. The parent/city and its citizen/siblings had failed Socrates, rather than he failing it/them, if he had committed the errors of which they accuse him. This composes the paradox of punishment: if I had been properly taught my moral lessons, then shame would have stopped me before I erred; if I had not been taught my moral lessons, the very party of authority that seeks to punish me for my errors is (at least in equal part) culpable for my error.

I have stated that shame is an internal *self*-relation that involves the turning of the soul toward the good. But shame is also a relation with the external world, a political relation, because my vision of the good is as it is, because I have internalized the ideas in force within a particular social order. So shame reaches beyond the self-relation and relates me to the political realm. Shame indicates my positioning within a broader social world, my attunement to power relations. Because shame is an instrument of moral education within a specific social arena, it functions to preserve that arena as a socio-economico-political cosmos. Shame illuminates a culture's power over the individual, its control over individual freedoms. But it also conscripts the individual in the army of the system's defenders.

Shame is a witness to social learning, and as such, it can be a salutary pedagogical tool. When it functions in advance to save an individual from going morally astray, it can save her a great deal of pain. But precisely because shame involves existential pain, it can also go very badly astray. The agony and grief caused by this powerful affect can be profound and extensive, because shame has the power to translate a momentary lapse of moral judgment into evidence of a failed self, a failure *of* self. Shame can effect an ontological fall that dehumanizes the agent. Though an unworthy act is about *what I do*, shame extends the social value of the act to the existential meaning of *who I am*.

Alcibiades (450 to 404 BCE) exemplifies the profoundly destructive effect that shame can have on its victims. Alcibiades was a prominent Athenian statesman, an orator, and a general. But in the *Symposium* we find him a drunken fool, wallowing in shame for loving Socrates the wrong way. As Alcibiades describes his agony to the symposiasts, who have been eulogizing the god of love at this party, he demonstrates the shame that has revealed his life as unworthy and unlivable. Shame has translated his moral failure in loving Socrates wrongly as evidence of *his* disgrace, his unworthiness of love. Shame propelled Alcibiades away from the philosophical life that Socrates desired for him, and will go on to propel him into a future of the most profligate actions—sacrilege, treason, exile, disgrace, and finally assassination by foreign barbarians. Shame can have a morally defeating effect, by leaving its victims so dehumanized that they have nothing to morally or existentially lose.

Alcibiades case, and countless others, evidence the fact that shame is a highly powerful tool of social learning that can sometimes do more harm than good. In Greek, "the shameful" (*aiskuron*) is named by the same word as "the ugly," and it means the opposite to "the beautiful" and "the shining" (*kalon*). The beautiful shines forth for all to admire, while the ugly hides itself in shame. Shame is the ontological glue that secures the building blocks of the social order. It leads one to live a certain kind of life, and to connect to certain ideals that configure a certain vision of the world.

It is crucial, therefore, that we step back from the prevailing truths of our system rather than blindly accept the assumptions of our societies and teach them to our children. Sick societies do exist and they line the pages of our history books. Their building blocks are toxic and they breed a distorted sense of shame. Sparta punished its young trainees, not for theft, but for being caught stealing. German officials shamed the officers who hadn't the stomach for killing Jews, gypsies, homosexuals, mental patients, and other victims. Shame may be conscripted in just societies to cultivate excellence in the souls of its citizens, but in unjust societies, shame carries the moral disease of the society and festers and poisons citizen souls.

These ideas are in no way as hegemonic as Marxians suggests. There are always local pockets of resistance to, and ironic appropriations of, the dominant truths. But appropriations notwithstanding, the lower classes of any society are the most likely to fully embrace the dominant truths. This may seem ironic but it makes perfect sense: none are so desperate for social inclusion as those who are excluded and marginalized. One of the primary ways that the excluded seek to claim social place is by absorbing knowledge and thus identifying themselves as repositories of truth.

Kenneth Grahame captures succinctly and humorously the tendency for the general public to jump on the bandwagon and gleefully affirm the rightness of the justice system that targets and oppresses them. In *Wind in the Willows*, Grahame depicts the troublesome toad being dragged from the courthouse to the prison, after being convicted of the crimes of auto theft, furious driving, but most significantly, "cheeking" an officer of the law:

> Then the cruel minions of the law fell upon the hapless Toad; loaded him with chains, and dragged him from the Court House, shrieking, praying, protesting; across the market-place, where the playful populace, always as severe upon detected crime as they are sympathetic and helpful when one is merely "wanted," assailed him with jeers, carrots, and popular catch-words; past hooting school children, their faces lit up with the pleasure they ever derive from the sight of a gentleman in difficulties.[3]

Everyone loves to hate a criminal, and especially the lowly many, the primary target of the law in any period. It is the one way that the poor can publicly demonstrate their existential distance from the shameful. The toad's crimes are not particularly heinous, but the punishment is so severe because his "cheek" has challenged the minions of authority. Every poor washerwoman, every snotty-faced school child, every exploited worker can feel elevated beside the criminal's moral fall—the very castle "frowns" upon toad's shameful behavior.

Grahame's description is amusing. But the reality of penal practices today, as in every age across the history of crime and punishment in the West, is far from a joke, as the last chapter has shown. Systems of justice generally give lip service to "corrections" and "reform" of their social deviants, but in reality, the justice they dish out remains faithful to the logic of *dikephoros* or vengeance justice, bequeathed to us by the archaic princes, but rendered significantly more harmful by the Protestant Ethic, that magnifies its dehumanizing effects on the poor classes that it targets. What is little appreciated is the degree to which the shaming that Grahame describes, the ridiculing and humiliating in which the public merrily participate to show their contempt for social deviants, helps to propel future cycles of crime, in much the same way that the shaming of heroic princes spurred cycles of vengeance against their enemies.

Shame can be a useful pedagogical tool, when it is self-administered. It can warn us against unworthy acts before we commit them, and teach us not to repeat our mistakes. Its warnings can build our moral self-confidence until goodness becomes an unconscious matter, a function of well-worn habit. Shame can have good uses, but can it be *put* to good use? When others use it on us, does it always constitute misuse?

Being shamed by others is certainly not philosophically significant. Looking ridiculous to others never counts toward a valid accounting of worth, in the philosopher's accounting. Socrates assures us, "A good man cannot be harmed by a worse." Similarly, La Rochefoucauld states: "Only the contemptible fear being treated with contempt." Ridicule from the morally unworthy is of no consequence to a philosopher's moral self-accounting. American Buddhist monk, Bhikkhu Nyanasobhano, also urges:

> We ought not to be ashamed of ordinary mundane disadvantages, such as being poor or lacking education, social prominence, beauty, or any number of conventionally admired characteristics, talents, and accomplishments.[4]

But few of us are philosophers and monks. What harms us has more to do with the insecurities we already harbor, the wounds we already carry in our psyches, before the arrows of ridicule strike us. If our society's worldview already casts us as shameful, and our social status makes us feel badly about ourselves, we are much more susceptible to the pain of our society's shaming rituals.

Shaming others is never helpful to their moral development, and as the example of Alcibiades demonstrates, shame can have devastating moral effects on the bearer. The shame Germans felt at their losses in the First World War rendered them vulnerable to Hitler's pride-bolstering racist ideology of Aryan supremacy; their shame was avenged in the brutal murder of tens of millions of innocent people. The Belgians shamed the Hutu with the Hamitic Hypothesis that demoted them as a lower breed of African than their neighbors, the Tutsi, deemed closer in genetic make-up to the white European; the Hutu avenged their social demotion by the slaughter of a million of their fellow Rwandans. These cases are far from home, so we may feel that shame and its avenging violences are somebody else's problem. However, we see that after the World Trade Center attack, a broad spectrum of law-abiding Americans jumped on the bandwagon of a vengeance slaughter of first Afghani, and later Iraqi, civilians. The war cry was, "You are either with us or against us!" and no one wanted to be against avenging the deaths of the New York victims.

Cycles of vengeance can elevate unscrupulous leaders into power and propel an excessive "will to punish" that often redirects the group's shame onto scapegoat groups. There is no great mystery in the fact that from time to time unscrupulous leaders find themselves at the helm of their states. The real mystery lies with the fact that they are able to incite whole populations on board their killing sprees. Genocides cannot be carried out without broad citizen support, and shame is a one of the most powerful forces in motivating populations to support or take part in radical violences.

Far more common, however, is the violence that rebounds from individuals, who have been shamed in early chapters of their lives. Research demonstrates unequivocally that in the vast majority of cases, perpetrators of violent crime, and especially domestic violence, suffered shame in their childhoods, either from browbeating and physical beatings personally suffered at the hands of a parent or other family member, or by helplessly witnessing the abuse of another intimate.[5] A much more recent discovery, however, that demonstrates the power of childhood shaming, is that those victims of domestic and intimate abuse, who make a life pattern of returning again and again to abusive relationships, have generally suffered shame in their childhoods, and find themselves returning to the scene of the crime, as it were, to try to put right their earlier failures and cure their sense of shame.[6]

If witnessing violence and suffering denigration leaves traces of shame deep in the psyches of individuals and causes them to perpetrate against others and commit all manner of crimes against decency and peace, then it is no great leap to understand why poor, uneducated, black men from urban ghettoes in the United States, having descended so recently from a history of slavery and now bearing the burden of shame for their poverty in a prosperous consumer society, still under the thrall of a Protestant Ethic, might carry heavy burdens of shame in that propel them into crime. It is no great mystery why they might turn to offending the society that shames them, and using crime to avenge themselves on a system rigged for their failure.

In modern consumer society during an advancing capitalist age, shame continues to be attached to poverty and low social status, not to mention to cultural difference and the color of skin. For those young people not schooled in monkish or philosophical tradition but educated by their society's constant barrage of advertisements for products they cannot afford, shame can come to be attached more to what people do not possess, than to the crimes they may commit to gain possession of desirable things. Crime is a mode of social communication and an act of revolution toward the social order.

There are a number of things we can do to reduce crime, if this is an actual objective in modern societies (and I am not at all convinced that it is). We can alter the definitions of criminality so that medical and mental health conditions, such as drug use and alcoholism, are met with medical responses instead of punitive measures. We can reduce crime by outlawing the sale of handguns offenders use in the majority of violent crimes. We can reduce crime by doing everything we can do to keep people out of prisons, proven training camps in criminal expertise, sites for the construction of criminal networks, and places where offenders are often initiated into drug use. We can reduce crime by reducing recidivism, by spending enough on each prisoner *once*, to improve his literacy and work skills and increase his chances of employment when he is released. Punishment and crime are directly linked, as Rusche and Kirchheimer confirm:

> So long as the social consciousness is not in a position to comprehend and act upon the necessary connection between a progressive penal system and progress in general, any project for penal reform can have but doubtful success, and failures will be attributed to the inherent wickedness of human nature rather than to the social system. The inevitable consequence is the return to the pessimistic doctrine that man's evil nature can be tamed only by depressing the prison standard below that of the lowest classes. The futility of severe punishments and cruel treatment may be proved a thousand times, but so long as society is unable to solve its social problems, repression, the easy way out, will always

be accepted. It provides the illusion of security by covering the symptoms of social disease with a system of legal and moral value judgments.[7]

There is not the slightest doubt that the best way to wipe out the crimes that land the majority of offenders in prison is by changing the social order, such that the poor have access to the advantages that give their life value and that give them something to lose by entering a life of crime. We can best reduce crime by detaching shame from the condition of poverty and attaching it where it most truly belongs—to the state of neglecting the poor.

Derrick Jensen explains what stands in the way of transforming the structure of modern societies so the common good is better served:

> One of the primary problems with our system of social rewards is its tautological nature. We grant communal responsibility to those who have accumulated wealth and power; but the primary motivation for those who are responsible for decisions affecting the larger community lies in the accumulation and maintenance of power. The good of the community does not matter.[8]

The logic of the system creeps down to the least powerful of the society, as the leaders' thirst for wealth and power becomes "institutionalized" across the system and absorbed by all its members. Jensen affirms that this is precisely what happens:

> In time, the community takes on the character of those esteemed leaders. This happens primarily through direct decisions, the inculcation of citizens to emulate those who receive this respect, and the institutionalization of the leaders' drive for power. Institutions—be they governmental, economic, religious, educational, penal, charitable—will mirror their founders' proclivity for domination. It's inescapable.[9]

If Jensen is correct that every institution assumes the corrupt orientation of the wealth- and power-seeking leaders who govern the society, and since these are the very institutions that are relied on to school the citizens in virtue, then it seems that the virtues the system will foster are identical to the two principles that French anarchist Sebastian Faure cites as governing all politics within capitalist systems: "first, the acquisition of power by all means, even the most vile; and second, to keep that power by all means, even the most vile."[10] Since the larger the institution, the more wealth and power is required to obtain a position at the top, the United States, largest power in the world, should expect its leaders to be more corrupt than most, and their system to be especially adept at teaching their vices to their citizens. From this perspective, then, it is clear that our poor, illiterate, urban youth who turns to corrupt methods to survive, thereby proves himself the most proficient student in the land, because it is he who has best learned his social lessons from the best teachers in the art (of corruption).

We are unlikely to acquit criminals because they mirror the vile means for acquiring power modeled by their leaders. But perhaps we are willing to admit that if the city/parent, responsible for the care and education of its citizen/children, has failed those dependents in flagrant and reprehensible ways, then "acting out" in criminal behaviors is a predictable means of protesting that parental neglect. Seen from this angle, the symptoms of the social disease of crime not only indicate the cause of the disorder, but they recommend a cure, the very cure that Plato urged in his *therapeuma* justice: educate the soul-sick in desirable virtues and surround them by appropriate models.[11]

Until the Protestant Ethic is undermined and the poor are valued for their human creative potential, given opportunities to succeed, and guaranteed employment at decent wages, then Western society can hardly be surprised if their impoverished classes rebel against the system that oppresses them and the ethic that shames them for their poverty. We would never think to avenge ourselves on our children when they go astray, stripping them of their worth and shaming them for their failures. Similarly, we must not humiliate and disgrace our offenders, even if, in cases of gravest danger to society, we must lock the few in cages. Instead we must create opportunities to promote the moral evolution of the wayward with the objective of welcoming them back into the community of the law-abiding. After all, they are always our children, no matter how far they may go wrong.

Notes

1. Alaine de Botton, *Status Anxiety* (New York: Vintage, 2005), 188.
2. Ibid.
3. Kenneth Grahame, *The Wind in the Willows* (New York: Aladdin Paperbacks, 1989), 124-25.
4. Nyanasobhano, *Available Truth*, 84.
5. Linda G. Mills, *Violent Partners* (New York: Basic Books, 2008), 93-97.

6. Ibid., 97-113.

7. Rusche and Kirchheimer, *Punishment and Social Structure* (New York: Columbia University Press, 1939), 207.

8. Derrick Jensen, *A Language Older than Words* (New York: Content Books, 2000), 213.

9. Ibid.

10. Cited by Jensen, Ibid., 214.

11. An example of *therapeuma* justice comes to us from an unlikely source, by many Western standards. Turki Al-Saheil reports that the Saudis are taking a most supportive role in rehabilitating their homecoming detainees, recently released from U.S. Guantanamo Prison in Cuba. Many of the suspected terrorists had suffered breakdowns, strokes and other medical emergencies, and many had attempted suicide, as a result of their treatment in the prison, and the uncertainty and despair that long incarceration without legal recourse had caused. Al-Saheil describes the official Saudi response to the returning "noncombatants": "The Interior Ministry is placing 23 former Guantanamo detainees through a rehabilitation program before granting them their final release. Interior Ministry officials have adopted a new method in dealing with former detainees whom they have finished investigating, which is to provide them with the opportunity to live outside the prison. It also provides schooling and involves them in different social programs" (Turki Al-Saheil, "Life After Guantanamo," *Asharq Alawsat* (August 6, 2010). The stated objective of the Saudi rehabilitation program is "to restore [the prisoners'] psychological, social and religious wellbeing and reintegrate them back into society." While we must grant that a report in English in an Arabic daily newspaper is likely to be at least as invested in propaganda as FOX news on any given night, the fact that the Saudis are allies of the U.S. should balance the usual anti-American bias that often plagues reporting in the Arab news world.

Afterword

Plato attaches the name of "justice" to the righteous acts of good persons. This permits him to determine that a soul lacking in justice must be a sickened soul. Injustice, for Plato, is a grave sort of soul sickness that robs the bearer of her happiness. The best state would take responsibility for its sick citizens, as parents care for their children and nurture them to health. Since justice, for Plato, composes "the definitive human virtue," not simply one virtue among all the others—beauty, temperance, courage, and so on—but the virtue that defines us as human beings, injustice is a grave illness of soul that demands our immediate attention, a *therapeuma* or curative response.

The only cure for injustice, in the Platonic view, is education. The two forms of education that work best in salvaging the soul's health are the company of fine exemplars who can model righteous conduct, and the constant practice of righteousness, until good conduct becomes a matter of habit. Studies of prison populations negatively bear out Plato's truth: nothing works but education and forced containment in bad company exacerbates the problem of soul-sickness, dehumanizing criminals and preparing them for lifelong careers in crime. As Foucault affirms, "The prison cannot help but produce delinquents. It does so by the very type of existence imposed upon its inmates."[1]

In general people seem to agree with Plato's definition of injustice; they believe that those scoundrels that populate our prisons are people who are morally and existentially sick. But Plato also voices, through the testimony of the political realist Thrasymachus, that what is named "justice" in our states—what ends up encoded in our laws, enforced on the streets, prosecuted in our courts, and punished in our prisons—is simply the good of the stronger. State systems of justice give only the "appearance of justice," rather than the real thing. What comes to be considered "criminal" in modern societies is what threatens to undermine the status quo of power relations. So the justice system seeks revenge on its enemies within the state.

In the aristocratic worldview, the nobles shamed *each other* for failure to live up to their birthright. Their *dikephoros* justice sought revenge for peer on peer offenses, shaming ignobility within their ranks. Modernity's petty bourgeois justice takes vengeance upon the poor for their poverty. It shames the unfortunate in the lowliest social ranks to raise themselves up by distinction, by their wealth, rather than by noble behavior. But as Foucault affirms in his brilliant study, crime bleeds out every level of the system; every social class has its peculiar brand of criminality. Prisons exist to mask this fact by highlighting the petty crimes of the poor.

If we consider that prisons exist to reform the soul-sickened children of the state, we will see modern prisons as an appalling failure. However, in the final analysis, Foucault has it right in affirming the success of the modern prison system: "the prison, apparently failing, does not miss its target; on the contrary it reaches it."[2] By isolating one particular form of illegality and placing this form in the full light of the public consciousness, prisons achieve the overarching goal: they "bring out a form of illegality that seems to sum up symbolically all the others, but which makes it possible to leave in the shade those that one wishes to—or must—tolerate."[3]

Notes

1. Michel Foucault, *Discipline and Punish*, Alan Sheridan, trans. (New York: Random House, 1977), 266.

2. Ibid., 276.

3. Ibid., 277.

Bibliography

Aquinas, Thomas. *Summa Theologica*. New York: Christian Classics, 1981.

Adkins, A. W. H. *Moral Values and Political Behavior in Ancient Greece*. London, Eng.: Chatto & Windus, 1960.

Allen, Danielle S. *The World of Prometheus*. Princeton, NJ: Princeton University Press, 2000.

Al-Saheil, Turki. "Life After Guantanamo." *Asharq Alawsat* (August 6, 2010). at http://www.asharq-e.com/news.asp?section=3&id=9700.

Aristotle. *Constitution of Athens*. London, Eng.: Elibron Classics, 2005.

———*The Ethics of Aristotle*. J. A. K. Thomson, trans. New York: Penguin, 1958.

———*Nichomachean Ethics*. New York: Cornell University Press, 2009.

Bonham, Elizabeth, "Adolescent Mental Health and the Juvenile Justice System." *Pediatric Nursing*. Vol. 32.6 November-December 2006.

Bouza, Anthony. *How to Stop Crime*. New York: Plenum, 1993.

Bowra, C. W. *The Greek Experience*. Aylesbury, UK: Hazzel, Watson, and Viney, 1973.

Brockett, Oscar G. and Franklin J. Hildy, *History of the Theater*. Columbus, OH: Allyn and Bacon, 2003.

Castoriadis, Cornelius. "The Greek and the Modern Political Imaginary" David Ames Curtis. trans. *Salmagundi*, 100 (Fall 1993): 102-29.

———"Radical Imagination and the Social Instituting Imaginary." *Rethinking Imagination: Culture and Creativity*, Gillian Robinson and John Rundell, eds. London and New York: Routledge, 1994.

Crawford, Michael and David Whitehead, *Archaic and Classical Greece*. Cambridge, Eng.: Cambridge University Press, 1984.

Dante, *The Divine Comedy*. Dorothy L. Sayers, trans. New York: Penguin Books, 1982.

De Botton, Alain. *Status Anxiety*. New York: Vintage Books, 2005.

Foucault, Michel. *Discipline and Punish: The Birth of the Prison.* Alan Sheridan, trans. New York: Vintage Books, 1995.

Frankfort, Henri. *Before Philosophy: The Intellectual Adventure of Ancient Man.* Harmondsworth: Pelican Books, 1949.

Franklin, James. *The Science of Conjecture: Evidence and Truth Before Pascal.* Baltimore, MD: Johns Hopkins University Press, 2001.

Gagarin, Michael and Paul Woodruff, eds. and trans., *Early Greek Political Thought from Homer to the Sophists.* Cambridge, Eng.: Cambridge University Press, 1995.

Garland, David. *The Culture of Control.* Chicago: University of Chicago Press, 2001.

Grahame, Kenneth. *The Wind in the Willows.* New York: Aladdin Paperbacks, 1989.

Hamilton, Edith, and Huntington Cairns. *Plato: The Collected Dialogues.* Princeton, NJ: Princeton University Press, 1989.

Harer, Miles D. "Prison Education Program Participation and Recidivism: A Test of the Normalization Hypothesis," Prepared for the Federal Bureau of Prisons, Office of Research and Evaluation Report (May 1995).

Hendricks, Cindy, James E. Hendricks and Suzie Kauffman, "Literacy, Criminal Activity, and Recidivism" available (June 26, 2010) at www.americanreadingforum.org/yearbooks/01_yearbook/html/12_Hendric ks,htm.

Homer. *The Iliad.* Robert Fagles, trans. New York: Penguin Group, 1996.

Jaeger, Werner. *Paideia: the Ideals of Greek Culture.* Oxford: Oxford University Press, 1967.

Jensen, Derrick. *A Language Older than Words.* New York: Content Books, 2000.

Kirk, G. S. *Myth.* Cambridge, MA: Cambridge University Press, 1970.

Lenin, Vladimir. *Lenin's Struggle for a Revolutionary International: Documents 1907-1916.* New York: Anchor, 1984.

Lorenz, Konrad. *On Aggression,* Marjorie Kerr Wilson, trans. New York: Bantom Books, 1967.

Mackenzie, M. M. *Plato on Punishment.* Cambridge: Cambridge University Press, 1981.

MacIntyre, Alastair. *After Virtue.* Notre Dame, IN: University of Notre Dame Press, 1984.

Marx, Karl. *The Communist Manifesto.* Helen MacFarlane, trans. London: Verso, 1998.

McGuire, James. *What Works: Reducing Reoffending.* Hoboken, NJ: John Wiley & Sons, 1999.

Mills, Linda G. *Violent Partners.* New York: Basic Books, 2008.

Nietzsche, Friedrich. *On the Genealogy of Morals.* Walter Kaufman, trans. Vintage Books, 1967.

Nyanasobhano, Bhikkhu. *Available Truth: Excursions into Buddhist Wisdom and the Natural World.* Boston: Wisdom Books, 2007.

PBS Special Report: "By the Numbers: American Prisons" Available (June 1, 2007) at www.pbs.org/now/shows/322/america-prsions.html.

Plutarch's Complete Works: Parallel Lives. New York: Thomas Y. Crowell & Co., 1909.

Porporino F. and D. Robinson, "The correctional benefits of education: A follow-up of Canadian federal offenders participating in ABE." *Journal of Correctional Education*, Vol. 43, No. 2 (1992).

Rancière, Jacques. *Disagreements: Politics and Philosophy*. Julie Rose, trans. Minneapolis: University of Minnesota Press, 1999.

Rowling, Marjorie. *Life in Medieval Times*. New York: Paragon Books, 1979.

Rusche, Georg and Otto Kirchheimer, *Punishment and Social Structure* New York: Columbia University Press, 1939.

Saunders, Trevor J. *Plato's Penal Code*. Oxford: Clarendon Press, 1991.

Sealey, Raphael. *A History of the Greek City States 700 to 338 B.C.* Berkeley, CA: University of California Press, 1976.

Sykes, Gresham M. *The Society of Captives*. Princeton: Princeton University Press, 1999.

Thucydides. *The Peloponnesian War*. Rex Warner, trans. Middlesex, Eng.: Penguin Books, 1985.

Verrall, A. W. "The Hymn to Apollo: An Essay in the Homeric Question" in *Journal of Hellenic Studies*, Vol. 14: (1894:1-29).

Weber, Max. *The Protestant Ethic and the Spirit of Capitalism*. Peter Baehr and Gordon C. Wells, trans. and ed. New York: Penguin Books, 2002.

Williams, D. "Project LEAD builds bridges." *Corrections Today*. Vol. 58 No. 5 (1996).

Index

About the Author

Wendy C. Hamblet, Ph.D., is a Canadian philosopher, who serves as Associate Professor at North Carolina Agricultural and Technical State University in Greensboro, North Carolina. She is also the Director of *Therapeia Ethics Consulting*, a firm which consults in the field of organizational ethics in government and business settings. Hamblet is a specialist in the research fields of conflict theory, genocide, and ethics. She has authored three books: *The Lesser Good: the Problem of Justice in Plato and Levinas* (Lanham, MD: Lexington Books, 2008); *Savage Constructions: The Myth of African Savagery* (Lanham, MD: Lexington Books, 2008); *The Sacred Monstrous: Reflections on Violence in Human Communities.* (Lanham, MD: Lexington Books, 2004). Her work is also extensively published in peer-refereed professional journals, such as *Monist, Symposium, Ratio, Prima Philosophia*, and *Existentia Meletai Sophias*, as well as in numerous anthologies and encyclopedia in her field. Hamblet holds editorial positions on the executive boards of four prestigious journals, including *Appraisal, Journal of Globalization for the Common Good, Newsletter of the Concerned Philosophers for Peace*, and the *Bulletin of Science, Technology and Society.*

Breinigsville, PA USA
10 December 2010
250985BV00004B/2/P